THE POCKET MBA

Everything An Attorney Needs To Know About Finance

THE
POCKET MBA

Everything An Attorney Needs To Know About Finance

MICHAEL SINGER

PRACTISING LAW INSTITUTE
NEW YORK CITY

9256

This work is designed to provide practical and useful information on the subject matter covered. However, it is sold with the understanding that neither the publisher nor the author is engaged in rendering legal, accounting or other professional services. If legal advice or other expert assistance is required, the services of a competent professional should be sought.

Copyright © 2005 by Practising Law Institute. All rights reserved. Printed in the United States of America. No part of this publication may be reproduced, stored in a retrieval system, or transmitted in any form by any means, electronic, mechanical, photocopying, recording, or otherwise, without the prior written permission of Practising Law Institute.

Library of Congress Control Number: 2005907293

ISBN: 1-4024-0632-0

TK

About this Book

PLI's Pocket MBA is the book form of the weekly email newsletter of the same name. PLI's Pocket MBA newsletter provides lawyers with an introductory peek inside their clients' businesses from a finance and accounting perspective. Every Wednesday since May 2003, Pocket MBA has provided an accounting or finance term, along with a definition and an example of how it applies or why it's relevant in the real world of business.

Foreword

During my third year in law school, I toyed with the idea of postponing my entry into the real world via a PhD in urban studies or a Masters in the burgeoning, but still speculative, field of something called "computer software." For some reason, going to business school never crossed my mind, although a number of friends and law school classmates had attended or were attending. In the end, I eschewed these possibilities, opting for a career path that has led me from courtroom to classroom to editing room. Some 15-plus years after I walked out of Boston University School of Law, Sandra Geller welcomed me to Practising Law Institute's (PLI) offices in bustling midtown Manhattan, tasked with developing and writing a series of lighthearted, and when possible, humorous, html eNewsletters, one of which was to be entitled *The Pocket MBA: Everything a Lawyer Needs to Know About Finance*, after the PLI program of the same name. My first thought was that each of those extra degrees would have come in handy at that moment. My second was, "I don't know anything about finance."

But of course, that was the point. Many lawyers, as students or after, had the foresight to learn about the businesses underlying their clients' legal concerns. Many others, including me, did not or felt we could not, either because to do so was too time-consuming or, as the old saw went, "Lawyers just aren't any good at math." Now, having researched and written three years' worth of *The Pocket MBA,* I realize that not only did I know much of this finance "stuff" already, but my trepidation about the rest of it -- including as to whether it could ever be humorous -- was largely (though not always) unfounded. *The Pocket MBA* is testament to that. And, as email is so easily deleted, I was excited when PLI decided to give the first 100 issues of *The Pocket MBA* eternal life via book form, a hard-copy roadmap of the weekly journey I take with thousands of readers.

For those who are new to *The Pocket MBA,* let me explain the methodology behind it, which is really quite simple. If a finance or accounting term is or has been in the news, legal or otherwise, it is fodder for an issue. There is no particular order to the terms discussed every week, just whatever seems both relevant and interesting at the moment. The original newsletter format of *The Pocket MBA* demanded brevity, and as such, I have never made any effort to be exhaustive on any particular subject. Rather, the discussion is an entrée to further study, if the reader so desires. To that end, there are occasional web links to relevant materials. Because there are references to what were current events at the time of publication, I have added "Author Updates" where appropriate to bring the discussion closer to the present.

Beyond that, researching and writing *The Pocket MBA* has led me to conclude that the economic and finance decisions people make everyday are not that different, other than as to scale, from those made by corporations. People may not be required to file audited financial statements, but we all keep a checkbook, as a paper-trail of our cash flow, and maintain records of our income, accumulated debt, taxes, depreciation, capital gains, stock holdings, etc. And even if we don't have to account for ourselves based on what the Financial Accounting Standards Board mandates, we comply, nonetheless, with a slough of IRS and other finance-related government regulations on a daily, weekly, monthly or annual basis. So, whenever possible, *The Pocket MBA* aspires to relate corporate finance to the reader's everyday life. As an example, it is this desire that has led me recently to incorporate the childhood lemonade stand as a test of various concepts. As a result I have come to realize that some seemingly complex aspects of finance are as simple as that lemonade stand.

And that's pretty much it. But before you get started on your Pocket MBA, I feel it important that you know *The Pocket MBA*, as a concept, was not my brainchild, and I would be remiss if I did not acknowledge and applaud those who laid the groundwork for this book and who were so confident that lawyers would want to spend a few minutes every Wednesday learning finance and accounting from another lawyer. I cannot say exactly what transpired before I arrived on the scene, but sometime during 2002, PLI's Executive Director Victor Rubino, Director of Programming, Sandra Geller and Director of Marketing Arlene Bein met with Internet marketing guru Andy Sernovitz of GasPedal. Together, they built the skeleton for what were to become PLI's eNewsletters. Sandy brought me on board in early

2003 and gave me a latitude in putting meat on the bones of that skeleton that an in-house writer can only dream of. In essence, she just let me fly, and it was her trust in my ability and judgment that propelled *The Pocket MBA* to its May 2003 launch.

But producing quality newsletters week after week takes more than a scribe with a computer. There is a small cadre of PLI marketing staff that read and produce everything I write, ensuring it's worthy of publication under the PLI banner. This group consists of David Smith, Nadine Hovan, Paula Gomprecht, Kim Russo, Josh McCuen and Brian Scott Mednick. Thanks also to James Silvestri, who makes sure I receive reader correspondence. And a special thanks goes to Arlene Bein, who assembled this group of people and whose inimitable wit, spirit and sincere friendship have inspired me and dragged me through the inevitable days when I felt like I just didn't have anything to say. Most of all, however, I thank you, the readers of *The Pocket MBA* -- for your supportive emails and your constructive criticism, for your clarification inquiries and your outright corrections. It is you who keep me motivated and on my toes, and who give me the fortitude to forage onward on a quest to earn my own Pocket MBA.

Michael Singer
New York City - August 2005

Table of Contents

About this Book vii
Foreword ix

Volume 1

Financial Accounting Standards Board (FASB) 17
Public Company Accounting Oversight Board (PCAOB) 18
Generally Accepted Accounting Principles (GAAP) 19
The 10-Q 20
Section 906 Certification 21
Earnings 22
Retained Earnings 23
Book Value 24
Goodwill 25
Repricing Options 27
Options Expensing 28
Inventory 30
Safe Harbor Statements 31
Reg. FD 32
Extraordinary Items 33
DIP Financing 34
Deflation 36
Free Cash Flow 38
Cash vs. Accrual Accounting 39
Going Concern Principal 40
Notes to Financial Statements 42
Current Assets 44
Non-Current Assets 46
Current Liabilities 47
Hedge Funds 48
Derivatives 50

Money Supply 52
Long-term Liabilities 54
Restricted Stock Grants 56
Market Timing 58

Volume 2

Budgeting 60
Capital Budgeting 62
Off Balance Sheet Arrangements 64
Earnings Restatements 66
Productivity 68
Fair Value Pricing 70
The Specialist System 72
Monetary Policy 74
Dutch Auction IPO 77
Just In Time (JIT) 79
EBITDA 82
Revenue Recognition 84
Burn Rate 87
Depreciation 89
CAGR 93
Investment Company 96
Break-Even Analysis 100
Liquidity Ratios 102
S Corporation 105
Inventory Financing 107
Accredited Investor 109
Price Elasticity of Demand 112
Depreciation Recapture 117
Trade-Through 118
Fair Value 122
CAP-EX 125
Commodities Futures Trading Commission 127
Auditor Report 129
Cost of Goods Sold (COGS) 132
Enterprise Value 134

Lower of Cost or Market (LCM) 136
Accretive to Earnings 138
Capital Structure 140
Debt/Equity Ratio 142
Capital Lease 143
Diluted Earnings Per Share 146
Stock Buyback 148
SWAP 150
Not-For-Profit Organization 153
CUSIP Number 154
Technical Analysis 157
Golden Parachute 158
Shelf Registration 160
Poison Pill 164
Barriers to Entry 167
Altman Z-Score 170

Volume 3

Forensic Accounting 172
Profit Margin 174
Deferred Revenue 177
FAS 151 & Accounting Divergence 178
Return On Equity (ROE) 180
Return on Investment Capital (ROIC) 182
Naked Short 184
FAS 123r 187
Road Shows 191
Efficient Market Hypothesis (EMH) 194
FAS 95 (Statement of Cash Flows) 197
FAS 117 200
SEC No-Action Letter 202
Down-Round Financing 204
Junk Bond 207
American Depositary Receipt (ADR) 209
Asset Turnover Ratio 212
Net Profit Margin 216

Return on Assets (ROA) 218
12b-1 Fee 222
Stock Appreciation Rights (SARs) 225
Inventory Turnover 227
Exchange Rate 230
Beta Coefficient 233

Appendix A

Appendix B

Financial Accounting Standards Board (FASB)

The Financial Accounting Standards Board (FASB) is the privately funded organization whose mission is (according to its web site, www.fasb.org) "to establish and improve standards of financial accounting and reporting for the guidance and education of the public, including issuers, auditors and users of financial information."

FASB IN THE REAL WORLD:

FASB was a big secret, as far as the general public was concerned, until recently. Now the organization is all over the news, as it has acted to revise reporting standards that were too easily abused and that failed to stop the corporate accounting scandals that have come to light in the past few years.

Ever since Enron, WorldCom and friends worked their accounting sleights of hand, FASB has publicly wrestled with issues including how corporations should account for options; the end to amortization of goodwill and pooling of interest accounting by merging corporations; and convincing investors that its pronouncements will stem the abuses. Of course, corporations rarely welcome most reforms (particularly things like the potential requirement that options be recorded as an expense), because they result in greater accounting cost, as well as increased financial transparency, and some companies (at least those that have things to hide) don't like that.

But here's the rub: although FASB sets the accounting standards and is recognized as authoritative by the SEC (which has the actual statutory power to set accounting standards, but defers to FASB), the organization has no enforcement authority (that belongs to the SEC also), and is funded by the very accounting firms for which it sets standards. That's quite a tightrope to walk. And now there's also the Public Company Accounting Oversight Board (PCAOB) to consider. Where does it fit in? Read on.

Public Company Accounting Oversight Board (PCAOB)

The Public Company Accounting Oversight Board (PCAOB) is a private, non-profit corporation charged with protecting investors in U.S. securities markets and furthering the public interest "by ensuring that public company financial statements are audited according to the highest standards of quality, independence, and ethics." See www.pcaobus.org.

PCAOB IN THE REAL WORLD:

The PCAOB is a creation of the Sarbanes-Oxley Act of 2002, and it is so new that nobody is quite certain how it will impact the auditing profession in the long run. So far, the Board's web site offers not much more than its mission statement and an opportunity to comment on proposed Rules. If the Board's initial actions are any indication, however, the accounting world is in for quite a shakeup.

On April 25, 2003, the SEC pronounced, pursuant to section 110(d) of Sarbanes-Oxley, that the Board had properly organized itself and had the capacity to carry out the requirements of the Act. The Board moved to adopt many of the pre-existing standards of the auditing profession, then quickly stripped the authority of the American Institute of CPAs (AICPA) to regulate the accounting profession; it has issued a rule requiring public companies and mutual funds to supply its principal funding; and has proposed a rule (publicly backed by the SEC) requiring foreign firms that audit U.S.-traded companies to register with the Board.

AUTHOR UPDATE: The PCAOB web site now has a special area that houses all current and proposed standards. See http://www.pcaobus.org/Standards/index.aspx. It has adopted three such standards, along with several rules and, as of this writing, has pending a fourth auditing standard.

Generally Accepted Accounting Principles (GAAP)

Generally Accepted Accounting Principles are the accepted rules, conventions, standards, and procedures to which most companies conform when reporting financial information. The responsibility for establishing GAAP and for keeping GAAP current and responsive to current needs falls on FASB.

GAAP IN THE REAL WORLD:

As with many areas in corporate finance and accounting, the relevance of GAAP to adequate financial reporting, or even more importantly, the relevance of non-GAAP financial reporting, took on new meaning after the passage of the Sarbanes-Oxley Act in July 2002, which directed the SEC to adopt rules regulating the release of financial information calculated and presented on the basis of methodologies other than GAAP.

Theoretically, when a company uses GAAP, anyone should be able to examine a financial disclosure and assess the financial condition of the entity. It's those non-GAAP disclosures that became so popular in the 1990s that were wreaking accounting scandal and investor havoc. (These most notoriously took the form of pro-forma earnings reports that often included speculative financial measures not normally found on a balance sheet and left out all kinds of potentially unpleasant financial news that should be on a balance sheet.)

Well, no more. As of March 28, 2003, there's a new sheriff in town: Regulation G. Regulation G requires public companies that disclose or release non-GAAP financial measures to include "a presentation of the most directly comparable GAAP financial measure and a reconciliation of the disclosed non-GAAP financial measure to the most directly comparable GAAP financial measure." So now, though there may be two sets of numbers to confuse the uninformed, at least one of them will be recognized as generally acceptable by someone.

The 10-Q

These are the quarterly financial reports the SEC requires all public companies to file within 35 days of the end of a fiscal quarter. The 10-Q includes relevant financial disclosures, such as operational results, highlights and acquisitions.

THE 10-Q IN THE REAL WORLD:

When people think about quarterly reports, they also often think of quarterly earnings and the prior estimates against which those earnings are measured--estimates that have often become the public face of corporate performance. But most people don't realize that these estimates are neither required nor necessarily esteemed by those who have to pay attention to them. For instance, Warren Buffet thinks companies should discontinue issuing earnings estimates. Why? Companies can easily manipulate data by, for instance, buying back company stock, to reach or surpass estimated results in any given quarter, and in some respects, the quest to beat these estimates led to the corporate accounting scandals of the recent past.

So it was big news in December 2002 when Coca-Cola announced that it would no longer issue quarterly guidance. This move was applauded in many circles because it reduced the pressure on Coke to achieve short-term operational successes at the expense of long-term business strategy. Also, reducing the emphasis on quarterly results attracts long-term investors, and tends to discourage short-term investors who care only about whether a company meets short-term estimates rather than whether a company is actually healthy for the long run. Some viewed Coke's move more cynically. Either way, if you want to know how Coke is doing in the future, you'll have to wait to read the 10-Q and figure it out for yourself.

Section 906 Certification

Sarbanes-Oxley Act requirement that CEOs and CFOs personally certify that a company's periodic reports (1) comply with section 13(a) or 15(d) of the Securities and Exchange Act of 1934; and (2) fairly present, in all material respects, a company's financial condition and operational results.

SECTION 906 CERTIFICATION IN THE REAL WORLD:

Talk about having to perform under pressure. When President Bush signed the Sarbanes-Oxley Act on July 30, 2002, Section 906 went into effect immediately, giving most CEOs and CFOs scant weeks to undertake the required certification of corporate results. The penalties for willfully filing results knowing they are false can reach as high as $5 million in fines and up to 20 years in prison.

Section 906 has been lauded and excoriated--hailed for its salutary effect on corporate financial responsibility and critiqued because the law contains no objective standard telling executives exactly what standards they are to apply in certifying their results. They're managing, of course, and as of this writing, no CEO or CFO has been hauled off in handcuffs for filing a false Section 906 certification, which may be more of an attestation to the fact that a few bad apples were spoiling the whole bunch during the go-go 1990s. In that respect, perhaps Section 906's most fundamental benefit is in confirming the essential ethicality of the overwhelming majority of people--CEOs, CFOs, auditors and attorneys--involved in the reporting process. And that's a good thing.

Earnings

Earnings are the revenues of a company, less its cost of sales, operating expenses and taxes during any defined time period.

EARNINGS IN THE REAL WORLD:

A couple years ago, it seemed as if corporate earnings as a major barometer of the financial health of a company were a thing of the past, bowing to such things as "buzz." Well, it turned out that the number of hits your web site gets matters not a whit, after all, and it seems so obvious now that the late 90s internet mania has died. Good companies make money, the best companies make lots of money, and the companies that make no money disappear, no matter how cool their Super Bowl ads are. Who can even remember any of the dot-coms that went public to high acclaim and then liquidated in ignominy? Here are a few: Boo.com, eCAMPUS.com and Toysmart.com.

Earnings as a snapshot of corporate performance are some of the first numbers the investment and finance crowd look to on a corporate balance sheet. Earnings took a back seat to market share, potential growth rates, and that "buzz" thing for most of the 1990s. Now, even new economy companies (the ones that survived) have come to the realization that, while those other things are important, long-term corporate health is premised upon solid earnings, either now or in the very foreseeable future, as opposed to "earnings in the so-distant future as to constitute a pipedream."

The only way a company can continue to grow over time is by actually being able to report earnings, which informs the capital markets of its long-term viability and credit-worthiness, and which can then be used to pay dividends, to pay down debt, or for reinvestment in the business. But even positive earnings can be classified qualitatively as good or bad. And anyone who regularly reads financial publications will note an increasing number of articles dedicated to the notion that the best earnings are those that result in increasing generation of "free cash flow." Pocket MBA will examine this later.

PLI's Pocket MBA Vol. 1, No. 7   June 25, 2003

Retained Earnings

Retained Earnings are the profits a company uses to reinvest in its business, to purchase other businesses or to pay down debt, rather than to pay out as dividends to shareholders.

RETAINED EARNINGS IN THE REAL WORLD:

With all the hoopla surrounding the push to reduce or eliminate individual income taxes on dividends and the supposed incentive that would give corporations to pay them, one would think that companies have no reason not to pay them other than tax policy. But, as the definition of retained earnings implies, a company has many options (even requirements) as to the disposal of its profits, like paying down debt (as if this could ever be optional) or financing growth by increased investment in research and development or through acquisitions, that can make more long-term economic sense at a given point in time than paying a dividend. And sometimes there simply isn't any profit left (or free cash flow), after required expenditures, to pay a dividend.

When a company is small and nimble, it can grow faster by plowing earnings into R & D. Established, but still growing, companies often seek to expand beyond their original markets by buying other companies that complement their existing business and add to the bottom line. This works better for investors than dividends if the company, say Cisco Systems, shows a substantial return on its reinvestment to the business. Cisco has retained all earnings throughout its history, and during the 1990s, powered its growth and increased its earnings by acquiring companies with the hefty cash cushion it had built up by that practice.

But if reinvestment in the business, whether through increasing R & D or by acquisition, doesn't accrete to the bottom line, a company can often end up with more debt, slowing or no growth, or scads of cash sitting in the bank, which lead to diminishing shareholder value. This is often why companies with slowing growth and hordes of cash change course and begin to disgorge earnings through a dividend. (Microsoft did this recently, although its reasons for doing so are hotly debated; the company does have some 40 billion dollars in cash on its balance sheet.) Other companies, for which heady growth days are simply over, pay out their profits because it's a way to attract investors whose aim is to receive income. In these cases, not retaining some of the earnings becomes the better investment.

AUTHOR UPDATE: Since this issue of Pocket MBA was published, the government slashed the federal tax rate on dividends to 15%, and as a result, many companies have instituted and/or increased payouts. Microsoft has continued to pay out dividends, though with the exception of a one-time $3/share jackpot special dividend, they have been relatively small. These payouts have not dented Microsoft's cash horde, which now stands around $70 billion. And despite slowing growth and a multi-billion dollar cash horde, Cisco Systems has still never paid a dividend.

PLI's Pocket MBA Vol. 1, No. 8	July 9, 2003

Book Value

This is the net tangible assets of a company--the value of a company's hard assets minus its liabilities. It's sometimes referred to as "the going out of business value," that is the shareholder equity remaining if the company were sold and its debt retired.

BOOK VALUE IN THE REAL WORLD:

For Pocket MBA purposes, book value has nothing to do with the most recent installment of *Harry Potter*. In the accounting world, book value has been used traditionally as a way of measuring a company's strength and value relative to its industry peers. (And along with its relative, share price to book value ratio, it is the denominator of just one of the many ratios--price/earnings, price/sales, price/earnings-growth are some others--analysts look to in evaluating these types of things, and which Pocket MBA will delve into in future issues.) It is a value that bespeaks of a bigger is better mentality: the more stuff you own, the better you must be. But book value is an increasingly illusory concept in an age where many companies' primary assets are intangible ones, such as goodwill, because these are excluded from the calculation. That is why some of the best-known and successful companies of the day have very low book values--traditionally a negative--relative to their actual size and strength (think Cisco Systems, for example, which has scads of intellectual property intangibles that don't find their way into book value).

Low book values can result in a deceptively high price to book value ratio, which traditionally was a signal that a company's stock was overvalued. Book value can also be distorted because hard assets are often valued as of their acquisition date, rather than at current market value. Nonetheless, book value and price to book value ratio persist as methods to get a general feel for the value of a company relative to a given peer group, possibly because in a given peer group, most companies will presumptively have a similar asset make-up.

Goodwill

Goodwill is the intangible value of a company, that is, the purchase value of a company above its book value. Goodwill can include any asset that provides a competitive advantage, such as a solid reputation, strong brands, patents and the like.

GOODWILL IN THE REAL WORLD:

Goodwill has grabbed headlines since FASB changed the way

companies have to account for it. In the old days (that is, before 2001), when one company bought another, the purchaser could treat purchased goodwill as a wasting asset, amortizable over a period of up to 40 years. But this practice had become increasingly archaic as goodwill evolved to often represent the most valuable asset many entities possessed. When a company (like many a tech firm) is primarily goodwill, goodwill cannot really be deemed wasting; rather it must be viewed as living indefinitely, otherwise some pretty large companies could conceivably have a value close to zero. Accordingly, FASB (via FAS 141 & 142) now requires companies to account annually for the value of goodwill and to write down, as a nondeductible loss, the value of goodwill that is "impaired," that is, that no longer exists or never existed in the first place (this may be the original "fuzzy math," but it makes perfect sense to those versed in the nuances of accounting).

Think about it in terms of paying $10 for what is otherwise a $.25 pack of gum solely because it is made by Wrigley's (as opposed to Bubble Trouble, an unknown company that sells a similar pack for $.25) and later realizing the Wrigley's brand only increased the resale value of the gum to $.50, thus rendering the price you paid too high by $9.50. Under the new FASB rules, instead of amortizing that amount, you now have to write it off all at once. The paper losses in such cases can result in a staggering blow to shareholder value--take AOL Time Warner.

When AOL purchased Time Warner (and not many recall that it was the now-marginalized Internet upstart that did the purchasing), it paid $147 billion (in stock), even though the value of Time Warner's hard assets (its book value) was only $51 billion--the excess $96 billion was deemed goodwill (attributable primarily to Time Warner's strong brands). Under the old accounting rules, AOL-Time Warner would have amortized that goodwill for a long, long time. Under the new rules, the drop in AOL-Time Warner's market value after the collapse of the stock market had to be accounted for. The result? AOL-Time Warner reported that it had lost $10.01 per share in the fourth quarter of 2002, even though it had earned $.28 per share from actual operations. Chalk up most of the difference (some $45.5 billion in all) to impaired goodwill. In the everyday-shopper's vernacular, that is how much AOL overpaid for Time Warner. And that's a lot of gum.

PLI's Pocket MBA Vol. 1, No. 10   July 23, 2003

Repricing Options

The practice of lowering the strike price (the exercise price) at which options may be exercised. It usually occurs after a company's stock price falls significantly below the strike price.

REPRICING OPTIONS IN THE REAL WORLD:

Repricing options became commonplace during the 1990s when new economy companies with minimal or no earnings and hence limited cash to throw down commonly offered options-based compensation as a lure to attract top-flight talent. When the company's share price dropped and stayed low (as happened to so many), these options became, in essence, permanently worthless. So companies began to reprice them. Unfortunately, the subsequent repricing often heralded the fading fortunes of these companies.

Executives often rationalized the practice by contending it was the only way to retain and motivate those employees who had been attracted by compensation in options that had sunk hopelessly "underwater" (the term used to indicate a share price below the strike price). In practice, repricing options had the primary effect of enriching option holders (assuming the share price rebounds at all) at the expense of common shareholders, who are left holding the bag of expensive shares purchased on the open market and who must sell them for the full loss.

In FIN 44 (Financial Interpretation 44), FASB reined-in post-1998 repricings of stock options by requiring companies to account for subsequent rises in the stock price as a compensation expense. Companies didn't find it all that difficult to get around the new rules, however. One way was to have employees give up their options in exchange for a promise to receive new ones at a much later date. Then if the company waited six months and a day, it could issue cheaper options to avoid the accounting requirements. Then there is the Microsoft solution. On July 8, 2003, it announced that it would cease issuing stock options as of September 2003, and that any employees with underwater options could simply cash them in--plain and simple. On top of that, the company declared it would restate its earnings for the past several years to expense the options it had issued.

PLI's Pocket MBA Vol. 1, No. 11	July 30, 2003

Options Expensing

The practice (currently voluntary) of treating the "value" of stock options issued during a reporting period as a business expense on the balance sheet, which reduces earnings. Companies that do not expense options report their value in footnotes to financial reports, which results in no impact to the bottom line.

OPTIONS EXPENSING IN THE REAL WORLD:

As the old song goes, "The times, they are a changing." On March 12, 2003, FASB announced that it would be deciding (sometime this year, for implementation in 2004) exactly what to do with the thorny issue of whether companies should be required to record the value of stock options as an expense.

The sides are drawn clear. Many corporate watchdogs and politicians are in favor of expensing because it would enhance corporate transparency. A slough of options-issuing corporations that wish to continue the practice without having it impact the bottom line are against. (You can subtract Microsoft from that group, as the company announced recently not only that it would cease issuing options altogether, but that it would restate its earnings for the past several years to reflect the expense of all the options it had issued.) But the opposing sides seem neither here nor there, as FASB will decide the issue one way or the other (probably in favor of expensing) and companies will have to live with it.

Of course, the real question is not whether to require expensing; rather, it is if expensing is required, how on earth does one value these things? FASB will wrestle long and hard with this one, because to date, there is simply no settled valuation method. Think about it. Employee stock options are issued on Day X; they are exercisable years down the road on Day Y. By that time, the make-up and value of the company may have changed drastically (and not necessarily for the financial better); many options-bearing employees may have left their jobs without having exercised their options. The initial valuation seems like guesswork at best.

So what happens when options are expensed? Well, naturally, reported profits decline. And investors and others become aware, balance sheet-wise, of the extent to which a company has issued options and the true impact on the cost of operations. Of course, those costs are already present today; most public companies already report options in the footnotes to their financial statements, so if one reads the footnotes, one can figure out what the impact of the options are if one knows how to calculate the value of the options. Which brings us back to square one.

In FAS 123 (issued in 1995), FASB declared that companies accounting for options (and there are many, including Coca-Cola, American Express, The Washington Post and, now, Microsoft) should use a "fair-value" estimation "using an option-pricing model that takes into account the stock price at the grant date, the exercise price, the expected life of the option, the volatility of the underlying stock and the expected dividends on it, and the risk-free interest rate over the expected life of the option. The fair value of an option estimated at the grant date is not subsequently adjusted for changes in the price of the underlying stock or its volatility, the life of the option, dividends on the stock, or the risk-free interest rate."

As critics have pointed out, this model can easily lead to overvaluation if an option is granted when a stock is at an unusually (and temporarily) high price. It also does not take into account the situation of options never exercised (in the case of employee attrition for instance). The expense sits on the books, but in retrospect, seems to stand as a fiction.

There are other valuation methods, but it is for FASB to figure out which will best reflect reality.

AUTHOR UPDATE: FASB did move eventually to require options expensing when it adopted FAS 123r, which is in the process of going into effect. For more information on FAS 123r, see Vol. 3, No. 8.

PLI's Pocket MBA Vol. 1, No. 12   August 6, 2003

Inventory

Assets intended for sale, being produced for sale or being used to produce goods for sale. During any given reporting period, it can be expressed as the value of the starting inventory plus net purchases minus the cost of goods sold.

INVENTORY IN THE REAL WORLD:

Inventory is a seemingly self-explanatory term, but oh the nuances. Here's the primary one. A company's inventory at the end of any given reporting period is dependent on its inventory valuation method, of which there are three in wide use: First In, First Out (FIFO); Last In, First Out (LIFO); and Average Cost. FIFO assumes that a company sells goods in the order in which they were produced or purchased. LIFO assumes that a company sells first the goods it produced or purchased last. And Average Cost assumes that each unit is sold for the average cost for producing or purchasing all the units on-hand during the period.

Each of these methods results in different financial results, unless inflation over time is equal to zero. In an inflationary world, the one in which we have traditionally lived, the use of FIFO will generally result in increased net-income in a given period relative to the other methods (and hence higher earnings) because the company is charging a higher price for goods it purchased at a cheaper level; concomitantly, FIFO results in a higher tax burden relative to the other methods. LIFO will result in lower net-income and taxes since the cost of goods sold is higher. In a deflationary world, the one into which many economists recently debated whether we might be entering, but didn't, the results will flip-flop.

By the way, if a company uses a particular method in its tax-accounting, it has to use the same method to report earnings to shareholders. So a company can't use LIFO to report low earnings to Uncle Sam, but use FIFO to report high earnings to the investing public. Also, if a company changes the valuation method it uses, it must report the financial impact of the change on its income statement for the period.

PLI's Pocket MBA Vol. 1, No. 13   August 13, 2003

Safe Harbor Statements

Statements made pursuant to the Securities Exchange Act of 1934, as amended by the Private Securities Litigation Reform Act of 1995 (the PSLRA), and that can be found in most company reports and press releases as a disclaimer of all forward-looking financial statements. They permit companies to make good-faith operational forecasts without fear of liability in the event the forecasts turn out to be wrong.

SAFE HARBOR STATEMENTS IN THE REAL WORLD:

The safe harbor was created to deter abusive and frivolous securities fraud claims. Since Congress enacted the PSLRA, plaintiffs must plead that companies issued forecasts with actual knowledge that they were false. There was a time, as recently as the early 1970s, when the SEC prohibited companies from including forward-looking statements from filings. Subsequently, the SEC began to recognize the importance of such forecasts to the financial and investing community. Safe Harbor rules followed accordingly, culminating in the provision of the PSLRA now relied upon in company reports. Since it is extremely difficult for securities fraud claimants to avoid the prohibitions of the safe harbor, most successful, recent litigation has posited that complained-of statements were not actually "forward-looking" and hence not protected.

In any event, under the PSLRA, companies have become masters at couching their reports with cautionary terminology that can take up pages of a 10-Q. Here's a recent example of a miniscule part of one company's safe harbor statement:

> Words such as 'anticipates,' 'estimates,' 'expects,' 'projects,' 'intends,' 'plans,' 'believes' and words and terms of similar substance used in connection with any discussion of future operating or financial performance identify...forward-looking statements. Those forward-looking statements are based on management's present expectations and beliefs about future events. As with any projection or forecast, they are inherently susceptible to uncertainty and changes in circumstances.

That statement was issued in November 2002 by a well-known conglomerate, and the company then listed all those possible uncertainties, most of which came to fruition, judging by the company's results in the following quarter.

Reg. FD

SEC Rule adopted in 2000 requiring public companies to disseminate "material" non-public information, relating to the company or its securities, simultaneously to both the public and to securities brokers, analysts, investment bankers and the like. Even when such information is disclosed unintentionally to brokers prior to the public, a company must disclose it to the public promptly (within 24 hours) thereafter.

REG. FD IN THE REAL WORLD:

Strike up another one for the Internet. Say what? Well, if it weren't for advances in technology that have made information ubiquitously available and easy to disseminate, securities information might well still be the repository of a select few analysts and brokers who might have less than altruistic relationships with issuers.

Now, an individual investor has the same shot at information that the big boys and girls have. Really, that's what the SEC said, but in more artful words. The actual words released by then SEC Chairman, Arthur Levitt, were as follows: "High quality and timely information is the lifeblood of strong, vibrant markets. It is at the very core of investor confidence. Regulation FD will bring all investors, regardless of the size of their holdings, into the information loop-- where they belong."

The SEC figured that given 21st century communications, a level investment playing field was actually possible so why not take advantage. Now, theoretically, anyone, be they analyst or individual, who wants an information advantage has to do the legwork themselves and do actual research into industries.

But the truly amazing thing about Reg. FD is that the SEC issued it before most of the scandal that bedeviled the markets in the early 21st century became public news. What prescience! Some don't like Reg. FD, arguing that companies now issue less information than before because of legal concerns that no one is certain of what makes information "material" and of whether the methods they use for public dissemination will satisfy the SEC. But quantity was not really the point. FD stands for Fair Disclosure, not more disclosure and, on that score, the SEC has probably succeeded.

Extraordinary Items

One-time, unusual and non-recurring events that impact a

company's operating results (either positively or negatively). They are usually accounted for separately and explained in notes accompanying the particular quarterly (10-Q) or annual (10-K) report.

EXTRAORDINARY ITEMS IN THE REAL WORLD:

If gains or losses resulting from 9/11 were not extraordinary items, then what would be? Well, a blizzard that causes a roof on a Toys "R" Us store to collapse could be an extraordinary loss; early payment of a debt could be an extraordinary loss; and receipt of that payment could be an extraordinary gain. But not gains or losses due to a one-time act of terrorism. Why not?

Well, according to an edict issued shortly after 9/11 by FASB's Emergency Issues Task Force (who even knew there was one), "the economic effects of the events were so extensive and pervasive that it would be impossible to capture them in any one financial statement line item." That is, a company has to be able to state the event and its impact simply and concisely, like, "On date X there was a blizzard and the roof collapsed, causing Y dollars of damage." As for one instance of the difficulty in the 9/11 circumstance, take the impact on the airline industry, as perceived by FASB: "Air carriers were unable to fly for two days [and] suffered the effects of rerouting and initiated layoffs in anticipation of lower passenger demand. No single line item can capture all of those effects." That is, the losses to the airline industry from 9/11 stretched indefinitely into the future and could not be concisely quantified. And if an event cannot be captured in such a manner, it is not extraordinary, from an accounting perspective, no matter how extraordinary it might be.

PLI's Pocket MBA Vol. 1, No. 16   September 3, 2003

DIP Financing

Debtor-in-Possession (DIP) Financing refers to the loans

companies entering Chapter 11 bankruptcy reorganization often arrange, with approval by a bankruptcy judge, to enable continued operations during reorganization.

DIP FINANCING IN THE REAL WORLD:

K-Mart had a DIP; United Airlines has a DIP; U.S. Airways had a double-dip; heck, even WorldCom had a DIP and American Airlines was lining one up, just in case, but decided it didn't need one after all. DIPs are so popular, you could have a reality TV show in which distressed companies compete for one.

DIPs are a fairly recent development, having come into existence along with the 1978 Bankruptcy Reform Act. Bankruptcy used to mean the end of business; now it can mean restructuring as a new entity. If you think about it, DIPs are essentially a lender's bet that a company will emerge from bankruptcy, and based, as they generally are, on a company's inventory and accounts receivable, they are a good bet, since the lender gets hefty fees and interest, not to mention dibs on the most liquid assets of the debtor in the event the process fails. DIPS don't help shareholders and other unsecured creditors of the pre-DIP entity, because their investments are usually rendered worthless in the reorganization.

Some have criticized the ready availability of DIP financing (almost 10 billion dollars in DIP financing was issued in 2002) because it postpones or avoids, altogether, Darwinian liquidations that would have an otherwise salutary impact on the overall economy. But it would seem intuitive that companies able to arrange DIP financing are more likely to restructure successfully, so perhaps it's best to let the bankers determine what are the best bets.

Of course, there are no guarantees, witness Pillowtex's 2003 decision to liquidate rather than go through a second reorganization, having successfully navigated a previous bankruptcy. In any event, here are some other well known companies that got DIP financing recently: Adelphia Communications; Conseco; Covad Communications; National Steel; Consolidated Freightways; and Kaiser Aluminum.

Deflation

Economic environment characterized by falling prices and a contraction in available money relative to capacity.

DEFLATION IN THE REAL WORLD:

Everybody is getting their dander up about the dangers of deflation. Whether there is really anything to worry about depends on who is doing the talking. Bureau of Labor statistics show that the U.S. annual inflation rate fell from 12.4 percent in 1980 to 1.5 percent in April 2003. Still, that indicates that our economy continues to be inflationary, or more precisely, disinflationary, which is characterized by a decline in the rate of inflation. And though the pricing power of some manufacturers (like computer makers) has declined, for others (homebuilders, oil suppliers) it is rising--each product operates on its own microeconomic law of supply and demand.

So what's all the fuss about deflation? Deep in everyone's heart of hearts, there is a microeconomic wish for a little deflation--who doesn't want a good deal, to spend a little less money to get the same basket of goods. But on a macroeconomic level, economists (and politicians) argue that deflationary pressures are arguably as bad as, if not worse than, inflationary pressures, if only because the government's primary tool for impacting inflation and deflation, tinkering with interest rates, hits a floor (zero percent) with deflation that doesn't exist on the inflation side. The Federal Reserve can always raise interest rates higher (anyone who lived through the late 1970s and early 80s remembers the sky-high interest rates designed to choke off spending and runaway inflation). And although lower interest rates are a disincentive to holding cash, if zero percent (short term interest rates are one percent now) doesn't get people to spend their money on goods and services, some argue there is little a government can do to fight deflation, except continue to flood the market with cash and wait.

Eventually, someone will produce something that everyone just has to have.

So how does deflation occur and what are its effects? Deflation occurs when the amount of supply on a macroeconomic level exceeds the amount of dollars available to soak up the supply. To oversimplify, nobody has money to buy what anyone is selling or already has enough of what is being offered. Producers are then forced to lower the prices of their goods to try and catch the available dollars. But when all producers are doing this, their profits decline, and then they have to lay off workers, which results in still fewer dollars available and yet further price declines, and so on. How does an economy extricate itself from that? Don't ask Japan. The last time this country experienced a deflation (the Great Depression) it took a New Deal and World War II (i.e. a lot of government deficit-spending) and plenty of individual sacrifice to end it.

Some have argued that in our current situation, deflation would not be a bad thing--it would just be the market working to find equilibrium, just as it does during hyper-inflationary times--that it would eventually cleanse the system of useless companies and prepare us for the next wave of growth, whatever that would be. (The explosion in computer and telecom technology arguably ended the economic stagnation of the late 1970s-early 1980s because there was new stuff that everyone needed, nobody had, and that had to be built, sold and serviced, and that was eventually, particularly in the telecom industry, overbuilt, oversold and over-serviced.) The history of markets is characterized by boom and bust cycles; they rarely have ended in deflation. And we haven't arrived there now either, and with the money spigot wide open, it's difficult to envision it occurring.

AUTHOR UPDATE: The feared deflation never occurred. Of course, now, with oil and commodities prices skyrocketing, American budget deficits soaring and with new entrants flying into the world economy and jockeying for a place among the economic first world (China, India, Latin America), the latest fear is...renewed runaway inflation. Hence, the Federal Reserve has been steadily raising interest rates since this issue appeared, and the end of these small raises is nowhere in sight.

Free Cash Flow

Amount remaining after subtracting operating costs of a business (e.g. investments in property, plant and equipment, working capital to support operations and tax payments) from cash derived from operations.

FREE CASH FLOW IN THE REAL WORLD:

Just think of "free cash" as corporate mad money. It's what's left after every conceivable cost of operating a business has been paid (this is what distinguishes it from retained earnings, from which nagging debt and taxes must be paid and which are definitely not earmarked for use as dividends). And think of the "flow" as the stream of free cash that piles up for very successful companies, quarter after quarter--it's kind of like leftover food, but it never spoils.

Free cash can be used at the corporation's whim (within legal constraints): it can be retained and used for acquiring other companies or for salting away in the bank (Microsoft is really good at this, having accumulated close to $50 billion of the stuff), to be drawn on in a pinch (Microsoft says it is hoarding cash until lingering antitrust disputes are resolved), or it can be paid out as dividends to shareholders. (Microsoft started doing this recently and is widely rumored to be considering increasing its dividend once those lawsuits are put to bed.)

Companies that have increasing free cash flow are often considered to be the strongest, from a long-term investment standpoint, because they have financial flexibility to meet future challenges. If you don't have money sitting around, and the market changes on you, all you can do is finance new plans through debt or sell your assets.

So how do you determine free cash flow? Well, you look at a company's statement of cash flow, which companies file quarterly along with their balance sheets and income statements. If you let your eyes drift down the statement of cash flow for the current quarter, you will see an entry marked "cash flow from operating activities." Close below will be a column marked "capital expenditures." Subtract that from the first number and you will have the total free cash. There are some caveats--some amounts, like cash derived from investments, aren't really cash from operations and should be excluded from that number. In any event, subtract the previous quarter's free cash total from the current quarter's and you can determine the free cash flow-- the increase or decrease for the quarter.

Increasing free cash flow over many quarters indicates a company on the move. Of course, if you're Microsoft, and you have all that free cash from prior golden years, it keeps piling up regardless of how fast current operations are growing. But then there's only ever been one Microsoft.

PLI's Pocket MBA Vol. 1, No. 19	September 24, 2003

Cash vs. Accrual Accounting

Cash and Accrual are the primary bases by which businesses record transactions. A cash basis company will record transactions during the tax year in which it receives or makes payment. An accrual basis company will record transactions during the tax year in which the right to receive or duty to make payment occurs without regard to whether payment has actually occurred. The IRS requires companies with sales exceeding five million dollars or that stock inventories for sale to the public to use the accrual basis.

CASH VS. ACCRUAL ACCOUNTING IN THE REAL WORLD:

The accounting method a business uses is, like many things in life, about timing and taxes. Over time, the methods will even out, with all income and expenses being recorded and taxes being paid. But, as most everyone would rather pay taxes later than sooner (although delaying a tax liability can be disastrous if you don't have the cash to pay it), the accounting method chosen does impact the year-to-year ebb and flow. Here is a fact pattern and some basic examples using cash and accrual methods to get you going.

Facts: Counselor's Corner is a company that embosses (but does not manufacture) legal pads with law firm letterhead. On September 30, it takes a $5,000 order for 10,000 pads from Big Giant Firm LLP. It immediately calls the manufacturer and places the order to have the pads delivered to it at a cost of 25 cents a pad. After receiving the pads on October 15, Counselor's Corner pays, on October 30, $1,250 to the manufacturer. Counselor's Corner embosses the firm's name on them and delivers them on November 30. Counselor's Corner receives Payment from the firm on January 15, 2004.

Cash Basis: Counselor's Corner gets to record the $1,250 expense on the day it paid the money, October 30, 2003. It doesn't have to record the income until January 15, 2004. Thus, it gets an expense deduction for the sale for tax year 2003, but doesn't pay taxes on the income until tax year 2004.

Accrual Basis: Counselor's Corner records the $1,250 expense on October 15, the day it received the pads and became liable to pay the manufacturer. Counselor's Corner records the income and a tax liability from its resale to Big Giant Firm arises on November 30, 2003, even though Counselor's Corner didn't receive payment until 2004.

This example demonstrates how the choice of accounting basis impacts timing and taxes. Of course, like anything, viewing one, isolated transaction distorts the reality of an ongoing business. You can get more useful tips on this issue in IRS publication 538, which is available from, surprise, the IRS.

Going Concern Principle

This is the assumption that a business will remain operational, and not liquidate, for the foreseeable future. It is the lynchpin of financial and auditing reports.

GOING CONCERN PRINCIPLE IN THE REAL WORLD:

The going concern principle is an assumption (and you know what "they" say about assumptions) that underlies all company financial reports. If either a company's management or its auditors has reason to doubt the assumption, that doubt will be reflected in company reports. The concept is crucial for many reasons, one of which being that the value of the assets of a going concern is generally higher than that of a company in danger of liquidation, in which case, it is often impossible to value many assets. For example, company letterhead (remember last week's issue) has value "x" if the company is a going concern, but has only scrap value if the company liquidates. Managers, accountants and auditors value companies assuming they are going concerns.

There are numerous circumstances that can undermine the going concern assumption, each of which can be roughly divided into one or more of three broad categories: financial, operational and legal.

Examples:

(1) A company that is not profitable or, though profitable, has incurred so much debt that it is not generating enough cash either to repay the debt or to enable it to obtain additional financing can be said to have financial going concern issues.

(2) A company that relies heavily on a particular individual may have operational going concern issues if that individual leaves the employ of the entity.

(3) A company that gets sued for patent infringement on the primary product it sells or finds that product outlawed by government regulation may have legal going concern issues.

When a company's auditor has doubt about the assumption that the company can continue as a going concern, that doubt will be revealed by the auditor in its reports and by the company in its SEC filings. Here is an example of how one company recently revealed its auditors' doubts:

Our auditors have included an explanatory paragraph relating to our ability to continue as a going concern in their Report of Independent Accountants included in our audited financial statements for the year ended December 31, 2002. Last year, we incurred a net loss of $19.5 million and negative cash flows from operations of approximately $20.0 million. We need to significantly increase sales to achieve profitability and positive cash flows. The auditors consider that these factors, along with the pending [XYZ Corp.] litigation, raise substantial doubt about our ability to continue as a going concern. The financial statements do not include any adjustments relating to the recoverability and classification of recorded asset amounts and classifications of liabilities that might be necessary should we be unable to continue in existence.

This company had both financial and legal going concern issues. Fortunately for the company, since that report, the company won its lawsuit and projected that it would achieve profitability by the end of this year. Hence, one would expect the going concern statement to disappear in future filings. And that's just the way assumptions work.

Notes to Financial Statements

GAAP prescribed disclosures that can be found at the end of a company's consolidated financial statement. They include disclosures and explications of events that impact upon a financial statement, but cannot be reflected by mere numbers.

NOTES TO FINANCIAL STATEMENTS IN THE REAL WORLD:

So, you've read a company's balance sheet, its income statement and its statement of cash flow. You see the bottom line numbers, and, if you're like most people, you scratch your head and say to yourself, "Those are interesting numbers; I can see this company makes money, but I still have no idea how they do it or even what they do." Enter the notes to the consolidated financial statements. This is where the actual disclosure of a company's function and condition are accomplished. They are more than mere footnotes because, within them, you will find (to a varying degree, depending how complex a company's structure and business are) information that will allow you to put the financial statement into the context of a going concern.

Notes covering the following subjects will allow you to assess the entity's current financial position, obtain insight into its future prospects, compare it to its competition and get a bird's eye view of how management sees the business:

- Company summary: short history and description of its business
- Summary of its accounting policies
- Information on acquisitions of other businesses or disposals of any of its own assets
- Dispositions or status of financial instruments, the change in values of which are reflected on the financial statements
- Restructuring charges
- Debt and borrowing arrangements (this could take many forms--credit facilities, warrants issued in company stock in exchange for cash, etc. These help you get a feel for a company's cost of borrowing and its ability to obtain additional financing)
- Pension and retirement benefits
- Explanation of stockholder equity, including options, commitments and contingencies

- Pending legal proceedings, including expenses
- Segment data (this is provided by companies made up of many product lines that generate separate financial information; it allows the reader to distinguish between a company's more and less successful lines)
- Subsequent events (these are events that occur after the date of the balance sheet that would otherwise have impacted the balance sheet)

As the above non-exhaustive list indicates, in a real sense, it is the notes that are the meat on the skeleton of the financial statement.

Current Assets

These are resources that a company may readily access, either because they are on hand as cash or because a company can reasonably expect to convert them to cash by sale or consumption within one business cycle (up to one year).

CURRENT ASSETS IN THE REAL WORLD:

Successful companies tend to run their businesses from current assets. Companies that don't have sufficient current assets to run their business have to do things like issue debt or shares of stock, which, of course, dilutes that value of the company to existing shareholders. Think of current assets in terms of your own budgeting. An individual's current assets are things like salary, savings and liquid investments. If these don't cover expenses, you turn to the plastic or other kind of loan. Of course, like people, who generally don't buy houses with current assets, businesses don't build factories with current assets. But a business will attempt to make due in its day-today operations from current assets.

Generally speaking, there are five categories of current assets:

(1) Cash & Cash Equivalents: Cash is cash, and equivalents are those instruments, like CDs and T-Bills with short maturities (90 days or less). Companies that have lots of cash and equivalents are also those that have the ability to pay dividends.

(2) Marketable (Short-Term) Securities: Companies that have more money than they need to run their businesses like to invest the money in debt and equity markets. When the investment is in issues with maturities of less than one year, or is one that the company intends to dispose of within one year, the security considered short-term and is reported at fair market value.

(3) Accounts and Notes Receivable: These are the debts (payable within one year) customers owe to the company for goods already delivered. Companies report these at "net realizable value," which is the amount a company actually expects to receive and excludes amounts the company does not expect to receive. The latter amount is reported as an allowance for bad debt. Sometimes when companies don't allow for enough bad debts, they later have to take a write-down of unrecoverable receivables to balance the books out.

(4) Inventory: These are goods a company has in production or holds for sale, or goods that the company will convert in the process of producing goods for sale. Inventory is the repository of manufacturing companies. Most service-based companies tend to have little, if any, inventory.

(5) Prepaid Expenses: When a company pays bills in advance, the amount is considered a current asset, even though it means the company has less cash and even though it is not particularly convertible into cash. Nonetheless, in terms of a balance sheet, which covers several months, money paid now doesn't have to be paid next month, so it is a current asset.

No doubt you noticed that the phrase "within one year" is very common in a discussion of current assets.

Non-Current Assets

These are the assets of a company that will not be converted into cash or consumed within a business cycle, or more generally, within one year.

NON-CURRENT ASSETS IN THE REAL WORLD:

Anyone can look at a manufacturing company, or even a bank, and see tangible non-current assets with their own eyes. Things like property, plant and equipment, whether purchased or leased, that a company uses for more than a year are often in plain view. (In the event of a long-term lease, it is the lease that is the asset.) You can even see the tangible depreciation of these assets--when a factory looks rusty and broken-down, you can sense the "accumulated depreciation"--the write-off of these assets that is a component of the non-current portion of the balance sheet. That's the easy stuff. It's those intangible non-current assets that confuse.

So what is an intangible non-current asset? It's an asset without particular physical form, but every bit as valuable as any hard asset. Intangible non-current assets are generally long-lived legal rights that a company develops or acquires, like patents, copyrights and goodwill. In the case of patents and other intellectual property, there is at least a piece of paper (or computer disk) to represent them ("specifically identifiable" in the accounting vernacular). Goodwill (the value ascribed to things like brands and customer lists), on the other hand, is largely invisible ("not specifically identifiable"). It is the value of a company above the fair value of the rest of the assets.

Like their tangible brethren, most intangible non-current assets waste over time. Patents and copyrights are amortized over their exclusive life. Goodwill used to be treated similarly. FASB changed all that recently, when it issued FAS 141 and 142. Now, goodwill is no longer deemed wasting. Instead companies have to account annually for the value of their goodwill. If the market value of a company is such that the world is ascribing a value to the company less than it would be if the goodwill were intact (that is, recorded at its original value), then the lower value of the company is considered an impairment of goodwill, and the impairment value must be recorded as a non-deductible loss.

PLI's Pocket MBA Vol. 1, No. 24   October 29, 2003

Current Liabilities

A company's current liabilities are obligations that are reasonably expected to be satisfied from current assets.

CURRENT LIABILITIES IN THE REAL WORLD:

Current liabilities is a relatively simple concept. If you think of it in terms of your own life, it's easy to grasp. These are the expenses you owe now: the phone bill; the electric bill; the cable bill; income taxes; current portion of a mortgage payment; the amount you pay as salary to the gardener (if you're lucky enough to have one--otherwise, maybe it's the "allowance" you give your kid for cutting the lawn, throwing out the trash, etc.). You get the idea. Companies have the same expenses, just more complex (though as most parents know, 21st century allowance structures can be as complex as any executive compensation agreement).

As the above indicates, there are several categories of current liabilities--well, actually seven or so:

- Accounts Payable
- Accrued Expenses
- Payroll Liability
- Dividends Payable
- Short Term Notes Payable & Current Portion of Long Term Debt
- Taxes

These are all fairly self-explanatory, perhaps with the exception of accrued expenses, which are simply the bills that have piled up but haven't yet come due. They are recorded on the balance sheet anyway. Income taxes are sometimes considered an accrued expense. The other twist is the current portion of long-term debt. Of course, most of a long-term debt is not a current liability. Assuming a company is in the first year of a 15-year mortgage, the payments for the 14th year are not a liability this year. However, the payments due this year are a liability this year and are therefore recorded as a current liability.

PLI's Pocket MBA Vol. 1, No. 25   November 5, 2003

Hedge Fund

Private investment vehicles structured as limited partnerships that are not offered to the public, and have historically been, by and large, exempt from the registration requirements of the securities laws. The general partner is usually the manager of the fund, and the limited partners are the investors.

HEDGE FUND IN THE REAL WORLD:

These days, most hedge funds are not really hedge funds, strictly speaking. According to Merriam-Webster Online, "to hedge" means "to protect oneself financially: as (a) to buy or sell commodity futures as a protection against loss due to price fluctuation (b) to minimize the risk of a bet." Indeed, hedge funds originated for just these purposes in 1949 when Alfred Winslow Jones purportedly created the first investment vehicle that hedged long stock positions with short positions.

Now, according to most published accounts, hedge funds are more about exotic investments and the exclusive investor, as opposed to a mere risk-modulator. Hedge funds go long; they go short; they arbitrage; they swap; they buy futures contracts. You name it, they're trying to profit from it. In its September 2003 report "Implications of the Growth of Hedge Funds," the SEC acknowledged that a hedge fund has no "precise legal or universally accepted definition," but is generally "an entity that holds a pool of securities and perhaps other assets that does not register its securities offerings under the Securities Act and which is not registered under the Investment Company Act." So as long as your fund isn't registered, it's technically a hedge fund.

Hedge funds have outperformed traditional investment vehicles (i.e. mutual funds) over the recent past. This is probably attributable in large part to the sophistication of the people involved in hedge fund investing. You can't just make a $500 investment into a hedge fund. These things have steep minimum investments (the lowest reported is $250,000) and are often limited to accredited investors (those who can prove minimum asset base and annual income). Hedge funds cannot advertise or publicly solicit, so they are kind of a private moneymaking club. Also, the fund manager has a great incentive to spend all of his or her time making sure that the fund performs well; hedge fund managers make their money from profits after the year is over, rather than the persistent management fees that their mutual fund counterparts receive.

But all is not wine and roses in hedge fund land. The USA Patriot Act raised concerns about unregistered investment companies because of their possible susceptibility to money laundering. The SEC expressed concern about the staggering growth in hedge fund assets because there is no way to monitor the trading practices (and their impact on markets) of the funds and, in the case of fraud, the SEC frequently can act only after "significant losses have occurred." Thus the SEC Report recommended, among other things, that the Commission consider requiring hedge fund advisers to register as Investment Advisers under the Investment Adviser Act, which may not sit too well with those in charge of the funds or those depending upon them for wealth creation. So stay tuned; things are just heating up.

AUTHOR UPDATE: New SEC rules that require compliance by February 1, 2006 will have the primary effect of requiring most hedge fund managers to register with the SEC under the Investment Advisers Act of 1940. See http://www.sec.gov/rules/final/ia-2333.htm

Derivatives

Financial instruments commonly used to hedge financial risks already undertaken. They take the form of contracts, the value of which are derived from the value of the asset underlying each contract, such as a commodity (oil, coffee, metals) or other financial instrument (stocks indexes, bonds, foreign currencies, interest rates) or anything else that can be bought and sold. (There are even weather derivatives.)

DERIVATIVES IN THE REAL WORLD:

Derivatives, as a concept, seem really scary, but they're not nearly so esoteric as the term might imply, and most laypeople, not to mention lawyers, have been exposed to derivatives in some manner or another. This is not to say that they cannot be incredibly complex financial vehicles; rather it is to say that you can get your arms around the basics if you simply read the business pages everyday. Then, you need merely apply the basics to the ever-increasing array of financial derivatives that are springing up. Of course, maybe that's easier said than done. But here are some basics to get you started.

Derivatives commonly take the following forms: forwards and futures (which are similar except with regard to various administrative and regulatory details), options and SWAPs. There, already it's easier. Anyone who grew up in the Midwest has a basic familiarity with futures from childhood because the morning news often led with the cost of a June corn contract on one of the Chicago Exchanges.

A forward/future is simply a contract that calls for the delivery of a commodity at a future date for a specified price. It's kind of like a bet on the outcome of a sports event. Here is a most basic example that has nothing to do with today's complex financial arrangements: Trader buys a corn contract (which stands for, say, 6,000 bushels of corn) to be delivered September 2004 for 100 dollars. If September 2004 comes and the actual price of corn is 120 dollars, the buyer profits; if corn is only 80 dollars, the buyer has lost. In today's financial derivatives world, futures contracts are for things like the future value of the S&P 500 (Just watch the stock ticker before the NYSE opens and you and you will see the readout on stock index futures.)

An option is a right (without accompanying obligation) to buy or sell a commodity or financial instrument (or anything else) at a specific price by a specific date. If an option is not exercised within the specified period of time, it expires. An option can take the form of a "put" or a "call." A put is an option to sell a stock or commodity at a certain price, while a call is an option to buy likewise. A stock option, like those granted to employees at many companies, is simply the right to buy a share of stock at a given price after a certain vesting date.

SWAPs are the derivative du jour. The market for SWAPs is currently figured in the tens of trillions of dollars. They are also the derivatives that are the most complex. They are the exclusive domain of institutions; individuals do not trade in SWAPs. At its most basic, a SWAP is simply an agreement to trade payments, and the most common form of SWAP involves interest rates.

Let's say Afraid, Inc. has borrowed money at a fixed rate of 5 percent over 25 years, but is now worried that interest rates will drop to 4 percent over the next five years. Similarly, Terrified & Co. has borrowed money at a variable rate for 15 years, starting at 4 percent, but is now concerned that rates will rise to 7 percent during that period, and would prefer to have borrowed at a fixed rate of 5 percent. The two decide to enter into a SWAP agreement lasting five years. Although each will continue to fulfill its obligations under its respective loan agreements, each company will pay the other company the amount that company paid to its respective bank. They have, in essence, swapped payments to hedge their respective concern about the direction of interest rates. Companies often do interest rate swaps involving differing markets; as such these swaps are often an effort to get the best of both worlds.

Money Supply

The aggregate amount of money that is in circulation at any point in time. The rate of growth or shrinkage in the nation's money supply is an important gauge of economic activity and inflation. The Federal Reserve Bank measures the United States' money supply on a weekly basis (Thursdays at 4:30 p.m.).

MONEY SUPPLY IN THE REAL WORLD:

The money supply is one of those terms that everyone hears regularly and about which everybody intuitively has a general idea. The money supply is, well, the supply of money. But when economists start discussing M1 and its relation to the inflation rate, eyes glaze over and a nagging desire to talk about one's next meal ensues. So what is this money supply, really?

According to the website of the Federal Reserve Bank of New York, www.ny.frb.org, the money supply, as reported by the Federal Reserve Bank, consists of three "money supply measures," M1, M2 and M3, each of which "reflect[s] the different degrees of liquidity--or spendability--that different types of money have." The Fed has used M1, M2 and M3 only since 1971; prior to that (back to the 1940s), the central bank reported the money supply in the aggregate.

- M1 is the narrowest and most liquid supply measure. "[I]t consists of currency in the hands of the public; travelers checks; demand deposits and other deposits against which checks can be written."
- M2 "includes M1, plus savings accounts, time deposits of under $100,000, and balances in retail money market mutual funds."

- M3 "includes M2 plus large-denomination ($100,000 or more) time deposits, balances in institutional money funds, repurchase liabilities issued by depository institutions, and Eurodollars held by U.S. residents at foreign branches of U.S. banks and at all banks in the United Kingdom and Canada."

Note that the value of securities traded on exchanges is not a part of the money supply.

Traditionally, economists have considered the rate of growth in M1 to be tied to increased economic activity and inflation. This is simple law of supply and demand. That's because if liquidity (demand) is increasing rapidly, but the amount of goods (supply) the liquidity is chasing is the same, there will be a squeeze on producers, and prices will rise. (Consider how much more willing you are to buy an expensive cup of coffee--and is there any other kind these days--when you have fifty dollars in your pocket as opposed to five dollars.) So historically speaking, a stagnant money supply has indicated a stagnant economy; rising money supply has indicated an expanding economy; and falling money supply has indicated a contraction.

These relationships have broken down somewhat over the recent past, so that the traditional relationship between money supply growth and economic activity isn't holding as true. For an example, think about all of the money that goes into stock and bond mutual funds--they are an incredible font of wealth, but their value is not included in M1, M2 or M3.

The Fed has noted that this money used to be held in small, time deposits like CDs and in savings accounts, which are part of M2. So M2 has been shrinking over the years, which would normally indicate a prolonged economic contraction. That has not been the case, which led Fed Chairman Alan Greenspan, (in 1993) to downgrade M2 "as a reliable indicator of financial conditions in the economy, and no single variable has yet been identified to take its place." Still if you were to extrapolate from this statement, if M2 is rising steadily and the stock market is rising steadily, you should have a pretty good economic expansion on your hands. This is why economic purists still put great stock in the money supply as a harbinger of economic activity: an expanding money supply is almost always an indicator of economic growth.

In any event, the Fed has various means (well, three) at its disposal to control the money supply and hence growth and inflation:

(1) by raising or lowering the reserve requirement for banks--that's the amount of cash a bank must keep on hand relative to its total assets;
(2) by buying and selling Treasury bills and notes; and
(3) by raising or lowering interest rates.

Each of these can expand or contract the money supply and represents an effort by the Fed to impose stability onto economic activity. For instance, when the Fed raises the reserve requirement, banks have less money to lend. When the Fed sells T-Bills, it removes money from the system and replaces it with securities. And then there's interest rate policy, the most public form of monetary control. Rising interest rates lowers money supply by deterring spending. And now, you can think about that next meal.

PLI's Pocket MBA Vol. 1, No. 28   December 3, 2003

Long-term Liabilities

Future obligations of a company that arise from current operations; they are not payable during the current operating cycle.

LONG-TERM LIABILITIES IN THE REAL WORLD:

If you've ever looked in the mirror and screamed at yourself, "I'm never going to get out of hock," you probably have some long-term liabilities weighing you down--things like a mortgage, student loans, maybe you borrowed money from Aunt Susie and gave her an

IOU stretching over five years. Maybe you tell a friend that if the Chicago Cubs win the World Series next year, you will pay your friend, on January 1, 2006, $10,000 plus an amount equal to the number of victories the Cubs have in all of 2004. These are all possible examples of long-term liabilities, and they can be reasonably equated to those that a company might report in some manner or another on its balance sheet.

And like yours, a company's long-term liabilities can impact upon its ability to order its affairs. For instance, if a company has long-term liabilities so substantial that its current and future operations look like they will never generate enough cash to cover the debts, the company will have increasing difficulty getting credit.

There are five categories of long-term liability:

- Long Term Debt (things like mortgages and bonds)
- Pension Obligations
- Leases
- Post-Retirement Benefits
- Contingent Liabilities

Each of these is plain enough, except that a long-term lease is recorded as both an asset and a liability, and a contingent liability is, well, contingent. Financial Accounting Statement (FAS) 5 governs the recording of contingent liabilities and generally requires contingencies to be disclosed and accrued when two conditions are satisfied:

(a) information available prior to issuance of the financial statements indicates that it is probable that an asset had been impaired or a liability had been incurred at the date of the financial statements, and

(b) the amount of loss can be reasonably estimated.

Take the Cubs...please! If the Cubs win the World Series next year, you will owe your friend $10,000 plus. Do you have to record this contingency on your Pocket MBA balance sheet? The amount of your debt can be reasonably estimated. It will be around $10,100, give or take a few dollars.

But the Cubs haven't won the World Series since 1908, and any diehard fan knows that there has been a curse on the Cubs since 1945 that pretty much ensures they never will. And though they had a decent shot this year, the chances of the Cubs winning the World Series next year remain remote, especially because their inability to hit Florida's Josh Beckett seems unlikely to change next year and because Beckett somehow pitches in all of Florida's games. But Pocket MBA digresses. The point is "remote" contingencies do not have to be disclosed at all currently, let alone accrued as a liability.

Now, what if come next August, the Cubs are sporting an 82-15 record and it's time to issue a new balance sheet? At that point, it would seem at least reasonably possible, even probable, that the Cubs would win the World Series (prior notable collapses by the team to the contrary notwithstanding, see 1969, 1984 and six weeks ago). "Reasonably possible" contingencies have to be disclosed, and "probable" contingencies have to be disclosed and accrued. So, at this point you might consider disclosing the contingency and accruing the liability. But check with your accountant. He might be a Boston Red Sox fan.

AUTHOR UPDATE: The Cubs are just, so bad.

PLI's Pocket MBA Vol. 1, No. 29   December 10, 2003

Restricted Stock Grants

Type of non-cash compensation issued by companies to employees, usually without cost to the recipient. The grants take the form of ordinary shares of stock, but the employee's control over them is limited by a vesting period.

RESTRICTED STOCK GRANTS IN THE REAL WORLD:

When Microsoft announced in July that it would cease issuing stock options and instead, thenceforward, grant restricted stock, the corporate world took a deep breath and waited for others to jump on the bandwagon. That hasn't happened yet. And it may or may not, but when Microsoft does something financially radical, Pocket MBA notices. So why did Microsoft do it and what are the implications?

Like other forms of non-cash compensation, the purpose of a restricted stock grant is to attract potential employees and rev up the performance of current employees with the promise of stock market riches. But whereas a stock option expresses a hope for rising stock prices (it gives the employee the right, upon vesting, to purchase stock at a predetermined strike price, even if the stock price has far surpassed the strike price; but the option is worthless if the share price falls below the strike price), a restricted stock grant is often a bow to reality, particularly given the experience of the recent bear market. The shares are always there and can be sold upon vesting for a specific value, even if the value is lower than the share price of the stock when issued.

Whether one is better than the other depends on your point of view. From the employee's perspective, when share price is skyrocketing, the option is arguably better, in terms of total potential gain. But when share prices are stable or falling, the stock grant can be the better value, as they can be unloaded anytime before zero, whereas the option-holder may be stuck with the options.

Some have argued that from the employer's perspective, stock grants are not as good a motivator as options because of that base value that exists in each share--why work harder when you already have the money. Perhaps that is one of the reasons the rest of the corporate flock have not hopped on the restricted stock bandwagon.

But from Microsoft's perspective, perhaps the bursting stock market bubble, which left many of the later-minted, ersatz Microsoft millionaires "broke" as their options sank further and further below the strike prices, became a disincentive. The new practice arguably guarantees that a repeat performance will not occur, as Microsoft is likely to stay in business, and stock grants will therefore retain their current value, and can increase in value over time. The stock grants become the incentive that many of the previously issued stock options no longer were.

Then there are the accounting considerations. FASB has not yet finalized its proposed changes to the rules for expensing of stock options, but the Board seems determined to make the practice, whatever form it takes, mandatory beginning sometime in the next year. Until then, there is no requirement that companies account for stock options as a compensation expense. Good deal for them. But stock grants like those issued by Microsoft are already accounted for as compensation, the value of the share being prorated over the vesting period. If the employee leaves before the shares fully vest, the company can recapture, as income, the amount already charged as an expense.

PLI's Pocket MBA Vol. 1, No. 30   December 17, 2003

Market Timing

Frequent securities buying and selling that traders engage in to take advantage of short-term market swings.

MARKET TIMING IN THE REAL WORLD:

To the extent that anyone was a complete stranger to the concept of market timing before the last several weeks, they are no longer. New York Attorney General Eliot Spitzer has made market timing a household term and the mutual funds that permitted it the latest bogeymen in what may turn out to be the ultimate dénouement of the stock market bubble-burst of 2000-2002. Some of the heretofore most trusted brand names in investing have succumbed to the inquiry into and exposure of this often-parasitic practice. (And denoting it as mere parasitism distinguishes it in kind from the late trading that some firms engaged in--trading that is blatantly unlawful. Market timing "merely" violates the company prospectuses of many of the funds that allowed special timing arrangements.)

So what exactly is so bad about market timing? Certainly it's good for the timers. They reap profits. And in trading individual stocks or mutual funds that are specifically geared toward market-timing strategies, this is simply free enterprise--anyone can buy and sell the same stock and fund all day long if they can afford the fees. But when it comes to the average mutual fund, market timing became the bastion of a lucky few who entered into special arrangements with fund companies. These arrangements permitted them to time funds and gain at the expense of those who were holding the funds for the long haul in reliance on the constraints of prospectus rules restricting or prohibiting such activity.

As noted in the October 31, 2003 edition of THE WALL STREET JOURNAL (Mutual Funds Vow to Fix Their Clocks, at C15), timers ply their trade most often in international stock funds. Why? Because those funds operate on the same schedule as domestic funds (4:00 p.m. close) even though the prices on stocks in those funds are often based on the prior day's trading. If you know foreign stocks are skyrocketing on Asian exchanges as the next day's trading begins there, you can hop into a fund in the United States, wait for the fund price to catch up to the news, then sell. The rapid purchase and sale impacts the amount of cash the fund manager has to keep for redemptions, which often requires that manager to sell more stock. This negatively impacts net asset value for long-term holders. Timing can also prompt fund managers to sell stocks to raise cash; this generates capital gains and tax liabilities, which are passed on to fund holders annually.

Of course, the fund managers did all this because they benefited from the timing agreements. So what will result? Certainly the proverbial heads will roll as the investigation expands and implicates more and more fund companies. And Spitzer promises criminal indictments to come. Then there will be the reforms, for this crisis is simply another challenge in the continuing corporate governance movement.

Some argue that no reforms are needed; all the SEC and fund companies have to do is enforce the rules on the books and in the prospectuses. Of course, that apparently hasn't worked, witness the SEC's action on December 3rd, 2003 proposing a new rule to firm up the previously not-so-firm 4:00 p.m. trading deadline. As for additional specifics currently on the table, many funds have already promised that they will repay management fees generated as a result of the timing arrangements. There are rumblings (and a House of Representatives bill) suggesting a legal requirement imposing short-term redemption fees (currently voluntary and limited to 2%, but which the SEC may raise), which many of the offending funds had in place already, and that funds be required to institute fair-value pricing, which is a way of averaging out those lagging international stock values. Only time will tell the entire extent of this, but it promises to play out publicly for quite a while.

AUTHOR UPDATE: Since 2003, the SEC has passed a slough of new regulations involving mutual funds, the most significant of which require funds to hire Chief Compliance Officers and increase the percentage of board members who must be independent. And in 2004, the SEC adopted a rule requiring mutual fund companies to disclose, via prospectus, "both the risks to fund shareholders of frequent purchases and redemptions of fund shares, and a fund's policies and procedures with respect to such frequent purchases and redemptions," its both of which are hallmarks of market timing. See www.sec.gov/rules/final/33-8408.htm

PLI's Pocket MBA Vol. 2, No. 1   January 7, 2004

Budgeting

Comprehensive process whereby an organization states its projected operational expectations in terms of revenues and expenses (and all other financial transactions) for a future period.

BUDGETING IN THE REAL WORLD:

Like many other things in finance, budgeting is deceptively complicated, especially given that everyone budgets, which makes the concept seem simple. Of course, everyone has the experience of creating a budget, only to find their expectations of what will occur dashed by changed circumstances. It was only a couple years ago that most governmental units were projecting surpluses; now changed circumstances have resulted in record deficits. And then there's

California. So the first thing to remember about budgeting is that it is all about projection; there is no particular reality about it, except the reality and predictability (to the extent that it exists) of human behavior, which is what allows individuals, corporate and government entities to create budgets in the first place.

So how do entities go about budgeting? Most organizations use what is known as baseline (or historical) budgeting. This means that a manager will take her current year's budgetary allotment, add the additional (or subtract the diminished) cost of doing business in the next year and arrive at a dollar figure. The base amount of this year's budget is not justified; it is simply assumed to exist as the fundamental (or baseline) cost of doing business. One of the great critiques of this type of budgeting (especially in the context of government spending) is that it results in waste and can result in the extrapolation of historical expenditure increases that have no current justification.

Baseline budgeting can be contrasted to Zero-Based Budgeting (ZBB), in which managers start their annual budget planning from a level of zero and must then justify all expenditures by creating "decision packages," (a fancy term for projects) ranking their importance and allotting amounts to be spent on them from most to least important. Many companies and governmental bodies have dabbled in ZBB, (President Carter instituted ZBB in the U.S. during his term in office) but it never really has caught on in any massive way. Why not?

Well, ZBB was touted as the most rational approach to budgeting because it requires that less useful/profitable operations be allotted less money. It is also said to create in managers a more intimate knowledge of their companies. But, there are a couple disadvantages to ZBB that have limited its usefulness.

The primary disadvantage to ZBB is that it is incredibly time-consuming (think about it, it's an annual, everything is on the chopping block mentality). ZBB Managers spend an inordinate amount of time creating their annual budgets; therefore the budgeting process can be an extraordinary expense in and of itself. A second disadvantage is related: many businesses are very predictable or have accumulated so much experience in determining demand--they know what they sell, how much and to whom--that given population growth and other macro trends, they can rather successfully forecast operations. Rather than recreate the wheel every year to end up with a budget very similar to what they would get if they simply used the baseline, they simply plan their budgets on the baseline method and invest the saved time to address problem areas of their operations.

Capital Budgeting

Process of determining whether and how to make capital outlays for a project, the benefits of which will accrue over many reporting periods.

CAPITAL BUDGETING IN THE REAL WORLD:

If you try to personalize capital budgeting, it's kind of like walking into a store, seeing a washer/dryer and, once having bought it, trying to figure out how many loads of laundry it will take before you will have saved exactly one quarter by not having to go the laundromat. In the corporate world, capital budgeting really boils down to that question: do the future benefits (cash inflows) derived from an asset justify the current outlays required to acquire the asset? And every company engages in this calculus on a recurring basis in order to determine whether to build new facilities and develop new products or to determine whether to replace old facilities or revamp or replace product lines. Boeing doesn't just decide to build the 787; Proctor & Gamble doesn't just repackage Tide. (Can you tell that Pocket MBA needs to do some laundry?) They determine whether the money they spend on these projects will be recouped over a specific time-period. If not, the project is probably a no go.

There are many techniques that companies use to determine whether to make capital expenditures. Among the more prevalently used are:

- Net Present Value (NPV): NPV is the amount by which the future cash inflows from the project exceed the initial investment. A discount rate is applied to the future inflows to express them in today's dollars (the so-called "time value of money"). When NPV > 0, an investment is worthwhile.
- Internal Rate of Return (IRR): IRR is the interest rate required to make the NPV of the future inflows equal zero. If the IRR is greater than the cost of your capital, the project is worthwhile.
- Accounting Rate of Return (ARR): ARR is the profit rate, determined by dividing the expected annual profit from an investment by the initial cost. The higher the ARR, the better the investment. Unlike NPV and IRR, ARR does not take into account the time value of money.
- Payback Period: Simple method of comparing the worthiness of different projects by determining the amount of time it takes to recoup the initial outlay. The shorter the payback period, the better the investment.
- Profitability Index: Slightly more complex method of ranking the investment-worthiness of differing projects. It is determined by dividing the NPV of a project by the initial investment. A profitability index greater than one signals a good investment.

You'll note that, as with most things economic, all of these methods require projecting inflows, outflows or interest rates or all three, and those projections can always turn out to be wrong. But nobody ever said economics was an exact science.

Off Balance Sheet Arrangements

Historically, any transaction, agreement or other arrangement that an SEC registrant has with an unconsolidated entity (e.g. any entity or person whose financial operations are not presented as part of the registrant's 10-Qs and 10Ks), the effects and risk of which are not plainly stated on the balance sheet.

OFF BALANCE SHEET ARRANGEMENTS IN THE REAL WORLD:

2003 was a year of transition for the infamous, Enron-destroying, scarlet letter wearing off balance sheet arrangement. Pursuant to the Sarbanes-Oxley Act, the SEC adopted new rules (see section 303(a) of Regulation S-K, 17 CFR sec. 229 et seq.) regarding quarterly and annual disclosure of these transactions, when "material," that became fully implemented for fiscal years ending after June 15, 2003 and December 15, 2003, respectively.

But the most overlooked detail in the public excoriation of these arrangements is that despite their slide into ill repute, a whole lot of companies have used and continue to use them legitimately (only now they will have to disclose them specifically). As stated in "MD&A 2003: The Off Balance Sheet Rules (a Mid-Cap Perspective)," by Marc Morgenstern (Kahn Kleinman LPA), they are "routinely used to minimize or reduce the financial risk and/or exposure of a company or other third parties," and they include "accounts receivable financing, synthetic leases and other real estate monetizations, parent guarantees of subsidiary debt, indemnification agreements and derivatives." (Each of these could merit an entire volume of Pocket MBA; for now, suffice to say they are all financing arrangements.)

The problems arose because (as always) a few bad apples (and you know who they are) spoiled the whole bunch by using them fraudulently (1) to disguise company-crippling amounts of debt as revenue or (2) to hide the crippling debt altogether. This was often done in an effort to maintain a debt-to-equity ratio low enough so that the companies could continue to tap credit markets (banks have this odd thing about not doling out money to those who may have trouble repaying) and to maintain the chimera of balance sheet health for investors.

For example, it has been reported that Enron had over 3,000 off balance sheet partnerships and arrangements. Most of these allowed it to shield incredibly risky investments from its investors by pushing the risks onto the investors of the infamous special purpose entities (SPEs) it and others created. As long as the stock market stayed aloft, making those SPEs look healthy, Enron appeared likewise, and nobody cared about the risk. But, when the economic bubble burst, these and other sleights-of-hand magically revealed themselves--down went Enron and in stepped Congress and, by SOX mandate, the SEC, to change the rules for all.

The new disclosure requirements, as synopsized by Morgenstern, encompass "a registrant's relationship with unconsolidated entities or other persons that either have (or are reasonably likely to have) a 'material current or future' effect on the issuer's 'financial condition, changes in financial condition, results of operations, liquidity, capital expenditures, capital resources or significant components of revenues or expenses.'" Companies have to reveal these arrangements quarterly, and as of the fiscal year ending the December 15 just past, they have to include in their annual reports a nifty little table disclosing certain financial obligations heretofore kept out of the bright lights.

Of course, the point of all this is transparency--investors should be able to discern the important financial activities of public companies. But, as always, the devil is in the details. Some have contended that CFOs will begin to over-report, by including not-so-material transactions in their reports, for fear of running afoul of the new rules. This could serve to confuse the average investors the rules were meant to help, as they wade through the summaries of endless, complex transactions (or, more likely, disregard them). Though as Morgenstern points out, "[c]onsistent with the SEC's drive for plain

English, transparency, and comprehensibility, the new required information must be presented so that a broad range of investors in the public markets (rather than only financial analysts, industry experts, or accountants) can understand the disclosure."

Additionally, as with many aspects of SOX, the impact on smaller companies is outsized. A relatively small transaction can be financially material to a small to medium sized company (and hence be required to be disclosed), but have no particular impact at all on a large company's financial condition (and hence be off balance sheet). This, of course, increases costs and impacts the bottom line of those smaller companies and says nothing about whether the transaction is above-board, in the Enron sense. But, this is all part of the grand experiment in corporate governance reform that is certain to play out and be revisited and refined over time.

PLI's Pocket MBA Vol. 2, No. 4   January 28, 2004

Earnings Restatements

Process whereby corporation revises inaccurate information (whether it was so due to intentional or accidental action) in its earnings release.

EARNINGS RESTATEMENTS IN THE REAL WORLD:

What do you do when you find $4.4 billion in your cookie jar? Well, you could ask Freddie Mac, the federally chartered issuer of low-income mortgage loans, which has said it will restate its earnings for the years 2000-2002 to account for just that amount. Of course, just how they "misplaced" that money is the $64,000 question FM is in the process of (very slowly) answering. And as its revelations seem likely to implicate investment banking firms as probably unwitting accomplices in its numbers games, these restatements may be the culminating events in the series of increasingly embarrassing earnings restatements that have plagued corporate America since Enron went belly up a few years ago.

An oddity of the Freddie Mac situation is that while most of the celebrated earnings restaters had to admit to overstating earnings--in addition to Enron, there were WorldCom, Tyco, Rite-Aid and AOL-Time Warner (which restated several times before reverting back to being just plain old Time Warner) and many others--Freddie Mac mostly understated its earnings for the years at issue (although it did overstate its first quarter 2001 earnings by $1 billion). Nonetheless, the inquiry that follows the restatements is always "Why?" And the answer determines whether and to what extent the company can earn back the trust of investors or stay in business at all.

Earnings restatements can be "innocent," that is they can result from any "math" error or innocent omission someone might make in a checkbook. They can also be prompted by non-fraudulent accounting errors or changes in accounting procedures (for instance, when Microsoft announced that it would no longer issue options and would exchange outstanding options for stock grants at the election of the employee, it said that it would revise its earnings statements for the years impacted). A company might have to restate if it has previously unreported losses or gains in a period resulting from discontinued operations or acquisitions. The list of innocent reasons could be endless, and in such cases, the company is generally not impacted in any material, negative way. (Of course, a restatement of earnings downward can always negatively impact stock price, even if the integrity of the company is not at issue.)

But the restatements in the public eye since 1999 have been almost exclusively the result of some kind of accounting manipulation or outright fraud, much of which was the catalyst for many of the governance reforms that have since become law. In the late 1990s, as pressure on go-go companies mounted to present ever-better earnings reports and forecasts, the guilty ones discovered that the easiest way to achieve inflated earnings was by manipulating the timing of revenue recognition or by inventing revenue altogether, often with incredibly complex balance sheet machinations.

So what happens when companies restate? Well, it depends on the level of chicanery. The punishment can range from "mere" decimation of stock price and reshuffling of the executive suite and/or boardroom (e.g. the former AOL-Time Warner) to bankruptcy, if the extent of the fraud is such that the revised balance sheet reveals an unstable financial condition (Enron, WorldCom). But there is always consequence, at least until Freddie Mac.

Freddie Mac's stock price has gradually fallen, but not in any drastic way, and its CEO has stepped down. But beyond that so far, not much has happened except bad publicity. The intriguing thing about Freddie Mac is that its Congressional charter exempts it from SEC regulation, so it is not in the same hot seat as other public companies. And there is some worry that if Freddie Mac reveals serious misdeeds and were to be punished (by its regulatory agency, the Office of Federal Housing Enterprise Oversight or by the NYSE, where its stock is traded), a major crisis in the housing market would ensue (Freddie Mac's mortgages back hundreds of billions of dollars in mortgages), potentially requiring federal intervention and bailout.

So it seems unlikely that Freddie Mac would be subject to the fate of some other celebrated restaters, regardless of the eventual revelations. Maybe that answers the question posed at the outset. When you find $4.4 billion in the cookie jar, well, you just keep going. When you have that much money, who's going to stop you?

PLI's Pocket MBA Vol. 2, No. 5   February 4, 2004

Productivity

The amount of economic output produced per given unit of input.

PRODUCTIVITY IN THE REAL WORLD:

Jaws dropped when the U.S. Department of Labor reported recently that productivity in the third quarter (2003) rose 9.4 percent from the second quarter; arguments ensued about whether this was a great event or merely a good one to be tempered by fears that such increases meant that the U.S. economy was producing more goods without a corresponding need for new workers (the so-called jobless recovery). Which is correct? Perhaps both. Perhaps more important a question is what is this "productivity?"

According to the Bureau of Labor Statistics (BLS), "[p]roductivity is measured by comparing the amount of goods and services produced with the inputs which were used in production. Labor productivity is the ratio of the output of goods and services to the labor hours devoted to the production of that output." http://www.bls.gov/lpc/peoplebox.htm#Q01. Of course, that's just fancy-speak for how many widgets each worker produces per hour. This is important because the BLS reports "labor cost represents two-thirds of the value of output produced," where unit labor costs = hourly compensation/output per hour. So if a worker earning $15/hour produces 5 widgets/hour, the unit labor cost is $3/widget. A rise in productivity by 9.4 percent, as occurred in the third quarter, means that the same worker produced 5.47 widgets for the same 15 dollars, resulting in a drop in unit labor cost to $2.74/widget. The company therefore earns an extra 26 cents per widget and puts that in the bank or back into the business or whatever.

The skeptical crowd argues that the company is able to forego new hiring because it is getting all the widgets it needs from the same worker making the same wage. But eventually, in every economic recovery, a tipping point is reached at which that worker cannot produce any more widgets per hour than she is already producing. If demand remains steady, no problem. But if demand increases, new labor is needed. And as anyone who runs a machine at full tilt for too long knows, eventually the machine breaks. If that worker continues to be strained to the maximum, her productivity might actually decline. Thus, in theory (and generally in practice) as worker productivity reaches the equilibrium between those two points (where worker capacity meets worker breaking point), new workers also have to be hired.

So in the beginning of an economic recovery, when demand is at its slackest and only beginning to rise, the skeptics are correct: current workforce can pick up new demand, and productivity tends to increase without a corresponding increase in employment. The result is that corporate profits soar, giving them the financial ability to hire, but which they don't do, making their profits soar even higher as demand increases. Only later, when demand eventually outstrips the current workforce's ability to produce, do companies begin to hire, spending some of that profit.

And that trend appears to have begun toward the end of 2003. Once that occurs, it theoretically begins a cycle of increasing demand and supply, as newly hired workers earn paychecks and begin to spend them. (This discussion, of course, does not address the effects of the outsourcing revolution, which arguably, does not change the calculus, but merely the location of the new jobs. Nor does it address the contentions of some that this is the first economic recovery of the computer age, and its impact on productivity is such that the old model may no longer apply.)

In the long run, increased productivity is, and always has been, a good thing for both employer and employee, even if in the short run, it gives the appearance of stifling employment growth.

PLI's Pocket MBA Vol. 2, No. 6	February 11, 2004

Fair Value Pricing

Method of calculating mutual fund net asset value that, rather than being based on the closing prices for all the equities in a fund, takes into account a variety of factors that impact the prices of those equities in the event the closing prices are not reflective of the actual value, were the fund to buy them at the close of trading on the NYSE.

FAIR VALUE PRICING IN THE REAL WORLD:

You would think, based on the hubbub of the mutual fund scandal and resultant calls for greater use of fair value pricing (FVP), that FVP was some revolutionary concept. Au contraire. FVP has been around as long as has been the Investment Company Act of 1940 (the Act) that spawned the modern mutual fund industry. Indeed, the Act requires a fund to make a good faith determination of the fair value of its securities when accurate market quotes are either unavailable or unreliable. And in a Proposed Rule now under consideration, the SEC is seeking to require funds to better explain the circumstances in which they use FVP.

Unavailability or unreliability can occur for a number of reasons, including the halting of trading for a domestic equity, or because events overseas that occur after a country's market closes (like an earthquake, political strife or even after-hours trading on bourses outside the country at issue), but during the NYSE's trading hours, render the closing price of a foreign equity obsolete.

Accordingly, the concept of FVP shows up in mutual fund prospectuses in many ways, but typically as in this excerpt from one mutual fund prospectus:

> The fund's assets are valued primarily on the basis of market quotations or official closing prices. If market quotations or official closing prices are not readily available or do not accurately reflect fair value for a security, or if a security's value has been materially affected by events occurring after the close of the exchange or market on which the security is principally traded (for example, a foreign exchange or market), that security may be valued by another method that the Board of Trustees believes accurately reflects fair value. A security's valuation may differ depending on the method used for determining value.

Of course, even after reading that, the question screams out: "What is the method of valuation?" Well, there could be many. For instance, if a stock closes at a certain price on foreign exchanges, but an event occurs subsequently that causes it to trade substantially higher or lower on other exchanges, the fund company might look to see if there is a dominant price in those after-hours trades. The bottom line is that FVP aims to achieve the fairest approximation of the true value of equities. Because the valuing of equities is a relative concept, whether FVP is at all possible is an entirely different question.

AUTHOR UPDATE: In 2004, The SEC adopted a rule requiring open-end mutual funds to explain in their prospectuses both the circumstances under which they will use fair value pricing and the effects of using fair value pricing. See www.sec.gov/rules/final/33-8408.htm

PLI's Pocket MBA Vol. 2, No. 7　　　　　　February 18, 2004

The Specialist System

Human element that maintains a "fair and orderly" trading flow on the auction-based New York Stock Exchange.

THE SPECIALIST SYSTEM IN THE REAL WORLD:

Today, five specialist firms reportedly have reached a tentative $240 million accord with the SEC to settle allegations of mishandling trades and skimming profits on the floor of the Big Board. This latest segment of the investment community to receive investigative scrutiny is also one of the most secretive and least understood. The specialist system, which has roots on the NYSE dating back to 1875, is comprised of a select group (there are only seven specialist firms employing over 440 specialists) of people who are members of the NYSE. One specialist represents each stock on the NYSE, and each specialist handles five to ten stocks. So "specialist," as a term, refers to the individual's specialization in a given stock.

When a person wants to buy or sell stock, they will generally place a "market" order, which means they will buy or sell at whatever price another individual is willing to accept. This process is fairly routine and does not require the services of a specialist. The "special" function of the specialist is to represent, as agent and broker, the purchase and sale of individual stocks assigned to him when that perfect match doesn't exist, that is, when there is an imbalance in supply and demand. The specialist does this by matching willing buyers with sellers when those buyers and sellers place "limit" orders (a price above or below which they will not buy or sell). So if X wants to buy 500 shares of XYZ Corp. for $10.23 a share and Y wants to sell 200 shares at $10.23 and Z wants to sell 300 shares at $10.23, but Q will not sell his 1,000 shares for less than $10.25, the specialist matches the willing buyer, X, with the willing sellers, Y and Z, and gets a commission. Q is left out of the deal. Simple enough.

But the specialist's true power arises when the imbalance in supply and demand for their assigned stocks is such that there is no supply or demand at all for a willing buyer or seller, as in the example above, where Q wants to sell 1,000 shares of XYZ Corp. for $10.25, but nobody wants to buy it for that price. When this occurs, the specialist wears the infamous moniker of "market maker," swooping in to buy (in the above example) or sell the unwanted shares, thus creating the market for them. They do this using their own personal accounts (which non-specialist NYSE members are not permitted to do). This can change the market price of shares, and the specialist then can turn around and sell (or buy) shares to whomever else at the market price. That is alleged flaw-of-the-system number one: there's an inherent conflict of interest when you can do your job by trading for yourself.

Alleged flaw number two? In order to understand the current clamor over the NYSE specialists, you have to understand that every other major exchange (e.g. NASDAQ) currently matches buyers and sellers electronically--without any human intervention. But the NYSE still uses the floor-trading system so masterfully portrayed in any number of films (Eddie Murphy's "Trading Places" comes to mind, though it involved futures trading: "Sell, Mortimer, sell!"), and thus specialists do the work of computers on the NYSE. As such, they are also in possession of the most precious "inside information" a trader could possible have: they know at what prices people want to buy and sell individual stocks before trades are actually made. So that is alleged flaw-of-the-system number two: temptation to take advantage of the informational advantage.

To combat the alleged flaws, the system relies on NYSE rules that require specialists to act in the interest of the customer and to cease trading for their own accounts when there is a price match between buyer and seller. Of course that only works if there is no corruption in the system, but that is exactly what has been alleged, not only in the investigation settled today, but also in a lawsuit filed by the California Public Employees' Retirement System (CalPERS). CalPERS' complaint alleges that each and every one of the seven specialist firms engaged in at least one of three types of fraudulent activity: freezing, front-running and interpositioning. Each is essentially a method of enabling the specialists to trade on their own accounts despite the pendency of matching buy and sell orders which would otherwise keep the specialists on the trading sidelines.

The CalPERS suit, filed in December 2003, was the culmination of months of controversy involving the NYSE that started with the resignation of former chairman Richard Grasso over allegations about his excessive compensation package. During that time there have been increasing calls for the NYSE to drop the human element in its trading system (the calls have come from leading investment figures, such as Fidelity Investments and Vanguard founder John C. Bogle). Until now, the NYSE has resisted change, but its new CEO, John Thain, has indicated a willingness to increase the amount of electronic trading on the Big Board. Indeed, momentum being what it is, some think it is only a matter of time before the specialist system is a thing of the past.

PLI's Pocket MBA Vol. 2, No. 8　　　　　　　　February 25, 2004

Monetary Policy

Federal Reserve Board's actions that influence the availability and cost of money and credit as part of its efforts to promote national economic goals.

MONETARY POLICY IN THE REAL WORLD:

On January 28, 2004, shortly after 2:15 p.m., stock prices plummeted. Nothing particularly earth-shattering had occurred, as far as the public was concerned: no terrorism, no indications that the economy was in any different shape from what anyone had imagined, no burgeoning corporate scandal (although the Martha Stewart trial proceeded apace). All was relatively quiet, except that the Federal Open Market Committee (FOMC), the policy arm of the Federal Reserve Board (the Fed), had issued its first statement of 2004, which included the following:

- The FOMC decided today to keep its target for the federal funds rate at 1 percent.
- The Committee continues to believe that an accommodative stance on monetary policy, coupled with robust underlying growth in productivity, is providing important ongoing support to economic activity.
- With inflation quite low and resource use slack, the Committee believes that it can be patient in removing its policy accommodation.

This can be contrasted with the FOMC's December 9, 2003 release, which was worded almost exactly the same except for the last bullet point above. In December, that part read "[h]owever, with inflation quite low and resource use slack, the Committee believes that policy accommodation can be maintained for a considerable period." According to market experts, both real and imagined, this change in language spooked the markets because it was an indication that interest rates would rise sooner rather than later.

That is a classic example of monetary policy at work. In reality, the FOMC did nothing, but in stating it would do nothing, it altered people's expectations about what it might do in the future and hence changed the market's view of what the costs of money and doing business might be down the road, leading to a shift in asset allocation. Also disproved by that single event were the theories of those who postulated that the Fed loses policy-making leverage as interest rates approach zero. Indeed, as the FOMC showed, its statements about how long interest rates might hover near zero are every bit as powerful as raising or lowering interest rates.

Monetary policy in the United States is a three-legged animal, of which the FOMC's open market operations (that is, the purchase and sale of government securities at specified target interest rates--the vaunted federal funds rate above) is the principal leg. The other two are the Reserve Market and the Discount Rate. Each merits its own Pocket MBA, but in brief, together they create supply and demand equilibrium in liquidity.

Banks are required to maintain a certain reserve of money in their own vault and at one of the 12 Federal Reserve Banks. When eligible banks need money to meet their reserve requirements, they can borrow it from the Fed for very short periods (usually overnight) at a specified interest or discount rate (so-called because it's less than the rate at which you or Pocket MBA or even big-shot corporations can borrow). Before banks borrow money from the Fed, they will usually seek to borrow it at the federal funds rate (also overnight) from other banks that have excess reserves at a Federal Reserve Bank. When disequilibria occur in this system, the open market operations take over, and the Fed will buy and sell government securities to adjust the amount of money in the system--it is this purchasing and selling that determines the federal funds rate. You can read about this very complex, but well-oiled, system in detail at the Fed's web site, www.federalreserve.gov.

Whenever the Fed changes monetary policy, there are eventual ripple effects throughout the economy. This is why traders of securities react so quickly to even the slightest hints of changes, such as occurred on January 28th. When the Fed acts in a manner that increases the fed funds rate, other short-term interest rates (like those on Treasury bills) begin to rise, leading to a reduction in the amount of money available for lending. This leads to higher costs of borrowing, which slows growth, etc. Slower growth translates into lower corporate profits, which makes smart traders sell stocks.

Back to January 28th. Many would say nothing happened on January 28th--that accommodative monetary policy (i.e. a low federal funds rate) remains intact. But those who are sensitive to changes in interest rate policy shoot first and ask questions later. To them, the wording of the FOMC release was a change in monetary policy because it signaled that the era of the one percent federal funds rate is finally coming to an end. Thus, doing nothing is akin to doing something huge.

And this is why, despite the fact that nothing happened on January 28th, stocks sold off. A caveat to this is that when Fed Chairman Alan Greenspan addressed Congress two weeks ago (in what used to be the Humphrey-Hawkins testimony, but is now just an annual tradition), his statements seemed to reassure investors that rates would remain at one percent for quite some time, and the Markets shot up, briefly. Change in monetary policy? Who knows?

PLI's Pocket MBA Vol. 2, No. 9	March 3, 2004

Dutch Auction IPO

An IPO in which the underwriter holds the issuers shares out for public auction, rather than selling the issue directly to its clients.

DUTCH AUCTION IPOs IN THE REAL WORLD:

Pocket MBA was doing a Google search on the largest IPOs of the past few years when it realized that Google's upcoming-out party will dwarf anything in recent memory, and not just in dollar amount, but in "buzz," which became a key component of success during the '90s IPO boom. And the latest buzz is that the Internet search portal is considering eschewing the traditional IPO route to go for a Dutch Auction IPO instead.

The pre-offering nuts and bolts of a Dutch Auction IPO are no different from that of a traditional IPO. The company still has to find an underwriter to handle the offering and still has to file a registration of its securities with the SEC, and then wait for the SEC to comment on the registration. Once satisfied with the company's response to any comments, the SEC will declare the registration statement effective. It is there that the similarities start to end.

Briefly, in the traditional IPO, the company and/or underwriters take their offering on the road to try and sell it to the underwriter's favored institutional clients. The clients tell the underwriter how many shares they are willing to buy at the price the underwriter has designated, which is somewhat below what the underwriter thinks the shares will fetch once they hit the open market. Assuming the underwriter finds a sufficient demand for the shares, it eventually buys them from the company and then turns around and sells them to the institutions, which distribute them to their favored clients and then the shares are unleashed on the market, at which time the public can begin to play. Of course, the public is usually paying a handsome premium to the offering price for their shares, a premium they may never recoup, as the price of the stock often never regains its initial highs once the insiders to the deal start to flip their stock (sell into the premium).

In the Dutch Auction IPO, on the other hand, the underwriter will essentially do an online road show for the world at large. Thus anyone who has a brokerage account with the underwriter can put a bid on the available shares. The bidding will stay open for several weeks, and at the end, everyone who bid at or above the "clearing price," that is the highest price at which the underwriter can sell all the shares, gets the shares at the clearing price. WR Hambrecht is the primary purveyor of the Dutch auction in the United States, and on its web site, it describes a hypothetical bidding process (which it calls "OpenIPO") as follows:

- IronBit.com offers 1 million shares at a projected price range of $8-$13. Mr. Smith wants IronBit.com shares, so he bids for 300 shares at $12 per share.
- After collecting all bids, WR Hambrecht & Co conducts the OpenIPO auction. Working from the highest bid toward the lowest, the auction finds that at $12, 1 million IronBit.com shares are bid for. So $12 becomes the "clearing price" because investors wanted at least 1 million shares at $12. This amount also represents the maximum public offering price for IronBit.com

shares. So Mr. Smith receives shares of IronBit.com - but how many?
- Because investors wanted exactly 1 million shares at $12, everyone bidding at least $12 receives the number of shares they bid for.
- If the number of shares bid for exceeds the number of shares in the offering, WR Hambrecht & Co allocates on a pro-rata basis. Under these circumstances, allocations will be rounded to multiples of 100 or 1,000 shares, depending on the size of the bid.

Both issuer and investor supposedly benefit from the Dutch Auction IPO. The issuer benefits because it doesn't have to give up the premium on the shares that the institutional clients earn when they flip their shares on the open market; the small investor because they don't have to pay the premium to get the shares--they get the same price as the big boys.

Despite these alleged benefits, Dutch Auction IPOs haven't really caught on. Traditional IPOs still rule the roost, due to a tradition that lands shares in the hands of investors who may hold a company's stock for long periods of time. Dutch Auction IPOs could potentially turn the IPO market into just another day trading event. But there really isn't enough data to determine their impact. Google may have a lot to say about that.

AUTHOR UPDATE: Google did, indeed, do its IPO via Dutch Auction, and on August 19, 2004, it unleashed its shares on the market. Still, despite the overwhelming success of Google's Dutch Auction, there has been no particular upsurge for this method of offering.

Just In Time (JIT)

Management philosophy that seeks to eliminate economic waste in the production and distribution of goods by manufacturing products as they are ordered by customers (or "just in time"), rather than in anticipation of orders by customers.

JIT IN THE REAL WORLD:

For anyone who grew up in the 1970s, there was a colossal and ongoing battle (that continues to this day to some extent) pitting McDonald's against Burger King for hearts, minds and mouths. The battle often dominated the public airwaves.

McDonald's, ever the industry leader, advertised its Big Macs with a cute jingle that everyone tried to sing the fastest (there were even contests): "Two all beef patties, special sauce, lettuce, cheese, pickles, onions on a sesame seed bun." The regular burgers came with ketchup, mustard and onions. When one walked into a McDonald's, one saw rows of these creations ready to go. Pity anyone who didn't like onions or mustard--that interrupted the assembly line and required a substantial wait because McDonald's inventory system assumed everyone wanted the product just the way they made it and so each McDonald's made dozens of standardized burgers for the anticipated number of customers who would arrive. And as long as the customer wanted that burger, the wait was close to nil--hence the moniker, "fast food."

Burger King was (and is) always number two. The chain, with its Whopper, could never really crack McDonald's dominance, though it had its fans. What to do? Well, Burger King came up with what seemed to be, to all observers, a marketing gimmick: "Have it your way." Thenceforward, when one walked into Burger King, one would see a few pre-made Whoppers and burgers for those who liked the works. But, when a customer ordered something different, the cashier's clarion call for the special burger would be announced over the PA system to the eager burger chefs waiting in the kitchen: "Whopper, no onion, no mayo." The order didn't throw the system off at all; it was designed to work that way.

In practice, Burger King's marketing effort to surpass McDonald's was a rudimentary, hybrid example of JIT production and inventory. The company produced the burgers as people ordered them. The burgers didn't sit around getting cold, so theoretically there should have been less waste. This has benefits and drawbacks, which Pocket MBA will get to below.

The development of JIT is accredited to the Japanese, Toyota Motor Corporation specifically. It swept through the American manufacturing landscape during the 1980s and has been applied to all manners of business models, including service businesses. In JIT management, inventory overhang is considered idle, and hence wasted, capital. Thus, JIT is, at root, an effort to reduce waste to a bare minimum. It requires companies to institute the most rigorous of quality control systems, because if there is no inventory backlog, there is no room for error in manufacturing.

Under a traditional, inventory-based system of production, it is assumed that a certain percentage of defective products will be produced and sold. The defects are made up for by having stock on hand that can replace the defective products. But the system is more costly to the company because in order to have inventory, the company needs storage space and employees to manage that space. In the ideal, JIT reduces the need for various layers of corporate expense, and relies on superior employee input to "save the day," as it were. This also simplifies the company's cost accounting, because instead of maintaining separate accounts to track materials and work-in-process, the two are combined into one resources account. This should also theoretically make the company more profitable.

Now, back to burgers. Assume two buses, racing across the country. They are prescheduled for a lunch stop at noon. One goes to McDonald's, the other goes to Burger King. McDonald's, with its inventory system, could accommodate most of these people faster because it had finished product on hand to serve. Burger King had to prepare each burger separately. Which bus will win the race? Some might argue that the people receiving the Burger King burgers got a fresher burger, but McDonald's doesn't serve really old, spoiled burgers, and if the aim is fast food, which company is serving its mission better? That's rhetorical, but it serves to point out that JIT may work in some industries or businesses and not in others. It all depends on various supply and demand calculi, like that unexpected busload of people, which could happen in many industries.

You can do a web search and find numerous stories chronicling entities for which JIT worked and entities for which it didn't and which later switched back to a traditional production style. As for Pocket MBA? The initial draft of this issue was finished on February 11, 2004 and placed into inventory. But production and copyediting was completed about five minutes before you received it. And that was just in time.

PLI's Pocket MBA Vol. 2, No. 11　　　　　　　March 17, 2004

EBITDA

Earnings Before Interest Taxes Depreciation & Amortization

EBITDA IN THE REAL WORLD:

Pocket MBA was reading some public company earnings reports recently and felt nostalgic for the days when countless companies' stock price would soar after issuance of fabulously exciting earnings releases trumpeting their EBITDA. The measure became a compliance bogeyman in the wake of the WorldCom scandal because of the belief that the use of EBITDA obscured investors' view of a company's actual bottom line. Of course, that was before passage of Sarbanes-Oxley and subsequently, SEC adoption of Regulation G, which requires public companies that issue non-GAAP pro forma financial disclosures, of which EBITDA is one, to note that point in their releases and to reconcile the non-GAAP information to the closest applicable GAAP measure. The companies must also report why they believe that the non-GAAP measure is useful for investors.

But just in case anyone thought that EBITDA, as a way of reporting earnings was dead since Reg. G went into effect, here's some news: statements like the following one, from NASDAQ-listed Workstream, have become a staple of earnings season on Wall Street:

EBITDA and EBITDA per share are non-GAAP financial measures within the meaning of Regulation G promulgated by the Securities and Exchange Commission. EBITDA is commonly defined as earnings before interest, taxes, depreciation and amortization. We believe that EBITDA provides useful information to investors as it excludes transactions not related to the core cash operating business activities. We believe that excluding these transactions allows investors to meaningfully trend and analyze the performance of our core cash operations. All companies do not calculate EBITDA in the same manner, and EBITDA as presented by Workstream may not be comparable to EBITDA presented by other companies. Workstream defines EBITDA as earnings or loss before interest, taxes, depreciation and amortization. Included, following the financial statements, is a reconciliation of net loss to EBITDA and EBITDA per share that should be read in conjunction with the financial statements.

So why is it that so many early-stage capital-intensive businesses and even mature business that have special circumstances impacting their bottom line still report EBITDA when it is agreed upon that it is not a true reflection of a company's cash flow? Well the answer, in part, is in the Regulation G disclosure above: "it excludes transactions not related to the core cash operating business activities [and] allows investors to meaningfully trend and analyze the performance of our core cash operations." Despite all the controversy, EBITDA can still deliver a pretty good sense of how well a particular business is functioning from an operations perspective and in relation to its industry peers.

Let's say you started a public company, Big Sales, Bigger Debts, Inc. (BSBD), which is in the business of self-cleaning windows. (Cool idea, huh?) Assume that the business borrows $10 billion to buy heavy machinery. (Don't ask who would lend that kind of cash; Pocket MBA remembers from Economics 101 that in demonstrating a point, outrageous assumptions are a necessity.) Further assume that the equipment is to be depreciated over, say 20 years (so the numbers are nice and round), that's $500 million per year. Also, there's interest on the loan to be paid annually. Assume the company owes no taxes and just ignore amortization for the sake of simplicity and outrageousness.

In BSBD's first year of business, it sells $100 million in windows at an ongoing operations' cost of $40 million and projects future sales increasing to the billion-dollar a year mark. On a GAAP basis, the company lost hundreds of millions of dollars. But on an operations basis, alone, the company made $60 million. This is important because, although the company will not be cash flow positive for several years, an investor can determine that there is a demand for self-cleaning windows that can be supported by the everyday cost of running the business. And that can coexist very nicely alongside Regulation G.

Revenue Recognition

The point in time when payment from a customer may be considered received.

REVENUE RECOGNITION IN THE REAL WORLD:

In the personal pocketbook world, revenue recognition seems like an incredibly simple concept. You go into a store, buy and pay for something that you take home, and the process is finished. So why is improper revenue recognition acknowledged far and wide to be the primary source of financial statement fraud? It's easy to create examples that show why. You agree to sell your car (to someone who answers your ad in the paper) for $500. (Don't laugh--Pocket MBA sold its Geo Metro to a nice lady in Lancaster, PA for $500 so her son could take it apart, which if you've ever seen a Metro, is like taking a Lego toy apart, but Pocket MBA digresses). The agreement occurs on Monday, the last day of your fiscal quarter (just pretend you use fiscal quarters), and you and the purchaser sign a contract at 2 p.m. Consider the following scenarios:

(1) You deliver the car on Monday at 2 p.m., and the buyer pays you at the same time

(2) You deliver the car on Monday at 2 p.m., and the buyer pays you a week later

(3) You deliver the car on Monday at 2 p.m., and the buyer pays you $200 at that time and the remaining $300 a week later

(4) The buyer pays you on Monday at 2 p.m., but you don't deliver the car until a week later

(5) You agree to the deal on Monday and money and car exchange hands, but your spouse, who also wants to sell the car for $500, but who holds joint title and must also sign the contract, isn't available to do so until the next week.

If you were a company, each of these scenarios would present a different issue in revenue recognition because, except in the first scenario, the deal, though contemplated, is not 100% complete until after the fiscal quarter has ended; hence the recognition of the receipt of the $500 may have to be delayed.

The SEC has summarized its views (which are an amalgam of various FASB and other accounting board publications on the subject) on revenue recognition in Staff Accounting Bulletin 101 (SAB 101). SAB 101 relies heavily on FASB Statement of Financial Accounting Concepts 5 (SFAC5), which defines "recognition" as the "process of formally recording or incorporating an item in the financial statements of an entity as an asset, liability, revenue, expense, or the like." SFAC5, Paragraph 83 provides that revenues cannot be recognized until they are (a) "realized or realizable," and (b) earned.

Revenue is realized or realizable "when products (goods or services), merchandise, or other assets are exchanged for cash or claims to cash," or when "related assets received or held are readily convertible to known amounts of cash or claims to cash." SFAC 5, Par. 83(a). Revenue is earned "when the entity has substantially accomplished what it must do to be entitled to the benefits represented by the revenues," that is to say, it has delivered the goods. SFAC 5, Par. 83(b).

SAB 101 interprets SFAC5, Paragraph 83 to mean that revenue

is realized or realizable and earned (and hence recognizable) when each of four criteria are met:

- Persuasive evidence of an arrangement (to sell something) exists
- Delivery has occurred or services have been rendered
- The seller's price to the buyer is fixed or determinable, and
- Collectibility is reasonably assured

You can apply these to the scenarios involving the sale of your car to get a feel for how revenue recognition works in an easy situation. This also demonstrates how easy it is for chicanery, not to mention honest uncertainty, to enter the calculus.

In scenario 1, the revenue can clearly be recognized in the quarter just ended. In scenarios 2 and 3, there is persuasive evidence of an arrangement; delivery has occurred and the seller's price is fixed and determinable. But, depending on your feelings about the trustworthiness of the buyer as to paying a week later, you may or may not be able to recognize the revenue in the current quarter. Under scenario 4, since you haven't delivered the car, the revenue is not recognizable, even though you have the money in hand. Finally, in scenario 5 (one which is based on a much more formal example in SAB 101), since your spouse is required to sign the contract and could theoretically nix the deal, the revenue cannot be recognized until the next quarter when her signature will demonstrate "persuasive evidence of an arrangement."

So there you have it, a revenue recognition primer. As always, Pocket MBA tries to make things simple and homespun. In your dealings with clients, obviously the scenarios will be much more complex and obtuse (heck, SAB 101 is 28 pages long--you know the SEC is way beyond selling broken down Metros) so check with your client's accountant and visit the SEC website or FASB's website for information on how to deal with sale of a fleet of Mercedes or multi-year gym memberships.

Burn Rate

For companies that don't earn a profit, it is the rate at which the company uses cash on hand, or its negative cash flow from operations, for a given period of time.

BURN RATE IN THE REAL WORLD:

Pocket MBA used to play a rudimentary computer game (this was back when computers fit neatly into an entire football stadium) that involved landing a lunar module on the moon. The idea was to use fuel at a rate that would maximize the possibility of making a safe landing. If you used too much fuel, you crashed to the surface with an empty tank. Ever the cagey Rocket Man (the Elton John song always seemed to be playing in the background), Pocket MBA conserved fuel so as to land with as full a tank as possible--alas, this was also futile, for not burning enough fuel led to crash landing as well because the module was weighed down by excess resources that should have been used to get to the promised land. Turned out there was an optimal range of fuel-use that would get you to the surface--don't burn too much but don't burn too little.

Not coincidentally, fuel use was called the "burn rate." And if you think about fledgling, unprofitable, cutting-edge industry companies, especially in terms of the lunar landing analogy (but it applies to established, but for-whatever-reason-no-longer-profitable companies, as well--think United Airlines as it flew into bankruptcy), you get an idea of how the burn rate works. Companies need to use fuel at a rate that allows them to reach positive cash flow. Use too much and crash landing (bankruptcy) ensues; hoard it and the business cannot stay on the cutting edge, inviting competitors to pass it by, resulting in declining sales, increasing negative cash flow and crash landing again. Quite a balancing act.

A new company (public or private) gets injections of venture capital in one form or another. That's fuel--stockholder's equity and borrowed capital mostly--to run and expand an unprofitable business. That works as long as the fuel tank doesn't reach zero. If the company realizes it will reach zero, it can seek more fuel, by issuing more debt or equity. The issue, for both companies and investors (who have the same vested interest in knowing if there is a point in the near future at which a company will need to seek new financing) is to figure out the burn rate so that zero won't come.

Burn rates can be calculated for any period of time, but generally, the monthly or quarterly burn rate gives a good picture (short- and long-term) of a company's expenses. However, when crisis occurs, burn rates can be expressed in days or weeks, if necessary. Refer to a company's statement of cash flow to determine its burn rate. Choose your desired time period, and add up cash outflows, including debt repayment (some analysts recommend including expenditures on capital investment to get a more complete picture of cash burn). That gives you the periodic burn rate.

For a hypothetical company, let's assume that number is $10 million per month. You can then determine how many periods a company can survive (without changing its behavior) by adding the amount of cash on hand and any additional capital that is coming in through sales or debt infusion; then divide that number by the burn rate. If our hypothetical company has $70 million, then it has seven months within which to secure financing or become cash flow positive. It can extend this period by reducing its burn rate.

The best tonic for slowing a burn rate is increasing sales. But, failing that, companies typically lay off employees or cut back costs in other areas, such as advertising and capital investment. But remember the lunar lander--no matter how many cutbacks the company makes, unless it becomes cash flow positive, the burn will force the company to eventually seek additional fuel or crash.

By the way, Pocket MBA never successfully landed on the moon.

Depreciation

The gradual expensing of the cost of an operational business asset (until zero) over its useful (estimated) life.

DEPRECIATION IN THE REAL WORLD:

Pocket MBA just filed for an extension to file its taxes. Things had been going swimmingly until the printer spit out IRS Publication 946: How to Depreciate Property. This prompted a trip to the refrigerator and several games of Spider Solitaire before Pocket MBA could actually face the 111-page tome. But after a few minutes, Pocket MBA was rejoicing at its newfound ability to fully write down the cost of every expenditure it made on business equipment in 2003. How did Pocket MBA do this? Well, clearly, this is not your father's depreciation anymore. In fact, it's not really depreciation at all, but rather a combination of depreciation and government-allowed deductions against the cost of business property that people think of as additional depreciation allowances.

Depreciation is one area in which accounting and the tax code are coconspirators in cooking up an expensing soufflé that benefits anyone who runs a small business. Between the Modified Accelerated Cost Recovery System (MACRS), Internal Revenue Code (IRC) Section 179 and bonus depreciation rules enacted last year, a small business owner can write off huge chunks of business equipment in the year it is purchased. While this stands traditional concepts of equipment expensing on their head, the policy justification for allowing this is straightforward enough: accelerating write-offs encourages small businesses to buy more equipment.

Nonetheless, depreciation, from an accounting standpoint, hasn't really changed a bit. So let's start from that basis (no tax-pun intended) and zip through to section 179 and the bonus depreciation rules now in place as a result of JGTRRA (that's the Job Growth and Training Relief Reconciliation Act of 2003) to see just what a small business owner can accomplish with a little work or a good tax accountant. (Pocket MBA apologizes in advance to all the accountants and tax lawyers for turning what should be a treatise into this short synopsis.)

Depreciation starts from the premise that when a business invests in a plant and equipment, the cost is an expense to the business and so should be deducted from income. But because the equipment lasts more than one year, it has to be expensed over the many years it is used (its "useful life"), which is traditionally a predetermined number of years for each piece of equipment. Once that useful life has passed, the asset no longer has value for accounting purposes, and it doesn't matter that a business might still be using the equipment; it's still worthless. So useful life engages a certain generally accepted fiction about how long equipment actually lasts in principle.

The depreciable cost of equipment is its acquisition price less salvage value, and there are numerous accounting methods for depreciating this cost, each of which subscribes to one of two different approaches to the value of an asset. First, there is straight-line depreciation--that's where an equal amount of an asset's life is considered used up every year. If a machine has a depreciable cost of $1,000 and has a useful life of ten years, the depreciation expense is 10 percent of depreciable cost per year, or $100.

Most other methods of depreciation operate from the premise that a larger percentage of an asset is used up at the beginning of its life. That's accelerated depreciation. (You know the old saying, "Once you drive a new car off the lot, it loses half its value." Same thing.) There are numerous methods of accelerated depreciation currently in use. (And there can be as many more as the human brain can cook up.) For example, the double (or 200%) declining balance method requires that a constant percentage (one that is equal to twice the straight-line percentage) be multiplied annually by the remaining value of an asset. So that a $1,000 machine with a 10-year life would depreciate 20% per year, as follows:

- Year 1 - $200, remaining value - $800
- Year 2 - $160, remaining value - $640

- Year 3 - $128, remaining value - $512

and so on through year ten, when the remaining value should approach zero.

Of course, depreciation (whether straight line or accelerated) is mostly relevant insofar as it relates to taxation. And the tax code historically permitted straight-line depreciation. But accelerated depreciation became a mainstay of the corporate tax landscape during the 1970s, when the government began shortening the useful lives of various assets. In 1981, as part of President Reagan's tax reduction plans (codified in the Economic Recovery Act of 1981), the Accelerated Cost Recovery System (ACRS) took effect and became a fixture of the small business landscape. The Tax Reform Act of 1986 modified ACRS, so that now it is referred to as MACRS. MACRS divides all property into class life, just like useful life except the classifications are broader. Take computers, for example. These are considered five-year property. Of course, the obsolescence cycle in the computer industry is much shorter than five years. No matter, computers are five-year property, even if you replace yours in three.

Leaving aside real property, MACRS provides for three-, five-, seven- and ten-year property, and provides a particular accelerated depreciation method for each, largely dependent on what method yields the greatest deduction early in the asset's life. For some property classes, the taxpayer is actually permitted to switch methods (from 150% declining balance to straight-line) in the middle of the class life when the second prescribed method would yield a higher deduction. You get the idea: our tax code encourages accelerated depreciation. And when that is not considered enough to spur investment in business equipment or to lower taxes sufficiently, Congress devises additional rules on top of depreciation allowances. This is where IRC Section 179 and the first-year bonus depreciation rules come into play.

Section 179 permits a deduction in addition to depreciation for property placed into service in the current tax year. After JGTRRA, the limit on such deductions has risen to $100,000. So for small business owners (you can only use Section 179 to the extent your purchases of equipment do not exceed $400,000, after which there is a set off provision, so it doesn't work for big businesses), the cost of most business property is fully depreciated or otherwise deducted in the first year, even if, for accounting purposes, the asset would still be in the process of being depreciated by the traditional methods. Certainly that $1,000 machine has no useful life, for tax purposes, after year one, if the taxpayer takes advantage of section 179. (Of course, the taxpayer can elect not to take advantage of Section 179.)

Periodically, Congress will pass short-term, stimulatory tax rules that grant yet further deduction allowances. JGTRRA contains bonus first-year depreciation rules that allow an additional 50% (or 30% at the taxpayer's election) for equipment put into service in 2003-04 with a useful life of less than 20 years. This deduction is calculated after Section 179 deductions. So where does that leave us? Let's see. Assume in 2003, a business owner bought and placed into service $250,000 of computer equipment. (That's five-year property eligible for 200% declining balance depreciation method. See IRS Pub. 946 at 29-34):

- Maximum Section 179 deduction? $100,000
- JGTRRA 50% bonus depreciation? $75,000
- First-year depreciation of the remaining $75,000? $15,000
- Being able to expense $190,000 of a $250,000 business investment in the first year? Priceless

Unfortunately, the preceding 10 paragraphs leave out just about everything you need to know about the ins and outs of depreciation and expensing. The point of this exercise, then? As always, to give you a start.

CAGR

Compound Annual Growth Rate (also known as "discount rate" or "internal rate of return").

CAGR IN THE REAL WORLD:

Pocket MBA tries assiduously to avoid math. Sometimes it can't. This week is one of those times. For your venture capitalist clients, CAGR is a crucial formula that helps them determine where to plunk their mad money. And for anyone, be they lawyer or client, who got sucked in by mutual fund advertisements touting annual performance averages only to find that they were completely divorced from mathematical reality, CAGR is a useful way to cut through the fog. So what is this CAGR? (Actually, if you say CAGR fast enough, it sounds like a fraternity party, as in "We had a double CAGR last night!")

For venture capitalists, CAGR smooths out the year-to-year returns of an investment over a determined period of time (venture capitalists like high CAGR). Unlike stodgy fixed-rate investments, most returns on investments in stocks or start-up companies are not the same every year. The growth rates jump around. So when you hear that a company is expected to grow at 15% per year, what you are really hearing is that the CAGR is 15%. Any given year's growth could be vastly different, and could even be negative. The most important part of CAGR is the C, which stands for compound and is the critical distinction between CAGR and the mythical concept of "average annual return."

For some mutual funds and their investors, there is a temptation to use averages when it comes to return because they are easy, and everyone knows how to calculate them. Some mutual funds used averages in their advertising, and it was one of the aspects of the industry that has irked many commentators because it was essentially dishonest or, at the very best, profoundly misleading.

If an investment of $1,000 in a fund returned 200% over three years (so it was valued at $3,000 at the end of the period), the fund might advertise an "average annual return" of 66.667%. Because the math is complex, nobody much questioned calculations like this. But to show you the ridiculousness of them, take a hypothetical $5,000 investment. If it returns 100% the first year, and loses 50% the second, you still have $5,000. An unscrupulous fund might claim an average annual return of 25%: (100% + (50%))/2. That's not right, especially when it is clear that the actual growth in that investment is ZERO! The problem with average annual calculations is they ignore the C in CAGR.

Indeed, everyone knows instinctively that average annual return is a mathematically disingenuous way to look at return. And in fact, any venture capitalist or investor who approached things that way would be heading for an adventure in being broke.

Think about an example that makes this easy for everybody to understand: your salary. If you make $50,000 and your salary goes up to $100,000 over five years, a 100% increase, you know that your average annual raise was $10,000, or 20% of your original $50,000. The problem with that formulation is you didn't average a 20% raise; in fact, assuming you received a $10,000 raise every year, you got 20% in year one; 16.67% in year two; 14.3% in year three; 12.5% in year four; and only 11% in year five. So in reality, the percentage increase in your raise declined every year, and you only received a 20% raise once in five years, even though your average annual raise over the period was indeed 20% of your original salary. If you had actually received 20% each year, you would have earned the following over five years:

- Year 0 - $50,000
- Year 1 - $60,000
- Year 2 - $72,000
- Year 3 - $86,400
- Year 4 - $103,680
- Year 5 - $124,416

So claiming an average annual growth rate of 20% overstates the actual growth by 24.416% after five years. Using CAGR, you would find that your salary during the period actually grew only 14.87% per year (on average), which isn't exactly chump change, but is far from 20%.

CAGR allows investors to see the true value of money they're putting up for, say, a new company that is expecting to grow sales from $50,000 to $100,000 over five years. (Not coincidentally this very small company earns as much money as the lawyer in the preceding paragraph.) So how do you figure CAGR? Well, you start from the finish line and work backwards. You take the amount you expect to end with (current value, or CV), the amount you started with (beginning value, or BV) and the number of years (5) and, if you're lazy or short on time, you enter them into a CAGR calculator, which you can find easily online. Of course, Pocket MBA eschews this type of shortcut, preferring to express CAGR as the following mathematical formula (here's that math Pocket MBA has been trying to avoid):

- CAGR = (CV/BV) to the Nth root (that's 1/N, where N is the number of years or periods you are using) - 1
- CAGR = $(CV/BV)^{1/n}$ - 1

It's not as difficult as that seems. If N is two years, you're looking for the second root, which is the square root; if N were three, you're looking for the cube root and so on. So for the hypothetical earnings or salary advance above, the formula is:

- $((100,000/50,000))^{1/5}$ - 1 =
- 2 to the fifth root (don't worry, you can input 2 to the fifth root into Microsoft Excel or any fancy calculator) - 1 =
- 1.14869835 - 1 =
- .1486935 or 14.87%

Presto magico, that's the same number as Pocket MBA figured out above. Who said lawyers couldn't do math; paste that formula on your desk for those times your high-finance clients start throwing around numbers. Now, bring on the surgery schedule!

PLI's Pocket MBA Vol. 2, No. 16   April 21, 2004

Investment Company

As defined in section 3 of the Investment Company Act of 1940 (the Act), an issuer engaged primarily in the business of investing, reinvesting, or trading in securities.

INVESTMENT COMPANIES IN THE REAL WORLD:

As the mutual fund scandal of 2003-04 continued to unfold, it was easy to forget (if you ever knew) that mutual funds are just one of the three types of investment company (IC) regulated by the Act. Certainly they are the most well known, but the shenanigans that have plagued the mutual fund industry have unfortunately tarnished ICs, in general, even though the two less-celebrated ICs--Closed-End Funds and Unit Investment Trusts--were not involved. Closed-End what, you ask? Unit Investment who? Pocket MBA had the same reaction, and so decided to probe what makes each type of IC. And as the IC is a creature of legislation, Pocket MBA is mindful that precision is crucial. Accordingly, Pocket MBA is happy to attribute most of the information that follows to no less an authority than the SEC itself. You can get more thoroughly acquainted with each IC at the SEC's web site, www.sec.gov.

Mutual Funds are companies that "pool money from many investors and invest the money in stocks, bonds, short-term money-market instruments, or other securities." Of course, you know that. Mutual funds are considered "open-end" companies, as opposed to the closed-end companies described in the next section. The distinctive features of open-end mutual funds are as follows:

- Investors can only purchase shares from the fund (or a broker for the fund). The shares cannot be traded on secondary markets like NYSE or NASDAQ. The price at which the fund sells shares is the Net Asset Value (NAV), which is determined by dividing the total value of all the assets held by the fund by the number of outstanding shares. The NAV is not related in any way to the perceived quality of the fund-- that is, unlike a share of stock, the NAV on any given day is irrelevant to the performance of the fund, and an investor cannot discern anything about the value of the investment from the NAV.

- Since the shares cannot be traded, they are redeemable only from the fund (or broker) at the next daily NAV.
- Funds sell new shares on a continual basis, though a fund may elect to stop selling shares, if it becomes too large or for other reasons.
- The investment portfolio of a mutual fund is managed by an Investment Adviser (as defined in the Investment Adviser Act).

That was probably old hat to many Pocket MBA readers, but it is important to restate what mutual funds are in order to place them in the context of the other ICs.

Closed-End Funds (legally, closed-end company) are a lot more exotic than mutual funds. In many respects, they resemble corporations in that they have an IPO and their shares are traded in secondary markets like NYSE and AMEX. But instead of using the IPO proceeds to manufacture widgets, the company uses them to invest in securities. So each share of a closed-end fund is made up of a pro rata piece of the investment portfolio. The underlying portfolio itself can be valued like a mutual fund, and so has a NAV, which is figured the same way as that of a mutual fund.

- Closed-end funds do not continuously sell shares. The IPO offers a fixed number of shares,

- the subsequent price of which are determined by the market demand for the shares.
- Importantly, the fund's price per share on the open market may be more or less than the NAV of the securities underlying the shares. The difference is referred to as the "discount to NAV" or the "premium to NAV." Whether a closed-end fund trades at a discount or premium to NAV is dependent on market supply and demand. Generally speaking, when a fund is trading at a discount to NAV, it is considered an attractive investment. Thus, unlike mutual funds, the price at which shares trade is one indicator of the value of the investment.
- Closed-end shares are not redeemable--that is the company will not buy them back from investors, as a mutual fund would. The shares must be sold in the secondary markets, although some closed-end funds have provisions to buy back shares at specified intervals. Not surprisingly, these closed-end funds are called "interval funds."
- The investment portfolios of a closed-end fund are managed by an Investment Adviser, as defined in the Investment Adviser Act.
- Closed-end funds are "permitted to invest in a greater amount of 'illiquid' securities than are mutual funds. Thus a fund company that seeks investment opportunities in markets where the securities tend toward illiquidity (like many emerging markets) will typically be organized as closed-end."

There are numerous additional web sites that explain the inner workings of closed-end funds, one of the more thorough of which is the Investor Awareness Series, available online from the Investment

Company Institute, www.ici.org.

Unit Investment Trusts (UIT) are the least well known investment company. Instead of being made up of shares, a UIT is made up of "units." The UIT will set the price of each unit. Like a closed-end fund, a UIT generally makes a one-time offering of a fixed number of units. Like a mutual fund, however, these shares are redeemable from the UIT at the NAV, which is based on the value of the underlying securities. Thus the UIT, in essence, operates its own secondary market for its units.

- A UIT will generally buy and hold a basket of income-producing securities, either equities or bonds depending on its investment strategy, and distribute the income periodically to investors. But a UIT can also focus on short-term capital appreciation.
- Unlike open-end and closed-end companies, UITs exist for a time-certain, after which they are liquidated, with the proceeds being distributed to the shareholders. The termination date is dependent on the types of securities held by the UIT. In the case of bonds, if the UIT holds bonds with a maturity of 20 years, the UIT will exist for 20 years. Equity UITs can last as short as a year, in the case of Dow UITs, which are baskets of the highest yielding stocks in the Dow Jones Industrial Index. Because those stocks change annually, Dow UITs tend to terminate at the end of each year.
- Because UITs buy and hold their portfolios, they are not managed by an Investment Adviser.

Break-Even Analysis

Business-planning tool that assists in determining the amount of revenue necessary to offset, exactly, both fixed and variable costs.

BREAK-EVEN ANALYSIS IN THE REAL WORLD:

Pocket MBA's favorite personal investment is in a company that turned a profit for the first time in the fourth quarter of 2003, only to sink back into the red in Q1 2004. The company had projected profitability throughout 2004, but one of the variables--revenue--that went into that determination changed, unexpectedly, due to a merger between two customers that rendered a large chunk of its sales commitments redundant. What that demonstrated to Pocket MBA is something that all good entrepreneurs know--that even the best break-even analysis is premised on projection and is, therefore, hypothetical. Nonetheless, nobody enters into business or adds new projects to an existing profitable business without conducting break-even analysis. And implicit even in any established business's financial planning is knowledge of its break-even point. Analysts also use break-even calculations in recommending investments. So how does one go about finding break-even?

Break-even analysis, like other business projections, can be done for any period of time. Pocket MBA's favorite time period is monthly because that allows it to consider some costs as fixed, like employee salaries, that might otherwise be variable over a longer period. (Employee salaries and number of employees fluctuate more over longer periods of time.) Break-even analysis is a function of several variables: fixed costs, variable costs per unit of production and projected revenue per unit. A monthly break-even analysis tells a business owner how much revenue she would have to take in each month to offset all costs.

Fixed costs are things like rent, insurance, employee salaries and debt-service that don't generally change from month-to-month. Variable costs per unit of production are the additional costs associated with actually producing a given unit of product. These costs are variable because, given economies of scale and the like, the cost of producing a unit increases or declines depending on how many units are produced. For instance, assume a business, North-by-Northwest Publishing, which produces case law digests in Braille. If the business has to buy $10,000 in materials in a month to produce anywhere from one to 10,000 units (books), then the variable cost of producing one book is $10,000. If the company produces two books, the cost drops to $5,000, and so on.

So assume North-by-Northwest has fixed costs of $5,000 per month. Further assume that it has investigated the market and determined that it can get solid commitments to sell 4,000 books and can probably sell another 1,000. Since it has storage space for 5,000 books, the company decides to produce that number. The variable cost per unit of production is therefore $2 ($10,000/5,000). Finally, assume that each book sells for $6 (that's the sales price or revenue per unit). How many of the 5,000 books does North-by-Northwest have to sell to achieve break-even? The following numbers are available for the break-even analysis:

- Fixed Costs (FC) = $5,000
- Revenue/Unit (RU) = $6
- Variable Cost/Unit (VCU) = $2

Break-even occurs when the Revenue from the total number of units sold (X) is equal to fixed costs plus variable costs, where Revenue = RU(X) and Variable Costs = VCU(X). So:

- $RU(X) = FC + VCU(X)$

All you have to do is solve for X (Hey wait, that's algebra! Sorry.):

- $6X = 5,000 + 2X$
- $6X - 2X = 5000 + 2X - 2X$
- $6X - 2X = 5,000 + 0$

- $4X = 5,000$
- $X = 1,250$ units

Thus, North-by-Northwest has to sell 1,250 of its 5,000 books (or $7,500 of books) to break even. Since it has a commitment for 4,000 books and can sell another 1,000, it is well above break-even. Of course, if that "commitment" falls through, and the company sells only 1,000 units, it will lose money, just like Pocket MBA's favorite company.

There are other ways to reach the same result. You can do it by dividing the "gross profit margin" into fixed costs. To do this, find the "gross revenue per unit" (this amount, which is simply the profit before subtracting fixed costs, goes by other more fancy names-- "average gross profit" and "contribution margin per unit" are two) by subtracting VCU from RU ($6 - $2):

- Gross Revenue Per Unit (GRU) = RU - VCU = $4

Divide GRU by RU ($4/$6), which gives you gross profit margin = .667 (or 66.7%). Then divide fixed costs by profit margin ($5000/.667) which equals break-even ($7,496). Close enough.

A final note. As Pocket MBA likes to keep readers up-to-date on technological advances, it must confess that, like CAGR in issue 15, there are break-even analysis calculators available online, and they confirm the above calculations. But who needs that when you can impress friends and clients with nimble algebraic ability.

Liquidity Ratios

Measures of a company's assets in relation to liabilities that indicate its ability to meet short-term debts.

LIQUIDITY RATIOS IN THE REAL WORLD:

Wall Street is coming through another earnings season, and if you pay attention to any of the gabfests on cable TV, you will have heard more than one reference to the pile of cash that Microsoft has hoarded over the years, at last count, somewhere north of $50 billion. That number leaves most mouths agape, but without considering the company's liabilities, it doesn't tell you that much about Microsoft's financial health. So what if Microsoft has $50 billion in cash and another $10 billion in other assets (Pocket MBA made up the second number, so don't take it seriously) if it has (again hypothetically speaking) $100 billion in liabilities? There might be a smaller company, let's call it Subatomicparticlesoft, that has a scant $30 million in assets, but no liabilities at all (or at least none that anyone could see) and a growing product line. Which company is better off under the circumstances? That's where liquidity ratios come into play.

Liquidity ratios measure assets against liabilities to arrive at a fairly standardized sense of a company's actual ability to use its assets (though every industry might have its own median liquidity ratios, depending on a number of factors, including whether the industry is inventory-intensive).

There are two primary liquidity measures in wide use: (1) the Current Ratio and (2) the Quick (or Acid Test) Ratio. Either or both can be useful depending on the circumstances of a particular entity. Both can and should be tracked over many time-periods--a one-month or one-quarter snapshot is not useful given the vagaries of business cycles (though Pocket MBA will engage that transgression in the next several paragraphs). If the trend of these ratios is negative over time, you are probably looking at a company with growing liquidity issues.

The Current Ratio is basic: current assets divided by current liabilities. (Turn back to Pocket MBA Vol. 1, No. 22 and recall that current assets and liabilities are those that can be converted to cash or that come due, respectively, within one year). Back to Microsoft.

Microsoft's June 2003 balance sheet showed current assets of $58.973 billion and current liabilities of $13.974 billion. That renders a Current Ratio of 4.22. That means that Microsoft could pay all of its bills four times over and still have cash left in the bank. Meanwhile, the company is generating more cash every month. From this, one can generalize what everyone already knows: Microsoft is in excellent financial health, but cannot figure out what to do with its excess money.

The next example is American Airlines. Its September 2003 balance sheet shows $5.076 billion in current assets and $7.132 billion in current liabilities for a Current Ratio of .712. Hmmm. American cannot pay all of its current liabilities without doing one of three things, all of which will raise cash: sell more seats fast, issue stock or borrow money. Again, the Current Ratio confirms what everyone knows: Legacy airlines aren't necessarily the healthiest businesses, despite the fact that we can't live without them.

Now, let's take one last example, everyone's favorite container maker, Tupperware. Its December 2003 balance sheet shows current assets of $411.4 million and current liabilities of $274.2 million. That renders a Current Ratio of a hair over 1.5. That means that Tupperware can pay all of its current liabilities and still have cash in the bank to expand a little or to increase its dividend or just to have for a rainy day. Incidentally, 1.5 is generally considered to be the minimal Current Ratio required to consider a business healthy in the short term (though some argue that a Current Ratio of 2 is optimal). So Tupperware is the average company, doing just fine, thank you.

The only caveat is that a good portion of Tupperware's current assets is presumably made up of plastic containers. And although generally speaking, Tupperware probably makes containers and then turns around and sells them relatively quickly, what would happen if (again hypothetically) Subatomicparticlesoft came up with a new storage device (like an invisible air bubble) that rendered Tupperware's containers obsolete. All of a sudden, Tupperware's current assets would not be worth anywhere near that $411.4 million, because $160.5 million is reported as inventory (which, due to Subatomicparticlesoft, no longer has much value).

The Quick Ratio is more useful in inventory intensive businesses, particularly in those industries where inventory tends to sit around for a while. Because it can only be converted to cash by being sold, it can't be used in a serious pinch.

The Quick Ratio eliminates inventory from the Current Ratio to give a greater sense of how much cash can be raised in that pinch--it shows just how liquid the current assets are. Commentators tend to agree that a Quick Ratio of one is optimal, and the formula requires only that you subtract the current value of Tupperware's inventory from current assets and divide what's left by the current liabilities: ($411.4 - $160.5)/274.2 = .915.

That's pretty close, and the company's next balance sheet might well show a Quick Ratio over one, so the company is in decent shape. But if that ratio steadily dropped over many quarters, you might conclude that Tupperware's fate is sealed (so to speak).

S Corporation

Corporation that, due to its structure, may elect to be taxed (much like a partnership) under Subchapter S of the Internal Revenue Code (IRC).

S CORPORATIONS IN THE REAL WORLD:

The Riddle of the Sphinx has many versions, but the gist is to the effect of "what walks on four legs in the morning, two legs at noon and three legs at night?" And the answer is human beings. (If you don't know why, figure it out for yourself.) Very existential...not really funny, but riddles are never funny after birthday number eight. (Although "Knock Knock. Who's there? Orange you glad I didn't say banana," challenges that notion.) Anyway, the S corporation could be the answer to a similar riddle: What gets taxed as a corporation in the morning, gets taxed like a partnership at noon and gets taxed like a corporation again at night if certain things happen? Still not funny, but it encapsulates the possible life cycle of an S Corporation as well as that riddle about legs, except that noon can last forever for an S Corporation.

An S Corporation starts out like any other corporation. But if the corporation meets all of the following requirements, it can make an election (IRS form 2553) to be treated differently from other corporations for tax purposes only.

- Is domestic
- Has no more than 75 shareholders
- Has only individuals, estates and a few other exempt organizations or certain trusts
- Has no nonresident alien shareholders
- Has only one class of stock
- Is not: (1) a bank or thrift institution that uses the reserve method of accounting for bad debts, (2) an insurance company subject to tax under Subchapter L of the IRC, (3) a corporation that has elected to be treated as a possessions corporation under section 936 of the IRC, (4) a domestic international sales corporation (DISC) or former DISC
- Has a permitted tax year (don't worry about that)
- Each shareholder consents

If the IRS accepts the election, the S form lasts indefinitely, or until terminated by the corporation.

As of the year 2000, there were 2,860,478 S corporations registered in the U.S. (compared to 2,184,795 C corporations – the standard corporate form). IRC Subchapter S was enacted in 1958 "in order to diminish the effect of federal income taxes in the organizational choice of small businesses, and to permit incorporation and operation of certain small business without the incidence of income taxation at both the corporate and shareholder levels." (Staff Report of the Joint Committee on Taxation, House Committee on Ways and Means, June 18, 2003 at 4.) Thus, the benefit for small business is that it gets the protection of the corporate veil without having to pay the corporate tax. And of course, this promotes entrepreneurial spirit, ease of management, uninterrupted operation in the event that an owner dies and other wonderful things (including the mediocre riddle that started this discussion).

S corporations are pass-through entities, and indeed, are taxed somewhat like partnerships without many of the complexities of the partnership form. This taxation method resulted from the Subchapter S Revision Act of 1982. Essentially, each shareholder reports their rata share of profits (or losses) and then reports it as income (or loss) on his or her personal income tax as a distribution of capital. Great right? You could make a lot of money in distributions of profits and not have any wages, which allows shareholders to never pay things like FICA and the like (and ask any sole proprietor--that's a lot of savings).

The IRS has begun to be more diligent in investigating such practices and is determined to look more closely at S Corporation shareholder tax returns that it claims disguise wages as distributions. This is especially the case where the shareholder provides services to the corporation that are the primary (or a major) source of corporate revenue. In such a case, the distribution of capital can seem more akin to wages, regardless of what the corporation calls it.

PLI's Pocket MBA Vol. 2, No. 20   May 19, 2004

Inventory Financing

A line of credit secured by a business's inventory.

INVENTORY FINANCING IN THE REAL WORLD:

Not so long ago, in an economy that seems light years away... In the original "Star Wars" trilogy, the third installment was supposed to have been entitled "Revenge of the Jedi." This was later changed to "Return of the Jedi." Pocket MBA prefers the discarded title, as it implies getting back at someone or something that has wronged you. In many respects, then, the rise of inventory financing in the wake of the dot-com bust has to be called "Revenge of the Business with Inventory."

For scads of Internet businesses that had originally been heralded precisely because they had no inventory (thus making them lean, mean service-business machines), declining economic fortunes (and the attendant declining advertising revenue, which was how they were reportedly going to earn profits) left them with very few financing options. And if you look at the stand-alone Internet businesses that remain, a large proportion has actual stuff in a warehouse located somewhere outside cyberspace (Amazon.com, Overstock.com). Most of those service-based Internet businesses were long ago liquidated. Really, after you've sold tons of stock and tapped all the debt you can, what can a few servers fetch in terms of credit?

Compare a small bottled water distributor, Splish-Splash, located in North Carolina. (BTW, Pocket MBA has created this business from thin air and an H_2 molecule.) Splish-Splash buys the water from some mountain stream owner somewhere else in North Carolina, bottles it and sells it to tourists looking for some homespun Southern charm. The company has little overhead--ten employees and a warehouse; it also has a couple bottling machines and some delivery trucks. And it sells a lot of water, like $1 million dollars a month, and plows through its current supply every 40 days or so. The problem is, it doesn't get paid upfront by its customers (they take a couple months to pay), but it has to pay the water company immediately for new shipments.

So even though Splish-Splash has annual revenues of $12 million, it has trouble paying its bills on time, which means that money is tight and the ability to grow constrained. In fact, the business could even hit a wall if larger competitors try to horn-in on Splish-Splash's territory. Without a lot of hard assets, there's not much to leverage. So is this a business doomed to eventual decline and failure? (This is where the "Star Wars" theme music begins to play).

Unlike all those defunct Internet businesses, Splish-Splash has something of value that replenishes on a regular basis and which keeps the company solvent and even profitable: it has a lot of bottles of water! This is increasingly attractive to a different breed of lender (though traditional banks are getting in on this action, also). These lenders issue revolving lines of credit to companies with inventory that is fresh and sells relatively quickly. The lender can have the traditional secured interest in something, and that something is those bottles of water that sell out every month-plus. With that revolving line of credit,

Splish-Splash can take more orders for water, pay for it up front and turn around and sell it. In no time, they'll have extra money that they'll need to buy more bottling machines and trucks. Voila, the inventory that seemed destined to doom a small business back in the whiz-bang 1990s is now the driver of growth and stability. The biggest risk is if people were to stop buying bottled water. And the bottled water craze is a trend that, though mystifying, seems unlikely to abate.

Of course, inventory financing isn't for all businesses. If the business doesn't have a track record of turning over a high volume of inventory, the purpose of inventory financing is defeated. As stale goods can become obsolete goods, their value can decline, which destroys the lender's interest.

So there you have it, a capsule look at inventory financing. But for those who want a more in-depth treatment, Pocket MBA directs you to Appendix A, where you will find the article *Inventory Financing* by Scott A. Lessne (FleetBoston Financial Corporation). Lessne offers some of the legal logistics (UCC definitions of inventory and collateral) that your clients demand. May the Force be with you.

PLI's Pocket MBA Vol. 2, No. 21   May 26, 2004

Accredited Investor

As designated in SEC Regulation D, Rule 501, a high net-worth person (or entity) eligible to participate in investments that are exempt from registration under Rules 505 and 506 of Regulation D.

ACCREDITED INVESTORS IN THE REAL WORLD:

It's a hedge fund world that we live in now. After the stock market cratered, followed by revelations that the mutual fund industry was racked by all manner of double-dealing, one could be forgiven for thinking that the only people who made money investing during the last few years (the last half of 2003 excepted) were those who were able to invest in vehicles outside the long arm of SEC regulation. It seems truly odd, in retrospect, that the people for whom the various

Securities Acts were designed to protect fared the worst in the market meltdown. A little tinkering is obviously in order, and the SEC has begun attending to that. And of course, the SEC's September 2003 Staff Report "Implications of the Growth of Hedge Funds" is an interesting part of the overall picture.

One of the more novel recommendations in the Staff Report was that the SEC explore the possibility of expanding the availability of absolute return (i.e. hedge fund) strategies to registered investment vehicles. The Staff Report made clear that this did not mean that the SEC should permit retail investors to invest in hedge funds. That will continue to be left to the accredited investor. If the average investor gets a crack at alternative vehicles, it will certainly be under the watchful eye of the securities regulator in chief.

So who exactly are these accredited investors that have unfettered access to the exotic? Are they wealthier than most? Yes. Are they smarter than everyone else? Some, maybe, but not necessarily all. Is the answer to that question even important? Let's take a look and see.

Pocket MBA's favorite FAQ on the SEC's web site is the following: What is the difference between an accredited investor and a sophisticated investor? The answer is that "accredited investor" has a legal definition and sophisticated investor is a term of art. So although one might assume that a person who is able to meet the legal definition of "accredited" must also be sophisticated and vice versa, that is simply not the case. For accreditation is based on wherewithal; sophistication is, well sophistication, and never the twain have to meet. Nonetheless, both terms generally refer to an investor who has such a high degree [of] financial knowledge and wherewithal that he or she does not need the protections afforded by registration with the SEC. But an investor who might otherwise be considered "sophisticated" still might not meet the definition of an accredited investor. It all depends on the circumstances.

Theoretically, one could have the investing acumen of Warren Buffet and be nowhere near wealthy enough to be eligible to invest, without limitation, in hedge funds and the like. Likewise, one could have the checking account balance of a Dupont and be a hapless investing hillbilly. Still under the SEC's rules, that person would be free to lose his money (and due to his lack of true sophistication, very well may), without limitation, in unregistered investment vehicles. That seems even more Riddle of the Sphinx to Pocket MBA than the situation with S corporations. See Vol. 2, No. 19.

So let's review exactly what factors render an investor accredited, and also what the SEC has to say about sophistication.

Accredited Investor is defined in Rule 501 of Regulation D. Regulation D Offerings are those that are exempt from the registration requirements of the Securities Act of 1933. Because they're exempt, the SEC seeks to protect the average Joe (read "not independently wealthy") from being enticed by promises of investment profits that are more than easily offset by the amount of risk involved. The SEC does this by limiting investment in these unregistered offerings primarily to investors of vast means. Thus, under Rule 501(a) of Reg. D, an accredited investor, as far as individuals are concerned (there are additional qualifications for banks and other entities), is:

> (4) Any director, executive officer, or general partner of the issuer of the securities being offered or sold, or any director, executive officer, or general partner of a general partner of that issuer;
>
> (5) Any natural person whose individual net worth, or joint net worth with that person's spouse, at the time of his purchase exceeds $1,000,000;
>
> (6) Any natural person who had an individual income in excess of $200,000 in each of the two most recent years or joint income with that person's spouse in excess of $300,000 in each of those years and has a reasonable expectation of reaching the same income level in the current year;
>
> (7) Any trust, with total assets in excess of $5,000,000, not formed for the specific purpose of acquiring the securities offered, whose purchase is directed by a

sophisticated person as described in § 230.506(b)(2)(ii); and (emphasis added)

(8) Any entity in which all of the equity owners are accredited investors.

That's interesting. The answer to the FAQ above states that the term accredited investor refers to someone with both financial knowledge and wherewithal. But, other than the reference to sophistication in subparagraph (7), there is nothing requiring that an accredited investor have financial knowledge. That is only required of someone directing a trust.

As described in Rule 506(b)(2)(ii), a sophisticated person is one "who is not an accredited investor either alone or with his purchaser representative(s) [but] has such knowledge and experience in financial and business matters that he is capable of evaluating the merits and risks of the prospective investment, or the issuer reasonably believes immediately prior to making any sale that such purchaser comes within this description." So if you're not really rich, but you're really smart, and as long you're directing a trust with assets of more than $5 million or as long as no more than 34 other really smart people are purchasing the specific unregistered offering that you are (see Rule 506(b)(2)(i) (limiting to 35, the number of non-accredited investors who can be involved in an exempt offering)), you're in. And just maybe, if the SEC Staff Report is any indication, there will be a day when the not so wealthy and sophisticated will have their own version of these same offerings.

Price Elasticity of Demand

Price elasticity is a measure of the extent to which the demand for goods and services reacts to a change in the prices asked for those goods and services.

PRICE ELASTICITY OF DEMAND IN THE REAL WORLD:

Pocket MBA discussed deflation in Volume 1, No. 17 because, at the time, Chicken Little had appeared proclaiming the sky was falling and that a downward pricing spiral was inevitable. Flash-forward to today, and now everyone is talking about the return of inflation. Everywhere one looks, it seems, businesses are beginning to feel greater freedom in charging more for the goods and services they purvey. As everyone knows, the past several months have witnessed geometric increases in the price of crude oil. But even ice cream manufacturers have warned that the summer of '04 will witness hefty increases in prices (ice cream is one of the few products for which elasticity is both an economic and weight control concept). The fears being expressed that the return of even modest inflation will squelch the economic recovery that has taken hold over the last year are a reflection of concern that consumers don't have much of an appetite for or, given the (until recently) shaky job market, high debt levels and you name whatever other concern, the ability to assimilate higher prices for most goods and services.

Only time will tell, but generally, these concerns relate to the concept of price elasticity--that is the pricing power of manufacturers and sellers, which had largely disappeared for a variety of reasons during the past several years (Fed policy, inventory gluts, etc.). There are two primary ways to measure price elasticity--price elasticity of demand and price elasticity of supply. Today's focus is on demand: the amount that a change in price impacts the demand for a particular good or service. As always, Pocket MBA apologizes for turning a chapter of economics into several paragraphs. Note that there are hundreds of online and print resources that can augment today's introduction.

All goods and services are either more or less price-sensitive-- that is they are either more or less elastic--meaning consumers will adjust their level of spending on particular goods or services at varying ratios in relation to the rise in price for each good or service. Goods or services that experience large changes in the quantity demanded in response to even small price changes are said to have a high elasticity. If the demand for a good or service is not appreciably impacted by a rise in price, the demand for that good or service is said to be highly inelastic. The designation is neither good nor bad; it just is. Generally, highly elastic goods are those that are neither rare nor necessary to daily life (like, say, cans of tuna), and highly inelastic goods are those that are generally considered essentials (think gasoline and, to a lesser extent, coffee, at least since the advent of Starbucks).

In modern society, people rely on fuel to run their cars, homes and businesses; therefore, it takes a fairly large increase in oil prices to change people's demand for oil, if it does even then. Therefore, it is axiomatic that oil is a very price-inelastic commodity, and this is somewhat borne out by present day events. Ice cream, on the other hand, is generally optional for most people. (Of course, Pocket MBA doesn't know any of these people.) If consumers are accustomed to paying $4.00 for a pint of Ben & Jerry's (Pocket MBA prefers Bovinity Divinity, which is white and dark chocolate-shaped cows mixed into chocolate ice cream), and the price suddenly rises to $7.00, one could surmise that consumption of Ben & Jerry's would decrease significantly. A valid conclusion from the change in behavior would be that premium ice cream is more price-elastic than oil.

You can apply the concept of elasticity by thinking about the economic decisions you make in your own life over a given period of time. Pocket MBA thinks back to a childhood baseball card collection begun when the price of a pack of cards was five cents (for five cards and gum). As the price rose (and the number of cards in the pack eventually stagnated and the gum disappeared) faster than Pocket MBA's allowance, the number of packages Pocket MBA bought began to decline. Consider how a rise in the price of something you buy impacts whether and how much you buy. When you do so, you can also develop a different perspective on the decision-process your clients go through in determining whether they can and will raise the prices of their goods and services.

Elasticity can be plotted onto a graph (price per unit on one axis and quantity demanded on the other) and will render either a more elastic or a more inelastic "demand curve." There are actually statistics kept on the elasticity of various goods and services.

These statistics are generated using the following ratio, where

E(D) is the elasticity of demand:

- E(D) = % change in quantity / % change in price

You can create your own products, input various price and quantity changes, then plot the results to develop a better understanding of how elasticity curves work. If you do this, note that, for economists, the general formula yields the five following cases:

(1) Elasticity = 0 (demand is perfectly inelastic)

In this case, a change in price results in no impact on demand.

(2) Elasticity < 1 (demand is price inelastic)

These goods are considered generally inelastic. A rise in prices will have a decreasing impact on demand as the ratio approaches zero.

(3) Elasticity = 1 (demand is unit elastic)

Demand changes proportionately to change in price.

(4) Elasticity > 1 (demand is price elastic)

These goods are considered generally elastic. As the elasticity increases, the drop in demand intensifies.

(5) Elasticity = infinity (demand is perfectly elastic)

In this case, any change in price results in a fall in demand to zero. When a good or service is perfectly elastic, it is impossible to raise prices.

Note that there are many factors that can impact elasticity that are not directly related to price. These include:

- Availability of substitutes - if the price of Ben & Jerry's rises because of rising cream prices, and sorbet is an acceptable alternative, ice cream will be highly elastic. However, if the rise in ice cream prices results from an increase in sugar prices, buying sorbet won't save money. In the scheme of sweet, frozen desserts, ice cream would then be more inelastic unless there were an acceptable frozen dessert that was also sugar free.

- Availability of income - if incomes are rising, then this can blunt the effects of elasticity because consumers will have more money to spend on nonessential products that have higher prices.
- Habitual goods - things like cigarettes, alcohol and oil tend to be more inelastic, as consumers are dependent on them.
- Time - Over a short period of time, goods and services tend to be more inelastic. The shock of higher prices cannot immediately overcome one's need or desire for a product. However, over longer periods of time, people may adjust their behavior so as to avoid the impact of high priced goods. For instance, a suburbanite who drives to work in the city could move downtown to avoid the increased cost of gasoline. These are changes that are made over time.

If inflation ever returns in any serious way, you can count on Pocket MBA to tackle some other issues involving elasticity.

Depreciation Recapture

The amount of income that a taxpayer must pay taxes on after selling a piece of business property sold at a price that exceeds the depreciated value.

DEPRECIATION RECAPTURE IN THE REAL WORLD:

Pocket MBA thanks a loyal reader for responding as follows to the issue on depreciation (Vol. 2, No. 14): "What about recapture," or something close to that. Indeed, that issue neglected recapture, but mostly because in Pocket MBA's world, after business property is fully depreciated, it continues to be used until it breaks and ends up out on the street, where some industrious entrepreneur rescues it from the trash collectors. In that case, recapture just isn't an issue. But it is for your clients, and maybe for you, as well. The concept is simple; the rules applying to it can be complex, if only because, like all things tax, what you're depreciating (and sometimes how) determines how and whether you recapture.

As to concepts, some have said of recapture, "what the IRS giveth, the IRS taketh away." But that's not really an accurate characterization. In reality, recapture merely keeps a taxpayer from "jobbing" the system by depreciating property and then selling it for more than the depreciated value without ever having paid taxes on the amount depreciated. Say Pocket MBA buys a trash compactor (it could happen) for $60,000 and depreciates $30,000 of that amount over a few years. The benefit to Pocket MBA is that its business income over the years of depreciation has been decreased by $30,000, on which no tax has been paid.

Now, assume Pocket MBA sells that trash compactor for $40,000. Technically speaking, it has been sold at a $20,000 loss ($60,000-$40,000). However, that doesn't take into account the fact that Pocket MBA took advantage of depreciation allowances to avoid paying taxes on other income. So the IRS takes some of it back, depending on whether you had a gain in light of the amount of depreciation you took. How to do it? Subtract the amount depreciated from the original sale price. This leaves a depreciated value of $30,000 ($60,000-$30,000), which becomes the adjusted tax basis for sale. Now comes the recapture. Take the resale price ($40,000) and subtract the amount depreciated/adjusted tax basis ($30,000), which leaves the recapture amount ($10,000). Note that this amount is not treated as capital gains, but rather it is added to ordinary income. You can think of it as subsequent, disallowed depreciation.

Note that this is a simplified treatment of recapture. There are different recapture rules that apply to different types of property, real estate in particular. See the IRS web site, www.irs.gov, for more details.

Trade-Through

Rule that is the main focus of proposed SEC Regulation NMS (NMS stands for National Market System). It seeks to ensure that investors receive the best price when they trade stocks. Currently, the rule does not apply to electronic exchanges, such as NASDAQ.

TRADE-THROUGH IN THE REAL WORLD:

You still have a week to comment on proposed SEC Regulation NMS, which tinkers with the current trade-through rule, but extends a new form of it to all exchanges. And if and when Regulation NMS becomes official, in whatever form that is, Pocket MBA will be on it; however, in order to understand the hubbub about Regulation NMS, a little background on trade-through is crucial.

As a preface, think of the following as food for thought. You're in your abode and you need a gallon of milk. You can get that gallon of milk at five places within walking distance of your home; those places are spaced at 1/5-mile increments. Each place charges a different price for milk and keeps you updated on their current price via your PDA. The closest store charges $3.00; the second closest charges $2.90; the third closest charges $2.80; the fourth closest charges $2.70 and the furthest away charges $2.60. Which one do you buy from and what are the factors that enter into that decision? If you are in a hurry, you may well opt for the $3.00 milk. If you have time to burn, you might walk the mile to the cheap place. Now what if you had hired someone to do the buying for you and instructed that person to always get you the best price available, even if you're in a hurry. That means you want $2.60 milk even if it takes an hour. Or maybe you told the employee to get the best price unless you were in a hurry, in which case you wanted to combine speed with price. In that instance, you might accept paying somewhere between $2.80 and $3.00 to get the milk faster, but you trust your employee to make that decision. That is somewhat akin to the debate over trade-through.

A trade-through is the execution of an order in one market at a price that is inferior to a price available in another market. And what are these markets? They are the various stock exchanges, such as NYSE, NASDAQ, AMEX, BSE (Boston), etc. Each of these markets accepts bids for buys and sells of the stocks listed on the NYSE. Those bids are not always the same. It is the duty of the specialists (see Pocket MBA, Vol. 2, No. 7) at the NYSE to fill an order at the best price available on any of the various exchanges.

Here's how it works, in more technical terms, according to the NYSE itself, in "Potential Costs of Weakening the Trade-through Rule," NYSE Research (February 2004):

> Companies listed on the NYSE are traded on the New York and regional stock exchanges, NASDAQ dealers, and Electronic Communications Networks. These various markets attract orders from stockbrokers by competitively quoting bid and ask prices, with orders flowing to the markets with the best-quoted prices. One or more markets can simultaneously quote the most competitive prices. Other markets may quote worse prices and consequently not receive many orders until

their quotes improve. If a market center displays a better quote than is available on another market, then specialists and market makers are generally required by SEC regulation ("trade-through" rule) to route orders to the market with the better price. This helps to assure that investors receive the best available price. At the same time it encourages the competitive vitality of markets by assuring that investors who provide the most competitive quotes and priced limit orders do not have their orders ignored ("traded through").

The trade-through rule has been around on the NYSE and AMEX for almost three decades. The philosophy behind it is simple: price is the most important thing for investors when they trade stocks. In fact, price is so important, it doesn't matter if trades don't happen quickly or at all, so long as an investor can get the price they want. One of the problems of the trade-through system is that the NYSE still operates "manually," for lack of a better term. Unlike its computerized brethren at NASDAQ, human beings are still required to do the price seeking and listing. As a result, the price an investor thinks is available might well not be the price a stock is actually trading at and hence the investor's order gets ignored, or he has to cancel his order and offer a higher price. It is for these reasons that NASDAQ, as a computerized trading center, is one of the chief opponents of the trade-through rule.

NASDAQ believes that the trade-through rule trumpets price over "best execution." Best execution combines factors such as price, speed, certainty of execution, accessibility and cost. NASDAQ, with its electronic-exchange affiliates believes that traders don't always want the absolute best price (especially when the difference is measured in pennies, as it now is, as opposed to the 1/8 dollar that it used to be measured by); rather, they want their orders executed in the best manner. NASDAQ believes that in the broad scheme of things, all things being relatively equal, aiming for best execution results in the best price available. According to NASDAQ, bids can languish on the NYSE while the specialist searches (and some argue manipulates) the system for the best price. NASDAQ guarantees swift execution, although you might get the second or third best price. To get a better feel for how NASDAQ views the trade-through rule, see www.nasdaq.com/newsroom/news/pr2005/ne_section05_013.stm.

Now comes the SEC, in the wake of allegations of specialist and other market abuses, and at the urging of players such as NYSE, Fidelity Investments and CalPers, to review the entire NMS to see if it shouldn't ban trade-through altogether. The result is Regulation NMS, proposed on March 9. 2004, which strikes a middle road approach. In its executive summary, the SEC stated as follows:

- Clearly, in a fully efficient market with frictionless access and instantaneous executions, trading through a better-displayed bid or offer should not occur. Yet the Commission believes that even in the current markets with linkages between markets and a range of execution speeds and fill rates, there is value in protecting a displayed price from trades occurring at inferior prices in other markets.
- The Commission therefore is proposing a rule intended to preserve the benefits of price protection across markets, while addressing the tensions in the operation of the current ITS trade-through rule.
- The proposed rule would require an order execution facility, national securities exchange, and national securities association to establish, maintain, and enforce polices and procedures reasonably designed to prevent the execution of a trade-through in its market.
- The proposed rule would have two major exceptions. One would allow customers (and broker-dealers trading for their own accounts) to "opt-out" of the protections of the rule by providing informed consent to the execution of their orders, on an order-by-order basis, in one market without regard to the possibility of

obtaining a better price in another market. The other exception would take into account the differences between the speed of execution in electronic versus manual markets by providing an automated market with the ability to trade-through a non-automated market up to a certain amount away from the best bid or offer displayed by the non-automated market.

- The Commission believes that the proposed rule would promote competition and order interaction between markets, provide an incentive for the use of limit orders and aggressive quoting, facilitate the ability to achieve best execution and help reduce the effects of fragmentation.

The sides are drawn and, in essence, a turf battle has ensued, with the NYSE staking out a position in favor of the proposal, with the exception of the opt-out; and the NASDAQ, realizing that it cannot win on the trade-through rule, urging that the opt-out is essential to the future survival and efficiency of the markets. This will surely play out in public view over the next year, as the SEC decides ultimately what to do. So keep watching.

AUTHOR UPDATE: In April 2005, The SEC voted 3-2 to adopt Regulation NMS in a somewhat controversial move on the eve of former Chairman William Donaldson's departure. NMS includes an order-protection rule that requires traders to obtain the best price for investors. So the trade through rule lives on.

PLI's Pocket MBA Vol. 2, No. 25   June 30, 2004

Fair Value

The amount at which an asset (or liability) can be bought (or incurred) or sold (or settled) in a current voluntary transaction (i.e.

outside of liquidation or other forced purchase or sale).

FAIR VALUE IN THE REAL WORLD:

The above definition comes from the Financial Accounting Standards Board's (FASB) Statement of Financial Accounting Concept 7. But nobody really knows what fair value means, except that it's one of those, "I know it when I see it" things. Pocket MBA has argued with many friends and family members about whether athletes and movie stars are worth the exorbitant amounts of money they are paid to, respectively, play games and just play. Pocket MBA always posits that if the market is willing to pay these amounts then that is what the athletes and actors are worth. The opposing argument is that it's just not fair that such value is attached to subjectively trivial activities, to which Pocket MBA responds, "If the market will bear it, then the value is fair."

If you really strip the concept of fair value down to its essence, it is just that: What is someone willing to pay for an asset in a voluntary transaction? Of course that begs the question--it's an unending loop of, "But what's fair and who decides?" And even if an agreement can be reached that any value arrived at after a fair and voluntary negotiation renders "fair value," left out are assets and liabilities for which there is no current market negotiation--those that an entity has and, for some reason, must assign value to. In those cases, who's to say?

The concept of fair value is one of the lynchpins of GAAP and is important to accountants and auditors. More and more accounting standards require that companies value assets and liabilities at fair value. For instance, accounting for business combinations (FAS 141) and goodwill (FAS 142) now require that these items be recorded at fair value. But the determination of fair value can be so nebulous that any lawyer, when confronted by references to fair value, will probably raise an eyebrow and mutter, "Objection." Indeed, GAAP doesn't specify how fair value is to be measured. In fact, the standards of the Financial Accounting Standards Board (FASB) starts from the assumption that "most accounting measurements use an observable marketplace-determined amount, like cash received or paid, current cost, or current market value." FASB Statement of Financial Accounting Concept 7.

As a result, FASB has raised that same eyebrow that you probably do. And so last June, FASB embarked on what could only be called a "fair value project." In a June 30, 2003 release, the Board stated that it plans to develop a Fair Value Statement--a "framework for fair value measurements, thereby providing a single reference source for fair value measurements required under other accounting pronouncements." FASB noted that its Concepts Statement No. 5 (Recognition and Measurement in Financial Statements) "provides only limited guidance for addressing measurement issues. Among other things, it does not identify fair value as a possible measurement attribute. It also does not provide an adequate basis for determining how that qualitative characteristics of relevance and reliability should be applied in selecting an appropriate measurement attribute." That's comforting. Many companies that have to engage in the assignment of fair value, but which lack personnel qualified to make the determinations, hire outside valuation consultants who specialize in fair value. And auditors are subsequently left to determine whether the assumptions made and factors used by these "experts" are legitimate.

FASB expects to issue a draft Fair Value Statement in the near future. Already, in relation to the standard, FASB has decided to modify the traditional definition of fair value, as restated above, to the following:

> The price at which an asset or liability could be exchanged in a current transaction between knowledgeable, unrelated willing parties.

Pocket MBA will continue to monitor the fair value project as FASB begins to determine how your clients should determine this most elusive, yet common sense, value.

CAP-EX

Amount companies spend to acquire and/or upgrade long-term assets like plant, property and equipment.

CAP-EX IN THE REAL WORLD:

After concerns about the jobless recovery (which, in light of the explosion in hiring over the past few months, seems to have ended), the biggest buzz in the economy is about when large-scale CAP-EX will return. And the reasons are clear. CAP-EX tends to involve very large sums of money, the ripple effect of which is felt across the economy. When companies spend large sums of money to acquire or upgrade long-term assets, they demonstrate confidence in the future, on top of any present success. In the current situation, it would also indicate that all that excess froth that remained after the 90s boom had finally been absorbed. And according to various news reports, CEOs seem generally sanguine, even if not rah-rah, about CAP-EX for the near future. The Census Bureau conducts surveys of expected capital expenditures in 130 industries on an annual basis. The Annual Capital Expenditures Survey (ACES) "is part of a comprehensive program designed to provide detailed and timely information on capital investment in new and used structures and equipment by non-farm businesses." You can access the 2002 ACES on the bureau's web site, www.census.gov/csd/ace, to get an idea of what it looked like back when things were truly dire.

That's all fine and good, but from a Pocket MBA perspective, the importance of CAP-EX is its impact on balance sheets and tax returns. Why? Well because unlike ordinary business expenses, CAP-EX must be capitalized, that is depreciated, depleted or amortized, over its useful life, rather than expensed during the year purchased. And, of course, this dovetails with the Pocket MBA issue on depreciation - Vol. 2, No. 14. A reasonable conclusion is that aside from tax implications, CAP-EX is merely a bookkeeping exercise because, in the end, whether fully deducted in year one or depreciated over time, the remaining business value at the end of the depreciation of any investment approaches zero. Of course, the IRS prefers that investments in plant and equipment be matched with the annual income they produce, and therefore, their value must be depreciated over time. This also has capital gains implications if the asset is sold, but that's another issue altogether.

Merriam-Webster Online dictionary defines capitalize as, in part, "to gain by turning something to advantage." So, by definition, CAP-EX connotes a long-term, positive impact on the balance sheet and, hence, tax return. That's because CAP-EX involves the purchase of capital assets--those items that last for more than one year and that increase the value of a business or extend the useful life of business property. Therefore, things like repairs to plant and equipment that merely maintain the status quo of operability are not considered capital expenditures, nor are assets that are used up in the span of a year, like a pad of paper or an annual license. These short-term expenses are simply deducted from the gross receipts during the year they are incurred, never to be heard from again. But things like company cars, new computer systems, new and upgraded plants, patents and the like, stick around and continue to produce income over a long period of time. Thus they are not expenses, in the accounting or tax sense. Indeed, another definition of capitalize is simply "to treat as capital rather than as an expense."

Usually it's obvious whether an expense is capital or not. This is not always so with regard to repairs and maintenance. That is the big, gray area of CAP-EX. When is a business repairing and maintaining, as opposed to improving by making the repair? Over time, the IRS has developed a list of what is and what is not a capital expense. IRS publication 535 (available at www.irs.gov) is helpful in nailing down (so to speak) what is and what is not an improvement:

- The costs of making improvements to a business asset are capital expenses if the improvements add to the value of the asset, appreciably lengthen the time you can use it, or adapt it to a

different use. You can deduct repairs that keep your property in a normal efficient operating condition as a business expense.
- Improvements include new electric wiring, a new roof, a new floor, new plumbing, bricking up windows to strengthen a wall, and lighting improvements. Restoration plan.
- Capitalize the cost of reconditioning, improving, or altering your property as part of a general restoration plan to make it suitable for your business. This applies even if some of the work would by itself be classified as repairs.
- Replacements. You cannot deduct the cost of a replacement that stops deterioration and adds to the life of your property. Capitalize that cost and depreciate it.
- Treat as repairs amounts paid to replace parts of a machine that only keep it in a normal operating condition. However, if your equipment has a major overhaul, capitalize and depreciate the expense.

Publication 535 offers more concrete examples, including expenditures on business vehicles, machinery parts, tools and, oddly enough, heating equipment. Apparently, one of the first things businesses do when a new CAP-EX cycle begins is to replace heating systems. Got to keep all those new employees warm.

Commodity Futures Trading Commission

Government Agency that regulates financial and commodity futures and/or options.

COMMODITY FUTURES TRADING COMMISSION IN THE REAL WORLD:

Pocket MBA has to admit that until today, it had no idea what the Commodity Futures Trading Commission (CFTC) was or did. The CFTC's mission, as stated on its website, www.cftc.gov, is "to protect market users and the public from fraud, manipulation, and abusive practices related to the sale of commodity and financial futures and options, and to foster open, competitive, and financially sound futures and option markets." The agency has only been in existence since 1974 (see the Commodity Exchange Act, 7 U.S.C. sec. 1, et seq.), although futures contracts for agricultural commodities had been traded in the U.S. for more than 120 years when the CFTC came into existence, and federal regulation of commodities began in the 1920s. Congress renewed and expanded the CFTC's mandate recently, via the Commodities Futures Modernization Act of 2000. The CFTC seeks to enable the futures markets "to serve the important function of providing a means for price discovery and offsetting price risk."

Futures and options are one of the final frontiers in investing, as far as lay-investors go. Nonetheless, one can't turn on the television or pick up a newspaper without being inundated by futures' related news. All those stories about rising, and then sinking, oil prices are, in reality, stories about futures contracts and the speculation that has been going on about the future movement in the price of the black goo. And although your institutional clients may have been involved in futures and options trading for a long time, as more and more individuals (recall the brouhaha over then-First Lady Hillary Clinton's pre-1992 killing in the futures markets) and pension funds have become active in trading them, the need for centralized oversight has increased accordingly. Not only are more investors involved, the CFTC observes that "in recent years, trading in futures contracts has expanded rapidly beyond traditional physical and agricultural commodities into a vast array of financial instruments, including foreign currencies, U.S. and foreign government securities, and U.S. and foreign stock indices." And as everyone knows by now, it's when a formerly obscure or specialized investing method goes mainstream that opportunities for chicanery evolve. Hence the instructional and cautionary reports on the CFTC's website.

Most recently (in 2003), the CFTC moved "to eliminate several regulatory constraints on pension entities, making it easier for pension funds to operate without direct CFTC regulation." That's good news for your pension fund clients. Still there are constraints that you need to heed. First, CFTC SWAPS exclusions still apply to pension equities. Second, Commodity Pool Operators and Commodities Trading Advisors "must register with the CFTC and meet other regulatory requirements absent an exemption or exclusion." To learn more about the CFTC, visit www.cftc.gov.

PLI's Pocket MBA Vol. 2, No. 28   July 28, 2004

Auditor Report

Report by an independent CPA opining whether a public company's financial statements present fairly its financial position, operating results and cash flows in accordance with generally accepted accounting principles (GAAP).

AUDITOR REPORT IN THE REAL WORLD:

On May 24, 2004, the PCAOB's Public Auditing Standard No. 1 (PAS1) went into effect. PAS1 "requires that auditors' reports on audits and other engagements relating to public companies and other issuers include a reference that the engagement was performed in accordance with the standards of the PCAOB. This replaces the previous reference to "generally accepted auditing standards," or GAAS. Curiously, this seemingly substantive break with the past has no particular impact on auditors' reports as they have been constituted until now. Why?

Well, as the SEC reported in approving PAS1, "[t]he PCAOB adopted those generally accepted auditing standards, including their respective effective dates, as they existed on April 16, 2003, as interim PCAOB standards. Therefore, changing the reference from 'generally accepted auditing standards' to 'the standards of the Public Company Accounting Oversight Board (United States)' does not change the substantive procedures performed by an auditor. Because GAAS and the standards of the PCAOB are one and the same for PCAOB-registered public accounting firms, the PCAOB believes that a reference to GAAS in auditors' reports would no longer be appropriate or necessary."

Given that nothing much has changed, what exactly goes into an auditor's report in an average 10Q? Well, the easiest way to illustrate a standard auditor report is to reprint the bulk of a standard one here. Pocket MBA has redacted the names of the company and auditor from this report, issued in February 2004, just prior to the effectual date of PAS1:

> To the Board of Directors and Shareholders of XYZ, Inc.:
>
> We have audited the accompanying consolidated balance sheets of XYZ, Inc. and subsidiaries (the "Company") as of December 27, 2003 and December 28, 2002, and the related consolidated statements of income, stockholders' equity, and cash flows for each of the two years in the period ended December 27, 2003. These financial statements are the responsibility of the Company's management. Our responsibility is to express an opinion on these financial statements based on our audits.
>
> We conducted our audits in accordance with auditing standards generally accepted in the United States of America. Those standards require that we plan and perform the audit to obtain reasonable assurance about whether the financial statements are free of material misstatement. An audit includes examining, on a test basis, evidence supporting the amounts and disclosures in the financial statements. An audit also includes assessing the accounting principles used and

significant estimates made by management, as well as evaluating the overall financial statement presentation. We believe that our audits provide a reasonable basis for our opinion.

In our opinion, such financial statements present fairly, in all material respects, the financial position of XYZ, Inc. and subsidiaries as of December 27, 2003 and December 28, 2002, and the results of their operations and their cash flows for each of the two years in the period ended December 27, 2003, in conformity with accounting principles generally accepted in the United States of America.

In this report, everything is hunky-dory. It offers what is known as "positive assurance" that XYZ, Inc.'s financial statements comport with applicable accounting standards. Other reports might not be so glowing. Then, they might conclude what is known as "negative assurance"--that is a statement to the effect that the auditor is not aware of anything that might need to be changed to bring the financial statements into comportment with GAAP. This is a hedge of sorts. And then there is the next step down, an "adverse opinion," which would indicate the financial statements are not in comportment with GAAP. And even if the financial statements comport with GAAP, an auditor might express an opinion that it has doubts about the company's ability to continue as a going concern, see Pocket MBA, Vo. 1, No. 20, meaning there are circumstances that, if they continued or came about, would put the company's very existence into doubt. A report like that would contain language like the following from a February 2004 report on a different company:

> The accompanying consolidated financial statements have been prepared assuming that the Company will continue as a going concern. As discussed in Note 2 to the consolidated financial statements, the Company has had recurring losses and used $18.5 million in cash for operations in 2003. These matters raise a substantial doubt about the Company's ability to continue as a

going concern. The consolidated financial statements do not include any adjustments that might result from the outcome of this uncertainty.

PLI's Pocket MBA Vol. 2, No. 29   August 4, 2004

Cost of Goods Sold (COGS)

The costs directly attributable to manufacturing or selling the inventory of a business.

COGS IN THE REAL WORLD:

Pocket MBA has worn Nike sneakers on and off since 1978. The retail price of these sneakers has jumped from around $29 then to $79 now, give or take (obviously you can buy a pair of Nike shoes for as little as $40 or upwards of $200 if you really want to, and there was probably a $40 pair back in the day). So, it came as no surprise to Pocket MBA after a quick peruse of Nike's statement of cash flows that Nike has been enormously profitable, by and large, generating hundreds of millions of dollars in free cash flow in the past year alone. That's a lot of swoosh. But, you'd think at $200 a pop, the company that taught everyone to "Be Like Mike" and to "Just Do It" would make even more. It doesn't because profitability has little to do with the price of a good or service. If that were the case, the airlines would be making buckets off those $1,300 business fares. But they're not. And that, in large part, is due to COGS, the costs of selling goods and services, or as it is referred to on an income statement, cost of revenue. There is no gross profit (and, eventually, net profit) for a business until after COGS has been subtracted, and it is generally the largest expense a company has.

If you take a look at Nike's most recent income statement, you will see COGS ($6,313,600,000) on the second line, just beneath total revenue ($10,697,000). Subtracting COGS from total revenue gives you a company's gross profit ($4,383,400,000). Of course, the COGS number doesn't tell you what goes into its calculation. But the term, Cost of Goods Sold, is somewhat self-explanatory if you think about it--it's simply the cost of making something you sell. That can include costs of materials, labor costs and other direct costs, like the cost of transporting materials, etc. However, COGS does not include items such as office expenses, accounting, advertising or other expenses that are considered indirect, as they cannot be attributed to the sale of a particular item.

So, the retail cost of one pair of custom-designed Nike Shox R4 iD running shoes is $165 if you buy it from the Nike store. Ignoring economies of scale, in order to make that one pair of shoes, Nike has to purchase various lightweight synthetics that make up the shoe, along with what the company calls BRS carbon rubber that makes up the soles. Then there are nylon laces and little pieces of plastic here and there. Those pieces have to be delivered to a Nike manufacturing facility, but even then, the shoe doesn't yet exist. Someone has to put all these parts together (including that swoosh). Add whatever Nike pays that person to the other expenses, and you're pretty close to the COGS for that pair of Shox.

Still, your average company has a large inventory, moving in and out of the warehouse, along with parts and employees, etc. How do you figure COGS, generally, without doing it item by item? Simple. You take the value of the inventory at the beginning of a fiscal period, add in purchases of materials that make up inventory, labor costs and other direct costs (freight and some overhead items), then subtract the inventory remaining at the end of the fiscal period. For shorthand:

- COGS = Beginning Inventory + Purchases + Labor Costs + Other Direct Costs - Inventory Ending

This enables a business to avoid having to flag every item sold and attribute cost to that item separately. You can use your newfound knowledge of COGS to understand your clients' finances better or, like Pocket MBA, you can use it to figure out whether you're overpaying for sneakers.

Enterprise Value

A measure of the value of a company calculated by adding to market capitalization the amount of debt a company has on its balance sheet and subtracting the cash and cash equivalents. It can be used as a neighborhood takeover price.

ENTERPRISE VALUE IN THE REAL WORLD:

If you flip on the television and turn to any business program, the moderators always talk about the market capitalization of companies to signify their size. For several years now, Microsoft and General Electric have jockeyed back and forth for the title of largest market cap (as of this writing, GE has a $25 billion lead) and, hence, according to the talking heads, largest company. But does market capitalization really tell you enough about a company to tell you the value or size of the company? If you remember back a few short years ago, when companies that have long since disappeared sported market caps in excess of $100 billion, you will likely conclude, "No it does not." And if you had taken those same companies and determined their enterprise value, you might have foreseen the bursting of the bubble. For you might well have made yourself privy to what many at the time warned: these companies weren't worth anywhere near the amount at which they were pegged. And that's where enterprise value comes in.

So what does enterprise value tell you that market capitalization does not? Well, market capitalization is simply the number of shares outstanding multiplied by share price. And of course, it is axiomatic that investors pay for a share of stock whatever they perceive the company is "worth" in terms of its future earnings power. But since share price fluctuates constantly, share price doesn't really tell you anything beyond the general "this company is doing well at this moment or we expect it to in the future." It doesn't tell you about how a company's earnings are impacted by some of the innards of the company. Enterprise value is an attempt to factor those innards into the market capitalization to give a truer statement of a company's actual economic value.

For instance, some companies have no outstanding debt to speak of. Others have loads of the stuff. All things being equal, if you take two companies with the same market capitalization, one of which is loaded down by debt into the foreseeable future and the other of which is debt free, which is really more valuable at the given moment? For which would you be willing to pay more? Obviously, it's the one without debt. Now it may be that the company with debt has some future prospect (like the potential secret to curing baldness) that may render it the most successful company in the recorded history of the world. But as that prospect matures, it will be reflected in market capitalization. If it isn't currently so reflected, the prospect is just that--a prospect without any guarantee. But, in a purchase of these companies, the current debt comes with the company now, so again, all things being equal, the one without debt is worth more at this moment. In fact, if you paid market value for the outstanding shares, you would in reality be paying, in addition, the amount of the debt.

Similarly, you can take those same companies and assume that both are debt free. But, in this example, one has $1 billion cash on its books and the other zero. If you or a client were to buy one of these companies, the cash comes with it--it's like a discount off the purchase price. It's almost like going to the grocery store and seeing those specials where a company sells a bottle of mouthwash and attaches a tube of toothpaste in shrink-wrap. If the price of the bottle of mouthwash is the same with or without the tube of toothpaste, which is worth more? It's the one that gives you the added value.

That's all enterprise value is. It secks to give the investor or purchaser a true sense of a company's value beyond mere earnings. And debt and cash, combined, have an actual economic impact on a company's value that is not reflected in market capitalization. So the next time someone tells you that you can buy a certain company for its market cap of $10 billion, check to see how much debt is on its balance sheet because that is an unstated premium on the price. Conversely, check if the company has a figurative tube of toothpaste attached. In that case, $10 billion might be a bargain.

Now, for a real life example. As Pocket MBA referenced Nike in the last issue, it seemed appropriate to go to the well one more time. As of this writing, Nike sports a market capitalization of $19.3 billion (that's approximately 257 million shares outstanding times its recent $75+ stock price). It's balance sheet shows short and long-term debt totaling approximately $700 million and cash and cash equivalents of just under $915 million. So:

- EV = $19.3 billion + $700 million = $20 billion - $915 million = $19.085 billion

What does this tell you? It tells you that Nike is a pretty fairly valued company. If you were to buy all the outstanding shares of stock at the going market price, you would, taking into account debt and cash, be getting a $215 million bargain. And that's at least one a couple pair of Nike Shox.

PLI's Pocket MBA Vol. 2, No. 31   August 18, 2004

Lower of Cost or Market (LCM)

Exception to the cost principle of accounting, applicable particularly in the case of valuing inventory, where stock is valued at the lower of cost or market value.

LOWER OF COST OR MARKET (LCM) IN THE REAL WORLD:

For accounting purposes, assets have been valued, traditionally, at their acquisition cost (cost of an item plus incidentals like taxes, installation, etc. associated with putting the asset into service). This is known as the "cost principle." So, if a company buys a trash compactor for $75,000 (taxes included), and it costs $1,500 to deliver and install it and another $1,000 in taxes, the asset is recorded at a cost of $77,500.

LCM is a departure from the cost principle, and it is accepted under GAAP premised on the guideline of "conservatism," that is, accountants like to err on the side of under-valuation of assets rather than overvaluation. If you think about accounts like inventory, the cost principle can easily overstate the value of an asset. The value of manufactured goods deteriorates over time. Think about your computer. It probably cost you the same amount as the last computer you bought. But you get a lot more for your money. Now, think about all those computer manufacturers, like Dell, HP, Gateway, Sony. They are subject to the same economics. Except they have thousands of computers, many of which are obsolete, damaged, returned or whatever. It cost the manufacturers $X to make each of those computers, but due to a variety of circumstances, they will not reap the benefit of selling them. Each computer is sitting on the company's books at $X. But the value of the computer is no longer $X--in fact, it's probably closer to zero. It is at this point that accountants eschew the cost principle for something that more approximates the real value of the inventory, and that is LCM, which shows up on the balance sheet as a charge against revenue or in a reserve for obsolescence.

So how do companies peg the market cost of their no longer full-value inventory? There are four numbers that come into consideration: cost, replacement cost, floor and ceiling. Generally speaking, the replacement cost will be the number that represents market value. Back to those computers. Assume the manufacturer has 1,000 laptops with 12-inch screens and Intel 486 processors sitting around--clearly obsolete. It cost the manufacturer $600 to make each one. That's $600,000. The cost of replacing those items is now $225 per unit (mostly labor). That's $225,000. So, generally, the company would write down $375,000 against revenues. However, when assessing market value, a company must also determine two other numbers, the floor and the ceiling. The selling price (or net realizable value) of the computers minus the disposal cost is the market value "ceiling." The selling price minus a normal profit margin is the market value "floor." If the replacement cost exceeds or falls below these numbers, respectively, then the middle number of the three is used as market value.

Confusing, huh? You can play around with numbers to see how this works for yourself, but that's not really all that important. What is important is to be aware that LCM is out there and being used by your clients everyday. Now, if anyone is interested, Pocket MBA has a Compaq computer with Windows 3.1, an Intel 386 chip and a 560 megabyte hard drive, fully loaded with solitaire and WordPerfect 5.0, that cost $1,795 back in 1993. Address all offers to Pocket MBA's e-mail.

PLI's Pocket MBA Vol. 2, No. 32   August 25, 2004

Accretive to Earnings

In the M&A world, a buyout is accretive to earnings if it increases the earning per share of the purchasing company.

ACCRETIVE TO EARNINGS IN THE REAL WORLD:

Whenever a company announces it is purchasing another company, somewhere in the press release will be a statement as to when the deal will be accretive to earnings. If the deal is immediately accretive to earnings, stockholders get excited because the value of their shares will undoubtedly get a boost. But why is it that when one profitable company buys another profitable company, it isn't always accretive to earnings? The combined entity will earn more money than each standing alone. But, in the world of public companies, earnings standing alone don't tell an investor or analyst that much about how much the company actually made for their shareholders. Huh?

Simple. Take two companies. They each earned $1 million in their most recent quarter. Each company's stock sells at $10/share. Company A has one million outstanding shares. Company B has ten million outstanding shares. Which made more money for its shareholders? Company A did. It earned one dollar per outstanding share of stock. Company B earned only $.1 per share of outstanding stock. When it comes to accretion, that figure is important. The Price/Earnings Per Share ratio (P/E) of Company A is 10, and the P/E of Company B is 100. If Company B buys Company A, the deal will be accretive--it will improve its P/E ratio. But if Company A buys Company B, the deal will be dilutive. This works because "accretive to earnings" really means "accretive to earnings per share." And if the P/E ratio of the purchasing company is less than that of the target, then the purchase actually dilutes the earnings per share of the purchasing company.

So if Company B buys Company A for stock (say it issues five shares of B for every share of A), New Company B will have $2 million in earnings and 15 million shares of stock outstanding. New Company B now earns $.133 per share of stock, and its P/E ratio (assuming the $10 stock price) is only 75. This deal is accretive--it adds to Company B's earnings. But if you flip it around and have Company A buy Company B and issue one-half of a share of New Company A for every share of Company B, look what results: New Company A will have $2 million in earnings and six million shares outstanding. Instead of earning one dollar per share, as did Company A, New Company A is earning $.33 per share, which results in a P/E ratio (again, assuming a $10 stock price) of 30.3. That's dilutive.

Now, a company may want a deal that is presently dilutive because it expects the deal to become wildly accretive at some future date. That's just combining growth rates with more calculations. For instance, maybe Company A's earning power has peaked, but Company B is expected to double earnings every year for the next five years. That means, in five years, Company B will earn $32 million dollars. Assume the same buyout now of Company B by Company A, and you can see how Company B's future growth is worth a current dilution in earnings for Company A. Five years from now, the combined entity will earn $33 million for those six million outstanding shares. That's over five dollars per share in earnings. And the deal would have gone from dilutive to accretive sometime during the five years.

There are all kinds of permutations on this theme, and the deals don't quite work the same when the deal is not all stock. But you get the idea.

Capital Structure

The permanent, long-term financing of a company, generally analyzed by looking at its mix of debt and equity issues, that is, the amount of money the company has borrowed (via bond issues and loans, but excluding short-term debt and accounts payable) and the common and preferred stock the company has issued, together with its retained earnings.

CAPITAL STRUCTURE IN THE REAL WORLD:

Here's something axiomatic. All companies have a capital structure, and all it really represents is the mixture of financing mechanisms (equity and debt) that a company has put together to propel its long-term operations. As will be explored more thoroughly in our next issue, companies like large airlines have capital structures heavily weighted towards debt. And new companies like Krispy Kreme are weighted more towards equity. But at any given moment in time, the capital structure of a firm is largely irrelevant (unless bankruptcy is looming) to short-term operations. The capital structure is very important when analyzing the long-term health of a company and impacts the relative advisability of a company borrowing money or issuing new shares of stock, as well as whether an investor should pony up for either.

Going public ABC: as all Pocket MBA readers know, when companies go public, they issue shares of stock and receive money for them--money they use to finance operations and which rewards, often very handsomely (see Google) the venture capitalists who fronted the company from the beginning. The new shareholders get a stake in future profits of the business (which they may or may not receive in dividends at some future date). When and if the company plows through all the cash it raised via the equity offering, and if it doesn't generate enough cash through operations to finance current or future projects, it can issue more shares. The problem with this is that shareholders tend to expect a certain return over time, and the more shares a company issues, the less return each individual share is entitled to. And this dilutive effect of continued equity offerings tends to decrease the amount of money the company can raise through them. So companies begin to borrow money, either from lending institutions or by issuing their own debt securities. These mechanisms work because issuing debt tends to be cheaper than issuing equity. Lenders or purchasers of the debt receive a guaranteed rate of return and priority over the common stockholders in the event of financial disaster. Also, debt can reduce the taxes a profitable company pays, as the interest can be deducted off of pre-tax profits.

It is only after this process plays out (after a company begins to borrow money) that a company's capital structure becomes important. Why? The same reasons that borrowing is important for individuals--if you borrow too much, and your income is not increasing (or, worse, if a recession hits, and it is decreasing) the odds of being able to pay all the obligations of the debt begin to decrease. If a company has more debt than it can handle, it may be required to return to issuing shares. But new investors may be wary of a company with a lot of debt, and hence will pay even less for new shares. Worse, the original investors may not wish to plow any more money into a company that has borrowed heavily subsequent to the initial share issuance. It can be quite a vicious cycle for a fledgling company and can lead to the financing well drying up. If you're Google, and you just raised a couple billion dollars, you don't worry; but if you're an airline, like Delta, that has run out of financing options, you go hat in hand, looking for ways to restructure your incredible debt load, so you don't crash and burn.

You can research capital structure using myriad resources, and all will state that there is no optimal capital structure for a company. The only thing that experts agree on is that a company should seek some kind of balance (whatever that is) between debt and equity. One of the most important factors that go into determining whether a particular capital structure is right for a particular company include the type of industry a company is in--if a company's revenues are unpredictable because it is in a volatile industry, then a company is better off with less debt and more equity. The particular tax structure of a company is also important--the more tax deductible a company's debt is, the more likely it is to prefer debt financing over equity financing.

This simplified, introductory pre-Labor Day weekend discussion of capital structure serves merely as a springboard to future issues of Pocket MBA, the first of which will appear two weeks hence. Until then, enjoy the "last" weekend of summer 2004.

PLI's Pocket MBA Vol. 2, No. 34   September 15, 2004

Debt/Equity Ratio

Indicator of a company's debt exposure that compares how much the company owes (debt) against how much it owns (equity).

DEBT/EQUITY RATIO IN THE REAL WORLD:

American Airlines' is 30.6; Continental's is 12.45; Delta's is nearly infinite. By contrast, Yahoo's is .74; Nike's is .68; and Krispy Kreme's is .46. No, this isn't another bash fest on the economic inefficiency of legacy airlines. (But it does point that out, albeit inadvertently, seeing as JetBlue's is only 2.26 and Southwest's is only .95). Rather, it is testament to the fact that the debt/equity ratio is a pretty good indicator of how safe a creditor can feel handing money to a company. As Delta has announced it may be heading into bankruptcy, that infinite debt/equity ratio is as bright a red light as could be imagined.

Of course, issuing or taking on debt is as American as public corporations themselves, and when an opportunity to make money by issuing debt or borrowing money presents itself (to finance a blockbuster project, for instance), well, good for the company. The problem with debt is that with it comes interest expense, and depending on economic times and a company's debt rating, that can be a godsend (if the company can use the money for a better return elsewhere) or a killer (if the economy hits the skids and profits decline, leaving the company with less cash to pay the interest). So a high ratio doesn't necessarily mean that a company is in trouble. But if a company has a debt/equity ratio that is rising over time (and Pocket MBA would wager that if you looked at big airlines' debt/equity ratios over time, they would be getting larger and larger), you get a pretty good sense that the business is declining insofar as its fundamental economic health is concerned. Of course, there are industry-by-industry caveats that apply here. Nonetheless, it seems to be agreed that the average industrial company should sport a debt/equity ratio somewhere between .5 and 1.5.

So how does one go about determining a company's debt/equity ratio? This is probably one of the easiest calculations to make in all of finance, so long as you have access to a company's balance sheet:

- Total Liabilities/Total Stockholder Equity

Of course, this is just the public company version of the personal debt/equity ratio determination that most people keep a running tab on in their daily lives. Everyone who has credit card debt or a mortgage can probably state how much debt they have relative to the amount of cash, cash equivalents and stocks they hold. Like public companies, this ratio determines, to a large extent, whether an individual can or is willing to take on more debt. And for those who have no money in the bank, borrowing is obviously quite difficult. It's the same principle with public companies. So next time you need some cash, figure your own debt/equity ratio; if it's lower than American Airlines', figure you've got a shot.

Capital Lease

As specified in Statement of Financial Accounting Standard (SFAS) No. 13, a lease that meets at least one of several criteria that results in the transfer of substantially all of the benefits and risks of ownership in the property to the lessee.

CAPITAL LEASE IN THE REAL WORLD:

Caution, Pocket MBA is entering the territory of copy machines, car fleets and heavy-equipment. People tend to use the terms leasing and renting interchangeably, and that's okay in the personal finance world. But in the business world, they are two completely different concepts because of accounting consequences. When a business rents something, anything, be it a car or even office space, it takes possession of the rented property understanding it will return the property to the owner at the end of the rental period, be it a day, week, month, year or whatever. In such a case, the lessee records the payments it makes as an expense. But there are certain arrangements by which a company, as far as accounting is concerned, takes possession of property by a lease but, due to the terms of the lease, is required to treat the equipment as if it has purchased it. In such cases, the company capitalizes the arrangement on its balance sheet (that is it charges the expense to its asset account). When this is the case, the arrangement is called a "capital lease."

In the personal finance world, car leasing is a close relative of capital leasing--you lease a car for three years for $X per month and you get an option to purchase the car at the end of the lease. The payment schedule is not unlike that if you were actually to buy the car...but you haven't. Of course, since individuals don't have to keep balance sheets like companies do, capital leasing is not quite that simple. Just because a company leases a piece of property with a buyout option doesn't render the lease capital. FASB requires that the lease arrangements transfer most of the rights and obligations of ownership to the lessee before a lease can be treated as capital. A copy machine is normally depreciated over five years. Assume a business wants to rent a copy machine valued at $5,000, and a company agrees to lease it for three years at $175 a month, $22 of which is designated as maintenance costs, with an option to purchase it for $750 at the end of the lease. Prior to leasing the copier, the lessor had previously leased it to another company for four years. The lease is not capital. Why?

SFAS 13, paragraph 7 sets out the criteria, at least one of which must be met, to classify a lease as "capital." They are as follows:

a) The lease transfers ownership of the property to the lessee by the end of the lease term
b) The lease contains a bargain purchase option (defined in paragraph 5(d) as "a price which is sufficiently lower than the expected fair value of the property at the date the option becomes exercisable that exercise of the option appears at the inception of the lease, to be reasonably assured")
c) The lease term is equal to 75 percent or more of the estimated economic life of the leased property. (SFAS caveat: criterion c is inapplicable if the beginning of the lease term falls within the last 25 percent of the total estimated economic life of the leased property, including earlier years of use)
d) The present value at the beginning of the lease term of the minimum lease payments equals or exceeds 90 percent of the fair value of the property to the lessor excluding such parts of the payment as can be designated insurance, maintenance, taxes or other executory costs (SFAS caveat: criterion d is inapplicable if the beginning of the lease term falls within the last 25 percent of the total estimated economic life of the leased property, including earlier years of use)

As far as the copy machine is concerned, paragraph 7(a) is clearly not met, as the lessee must pay $750 to get the copier at the end of the lease term. As the economic life of the property will have expired by the end of the lease, paragraph 7(b) is not met because the purchase option is not a bargain. Also, because the lessee took possession of the copier in the last 20 percent of its economic life, paragraphs 7(c) and 7(d) do not apply. Thus the company will have to treat its payments under the lease as expenses.

Of course, Pocket MBA rigged this example just to give you an example of how SFAS 13 works at its most simple. It's obviously a bad deal for the lessee because, as anyone who has ever tried to use a copy machine more than a couple years old knows, they need constant maintenance, so you wouldn't want to pay any amount for one. If you want to see how paragraph (7)(c) and 7(d) operate just make the copier a new one and assume an interest rate of whatever to borrow the money for three years.

PLI's Pocket MBA Vol. 2, No. 36   September 29, 2004

Diluted Earnings Per Share

A company's earnings per share after assuming that all outstanding stock options have been exercised.

DILUTED EARNINGS PER SHARE IN THE REAL WORLD:

Now that the Google hullabaloo is subsiding, the company will have to start reporting earnings like every other public company, and there is already a wrinkle in the equation, which relates to the separate classes of stock that Google issued, the one that investors bid up in the public auction (but not quite so much as the company had expected) and the one held by company insiders. This insider class of stock has ten times the voting power of the publicly issued stock, but that doesn't mean it will be counted ten times in figuring the company's earnings, or at all, for that matter. So if Google reports that it earned a google dollars per share of common stock outstanding, be wary.

Generally, when a company reports earnings, it is reporting what is referred to as "basic earnings per share," which is figured by dividing the company's net income (less any dividend owed to preferred shareholders) by the weighted average of common stock outstanding. The result represents, theoretically, the portion of the earnings each shareholder would be entitled to if the company closed the doors immediately. But capital structures being what they are, shares of common stock outstanding aren't always the only shares that a company has "issued."

Companies issue all manner of convertible preferred stock (preferred stock that can be converted into common stock), stock options, stock warrants (like a stock option, except issued in conjunction with a bond offering) and convertible debt (bonds exchangeable for a specified number of shares at a specified price). Generally, speaking, when the headlines blare that Company B earned $3.57 per share, you are getting the basic earnings per share. But if you read an earnings report closely, you might find out that the company only earned $.25 per fully diluted share. That would mean that the company took its net income (less any preferred dividend) and divided it by the weighted average common stock outstanding plus all those dilutive securities (assuming they are exercised). The resulting number gives a truer picture of a company's earnings because, in fact, any or all of these options could be exercised at any time, thus increasing the number of shares outstanding and reducing, or "diluting" the current shareholders' claim on a company's earnings. Even if a company reports diluted earnings per share, the number can be misleading if the company has previously issued a large number of stock options that are currently underwater (valued below the strike price-- see Pocket MBA, Vol. 1, No. 10) and doesn't include those options in its report (and they generally don't). Since options have a long life, these currently worthless options can spring back to life with a change in company fortunes, thus bringing the possibility of further dilution.

A good annual report will make very clear the difference between the basic earnings per share and the diluted earnings per share. All you need do is turn to the financial statements and it will all be spelled out for you. For instance in the section of Cisco Systems 2003 annual report entitled, "Financial Review - Selected Financial Data," the company lays it out in black and white (and because it's an annual report, there is some yellow and green thrown in, as well):

- Net income (loss) per share--basic   .50

- Net income (loss) per share—diluted (1) .50
- Note 1: Diluted net income per share is computed

using the weighted-average number of common shares and dilutive potential common shares outstanding during the period.

In Cisco's case, the dilutive shares did not actually dilute its 2003 earnings. But the same report indicates that Cisco's earnings in 2002, after taking into account dilutive shares was .25, as opposed to .26 basic earnings per share. That may not seem like much difference, but with billions of shares outstanding, that single penny adds up to millions of dollars. That's somewhat less than a google, but it ain't chicken feed.

PLI's Pocket MBA Vol. 2, No. 37   October 6, 2004

Stock Buyback

Corporation's purchase of its own shares on the open market or through a tender offer to current shareholders.

STOCK BUYBACKS IN THE REAL WORLD:

When Microsoft announced on July 20 that it would pay out a special, one-time dividend of three dollars per share (amounting to approximately $32 billion) and that it would repurchase up to $30 billion of its own stock over the next several years, many long-term investors in the company probably sighed in relief and said, "So that's what they're going to do with all that cash." But many who bought the company's stock as a growth vehicle toward the end of the 1990s boom or thereafter probably asked, "So that's what they're going to do with all that cash?" You see, life all depends on your perspective. Microsoft has upwards of $60 billion in cash on its books, an amount that increases quarterly. As Pocket MBA readers know, it is an executive team's and board of directors' duty to make the best use of the cash, and having it sitting around accumulating is not particularly efficient. A company can do one of very few things with cash, aside from letting it sit idle: it can buy other businesses; it can reinvest in the business by expanding R&D or paying down debt; it can pay out cash dividends. Or it can buy back outstanding stock. If the latter is the choice, management is telling shareholders it cannot think of anything better for the business than retiring shares.

Of course, Microsoft is not the only company to buy back shares. Buybacks were especially popular before the recent reductions in dividend tax rates because the capital gains tax on the sale of shares was less than the tax on a dividend. Smaller companies do it all the time, and the reasons a buyback is the best use of cash can generally be one of three. Management might believe that the stock is undervalued, and hence a good investment. If a company's shares are trading at a discount to the company's performance or its future prospects, management can step in and buy the cheap shares, as would any other investor. Management might also buy back shares because the amount of dilution that has occurred as a result of its issuance, and employees' exercise, of stock options has rendered the share price stagnant due to the sheer number of outstanding shares. Finally, companies often engage in buybacks as a stealth method to jump-start their share price upward. Although this rationale for a stock buyback is often criticized (can jump-starting share price really be the best use for cash?), the evidence compiled by numerous research outfits shows that, in fact, the shares of companies that announce buybacks tend to outperform the market.

When a company buys back stock, it generally (but not always) retires the shares, which increases the companies earnings per share, and hence its relative performance (even though performance hasn't changed one iota). So how does it all work? Assume a company that earns $1 million per year and has 100,000 shares outstanding. The company is therefore earning ten dollars per share. Assume also that the company has $5 million in total assets (consisting of $1 million in cash and $4 million in various other assets). That should render something close to a $50 dollar share price ($5 million/100,000 shares). The company's return on assets is 20% ($1 million earnings/$5 million assets). If the company decided to take half its cash ($500,000) to buy back stock at market price ($50), it could buy 10,000 shares ($500,000/$50) and reduce the number of shares outstanding to 90,000. Then its earnings would increase to $11.11/share and its return on assets would increase to 22.2 percent. Thus each share is worth 10.11 percent more than it was prior to the buyback. Investors might well see their shares gradually rise to this new level, around $55. Not a bad return considering nothing really happened.

SWAP

Derivative investment vehicle in which the participating parties trade a stream of payments on a specified principle, but at differing terms.

SWAPs IN THE REAL WORLD:

As Pocket MBA reported in last year's derivatives issue (Vol. 1, No. 26), the current SWAPs market, which sprung up in the 1970s as a hedge against currency exchange shock, is valued in the tens of trillions of dollars. So Pocket MBA thought it wise to revisit the issue in a little more detail. At its most simple, a SWAP is simply an agreement between two parties to trade payments on some specified principle. SWAPs are engaged in by institutions only, but perhaps the best way to simplify the concept is to take it out of the institutional investment world and into the world of shopping, which everyone understands.

Imagine you and a friend each carry a $1,000 balance on a business credit card. Neither of you are paying off the balance in full currently; rather, you are each making the minimum monthly payment. Your friend's interest rate on the balance is a 7.9% floating rate (meaning it rises and falls with the market), and the interest rate on your card is a 5.9% fixed rate for life. Now, it may seem counterintuitive, but you may have a reason that you wish to pay 7.9% interest every month. Perhaps you think that interest rates will fall precipitously, and the credit card company at issue will offer rates substantially lower than 5.9% in the future (suspend disbelief now) and you'll be stuck at 5.9%. Your friend, on the other hand, gains an immediate 2% advantage by taking on your payments in exchange for his. So you agree to pay your friend the amount of interest he owes on the monthly bill and he agrees to pay you the interest amount you owe for two years. Each of you pays off the principle amount on your own at a specified rate per month, transmitting the monthly payment as usual. You've now swapped payments. That's how simple the concept of SWAPs is. And yet, that explanation nearly makes a mockery of the complexity of SWAPs.

There are numerous varieties of SWAPs into which institutions enter. There are interest rate SWAPs, currency SWAPs, equity SWAPs and SWAPs for any other kind of asset you can imagine. But the first three listed are the most common. Here, then, briefly, is an introduction to all three:

- Interest Rate SWAP (also known as plain-vanilla SWAP): This is the most common form of SWAP, and it is simply an agreement between two parties under which each agrees to make a periodic payment to the other for an agreed period of time based upon a notional amount of principal. The principle is only notional because when only interest payments are being swapped, there is no need to exchange the principle. Interest Rate SWAPs are used as a hedge against interest rate instability and uncertainty. These arrangements can be of the fixed for floating rate type (as in the credit card example) or an exchange of floating rates.
- Currency SWAP (also known as Cross-Currency SWAP): Currency SWAPs involve the exchange of interest payments denominated in one currency for interest payments denominated

in another. As this is somewhat complex, Pocket MBA consulted an expert, Wachovia's corporate and institutional investment glossary (www.wachovia.com). Currency SWAPs "permit a corporation with recurring cash flows in a foreign currency, or one seeking financing in a foreign country, to eliminate exchange rate risk. With a currency swap, you simultaneously purchase and sell a given currency at a fixed exchange rate and then re-exchange those currencies at a future date allowing you to convert a stream of cash flows in one currency into another currency at a fixed exchange rate." Unlike Interest Rate SWAPs, the principle amounts are exchanged, both at the beginning and at the end of the contract.

- Equity SWAP: A SWAP in which the exchange of payments on one or both sides of the agreement is pegged to the performance of some equity index, like the S&P 500. The payments depend on what happens to the price of the equities involved. Institutions use these to get the benefit of equity ownership without actually buying equities.

In researching this issue, Pocket MBA has discovered that there are all manner of SWAPs, including cocktail SWAPs, which have little to do with imbibing; rather they are a combination of interest rate and currency swaps. But Pocket MBA's favorite SWAP has to be the ZEBRA (or Zero Basis Risk SWAP), which involves a municipality paying a fixed rate of interest to a financial institution in exchange for a floating rate. This is not nearly as exciting as Pocket MBA's initial image: herds of actual zebra trading the chance of being eaten by a lion on the Discovery channel.

Not-For-Profit Organization

Incorporated, unincorporated or trust entity organized under a state's laws for purposes other than distributing income and profits to private owners.

NOT-FOR-PROFIT ORGANIZATIONS IN THE REAL WORLD:

Pocket MBA was tooling along recently when it dwelled for a moment on the fact that its publisher is a nonprofit organization and that the subject had never come up in an issue. Sometimes, it's just right under your nose. So here goes. First things first: is there a difference between a nonprofit and not-for-profit organization? Technically, yes. A nonprofit organization is one that does not generate a profit (insert your own airline joke here); a not-for-profit organization is one whose raison d'etre is something other than making a profit. The two are used interchangeably, most likely because, despite the state law origins of the entity, underlying either type is its eligibility for federal tax-exempt status under the Internal Revenue Code (IRC) section 501(c)(3). So both nonprofit and not-for-profit organizations fall under the larger umbrella of federally tax exempt organizations.

In fact, many not-for-profits earn profits. Like any good business, an incorporated not-for-profit may strive mightily for profits. It's just that unlike a for-profit entity, there aren't shareholders or venture backers to whom the profits are owed. Rather, the profits are used to perpetuate the charitable operations of the entity or to build an endowment or reserve fund with which to keep the organization running in good times and bad.

As a general matter, reference to a state's laws will tell you how to establish a not-for-profit organization. For an incorporated not-for-profit, as with any other corporation, an organization will file articles of incorporation, establish a board, adopt bylaws and set annual meetings. After that, it's just business as usual, consistent with the organization's mission. Most not-for-profits are indeed incorporated to take advantage of the federal tax exemptions. One of the primary policy reasons behind the exemption is that each not-for-profit is providing a service beneficial to the community that government might otherwise be forced to provide.

According to the IRS's website, www.irs.gov and IRS publication 557, in order for a not-for-profit to be exempt, it:

> must be organized and operated exclusively for one or more of the purposes set forth in IRC Section 501(c)(3) and none of the earnings of the organization may inure to any private shareholder or individual. In addition, it may not attempt to influence legislation as a substantial part of its activities and it may not participate at all in campaign activity for or against political candidates.

The eligible purposes are as follows: charitable, religious, educational, scientific, literary, testing for public safety, fostering national or international amateur sports competition, and the prevention of cruelty to children or animals. "An organization will be regarded as 'operated exclusively' for one or more exempt purposes only if it engages primarily in activities which accomplish one or more of the exempt purposes specified in IRC Section 501(c)(3). An organization will not be so regarded if more than an insubstantial part of its activities is not in furtherance of an exempt purpose." Most exempt organizations must file IRS Form 990 annually. (IRS Publication 557 specifies which do not). The form includes basic financial disclosures and is available for public perusal.

CUSIP Number

Identifying number issued to all registered securities in the United States and Canada by the Committee on Uniform Securities

Identification Procedures (or CUSIP). International issues also receive an identifying number, but under the name CINS (CUSIP International Numbering System).

CUSIP NUMBERS IN THE REAL WORLD:

Pocket MBA recalls seeing, and glossing over without much thought, a nine-character string to the right of the strange sounding word "CUSIP," on stock trade confirmations. Pocket MBA never bothered to compare one to another to see what each might represent or to look up the word CUSIP. In fact, the CUSIP Number (which can actually include letters, as well--see below) is one of those things that anyone who has ever bought or sold a security has experience with, but ignores. They are that quiet. Yet, they are crucial to the orderly clearance and settlement of buy and sell orders for stocks and U.S. government issued and municipal bonds. Given this centrality, one would think that the CUSIP Number has been around for ages. But the truth is, the system didn't come into being until 1967.

CUSIP stands for Committee on Uniform Securities Identification Procedures. It is a subcommittee of the American Bankers Association (ABA). As the securities markets grew throughout the middle of the 20th Century, dealing with increasing volume became a threat to efficient order clearance. In 1962, according to CUSIP's web site (www.cusip.com), the New York Clearing House Association's Securities Procedures Committee decided that a uniform securities identification system was both necessary and feasible. The Clearing House approached the ABA and, in 1964, CUSIP was established. Its goals "were to develop specifications for a uniform security identification system, for devising a format for imprinting the identification number on the certificate in man/machine readable type font, and to establish an agency to administer the identification system according to specifications." In doing so, CUSIP sought to address two main technical needs: 1) that the number should contain as few characters as possible, and 2) that it should be linked to an alphabetic sequence of issuer names. What has resulted is the nine-digit CUSIP number, now overseen by Standard & Poor's under a license from the ABA.

So what's in a CUSIP? Well let's take a look at 316345305, which belongs to a mutual fund, Fidelity Low-Priced Stock (FLPSX). According to CUSIP, in this string, the first six characters, 316345, "uniquely identify the issuer" in a manner that results in an alphabetic listing of issuers. (Obviously this means that some numbers are left unused because new issuers need to have space in the alphabetic system.) Of these initial six characters, the first three are always numeric, but characters four through six can be either alpha or numeric. Each issuer receives one issuer number, except for those issuers (like Fidelity) that have so many different issues that one issuer number cannot accommodate all the issues the issuer has. Accordingly, FLPSX has the issuer number 316345, but another Fidelity offering Fidelity Fifty (FFTYX) carries the issuer number 31617F.

The seventh and eighth characters identify each particular issue (numeric if an equity issue; alphabetic or mixed alpha/numeric for fixed income issues). Issue numbers are assigned in sequence as issues originate. So FLPSX is issue 30, which doesn't mean it's the 30th issue. See CUSIP's website for the complete explanation of how the issue number is determined.

The ninth character is a check digit. What is a check digit, you ask? Take it from CUSIP:

> In data transmission, when accuracy of the number may represent the only means of identification, the use of a check digit becomes mandatory as it provides the means of mathematically determining the accuracy of the whole number transmitted. For this reason it is necessary to use the full nine digits of the CUSIP code.

CUSIP provides a mathematical explanation of how it determines check digits that is far beyond the ambit of the Pocket MBA series. Anyone who wants to play with it can take all but the last number in FLPSX's CUSIP Number, go to CUSIP's website and have at it.

Technical Analysis

Market-activity based method of determining whether a particular security will appreciate or decline in value.

TECHNICAL ANALYSIS IN THE REAL WORLD:

Anyone with investment clients eventually hears one or more of them referring to things like "head and shoulders," "candlesticks" and "double bottoms." But they are not talking about, respectively, dandruff shampoo, lighting alternatives in the event of massive blackout or a reason to go on the Atkins diet. Rather, they are noting three varying types of stock chart patterns, any of which can (according to them) indicate the direction a particular equity is destined to go. True, the stock market meltdown of the late 1990s taught many investors, inexperienced or otherwise, about the value of analyzing the fundamentals of a company--its balance sheet, the quality of its earnings and whether it has positive cash flow--hence the term "fundamental analysis." And Pocket MBA has been largely dedicated to these propositions over the past two years. For as the disclaimer goes, "Past performance is not a guarantee of future results." But for some, those committed to technical analysis, past performance is all that matters. You could say that these are the sports enthusiasts of the investing world. For them, investing is about winning, and that means buy low, sell high (or if they're shorting, borrow high and repay low), rather than which company has the best bottom line. So what does a technical analyst do, anyway?

Technical analysts watch the investing public, through the proxy of a performance chart, to try and predict whether people will buy or sell a security, and then to try and beat the herd to the punch. They do this by looking at things like trading volume and use terms like "support" and "resistance," the prices at which demand for stock tends to, respectively, increase and decrease.

And while Pocket MBA does not have fancy graphics to

demonstrate the different types of charts, you can muse over the names of the three mentioned above and get an idea of what to look for. An advocate of the head and shoulders approach seeks a stock chart that has had a moderate rise and fall before a somewhat higher rise and fall, followed by a rise to just at or below the initial rise and subsequent drop. To a technical analyst, this is a bearish indicator and means sell. Assume a technical analyst committed to head and shoulders patterns bought shares of Look Out Below, Inc. at $5. The investor then watched it rise from $5 to $10 and then fall back to $5.25, then saw it rise to $12 and fall back to $5, and then rise yet again, but only to $9.95 and start to decline. The analyst would sell on the beginning of the decline, reasoning that the stock was headed back toward $5 once again, and it was, therefore, time to take a profit. (You can plot a chart of this action with share price on the vertical axis and passage-of-time on the horizontal axis to see how the name head and shoulders evolved.)

All technical analysis is a variation of the preceding. It is essentially a momentum strategy: get in or out before everyone else. Whether a company is viable enters into the equation not a whit. A technical analyst will tell you that they can trade worthless companies every bit as well as they can trade the best companies in the land using the various technical methodologies. You can get more information on technical analysis from a variety of web resources. Or you can just ask your investment clients. Most will probably scoff while explaining it, but you might find one or two who light up and show you how to find the latest stock making a double bottom. In that case, if you then go out and find one, you should buy with abandon, then cross your fingers and hope that technical analysis works.

PLI's Pocket MBA Vol. 2, No. 42   November 10, 2004

Golden Parachute

Pay packages included in many executive contracts that are contingent on a change "(I) in the ownership or effective control of the corporation, or (II) in the ownership of a substantial portion of the assets of the corporation." See Internal Revenue Code Section 280G.

GOLDEN PARACHUTE IN THE REAL WORLD:

Here's a twist on golden parachutes. When software-maker PeopleSoft's board announced that it had relieved its CEO, Craig Conway, of his job because the board had lost confidence in his ability to lead the company, news reports revealed that he could receive up to $20 million in cash and stock awards as part of a severance package that included a change in control clause. Of course, PeopleSoft has been fending off a hostile takeover by rival Oracle for quite some time, since late 2002, actually. Conway has strenuously opposed the merger, and so he got the boot, which some believe might pave the way for a friendly combine. The question is whether Conway's change in control clause would kick in if the merger came off in the wake of his termination. That would bump up his severance package (which without a change in control was a mere two years' base salary, plus bonus and accelerated vesting of various stock options and awards-- somewhere north of a couple million dollars) into full open parachute mode. Now, Pocket MBA has never jumped from an airplane, but imagines if Conway were actually jumping from one, it would be a case where the parachute didn't initially open, but the emergency chute would have to save the day.

Pocket MBA leaves to the M&A lawyers the ins and outs of what will actually happen with Conway's pay package if Oracle and PeopleSoft merge. But if the change in control clause kicks in, the situation will surely demonstrate the difference between a "mere" severance package and the golden parachute.

Severance packages are for everyone. You get a few weeks pay and sayonara, hasta luego. Pocket MBA got one of these once and it was far from a parachute--it was more like a pair of worn brakes. The image-conjuring golden parachute, on the other hand, is inserted into executive pay packages for a variety of reasons that, generally, only come into play when a company is involved in a takeover. The parachute (or payment in the event of a change in control of the company) cushions the fall of losing one's high paying, prestigious, executive job. But the companies involved in the payout also have good reason to offer them. The golden parachute is seen as an incentive for an executive to be objective about takeover bids. If you know you're going to get a big payday when you lose your job, you won't try and stonewall a takeover that is otherwise beneficial for shareholders in order to save your job. A corollary is that, as job insurance, golden parachutes enable companies to attract the best managers. Others see the golden parachute as a form of "poison pill" that acts as a disincentive to hostile takeover bids. (Although given the total size of a hostile takeover bid--Oracle bid $7.7 billion for PeopleSoft--paying out a golden parachute involving a few extra million wouldn't seem to be that much of a hindrance.)

In any event, some golden parachutes are extraordinarily (some would say obscenely) large, which moved Congress, back in 1984, to impose penalties on "excessive" golden parachutes. (Hence, the reference in this week's definition to IRC section 280G, which, along with IRC section 4999, is the home of these provisions.) At the time, Congress viewed golden parachutes as a detriment to merger activity. The reason all of this is relevant now is because the IRS recently issued its final regulation under section 280G relating to the denial of a deduction to a corporation for excess parachute payments. This is a process that has spanned years upon years (The initial proposed regulation was promulgated in 1989!) Luckily, Pocket MBA is fortunate to be able to turn to an expert in the area of executive compensation, Max J. Schwartz (Sullivan & Cromwell LLP), who penned an article that includes a section on the final golden parachute regulations and which you'll find in Appendix B.

Shelf Registration

Registration of a public offering when the company has no current intention to actually sell the securities at issue. Authorized by SEC Regulation C, Rule 415.

SHELF REGISTRATION IN THE REAL WORLD:

Pocket MBA was perusing the financial pages recently and saw that a company it was following had issued a press release stating the following (the name of the company has been changed to "Too Smart By Half, Inc."):

> Too Smart By Half, Inc....today announced that it has filed a shelf registration statement on Form S-3 with the Securities and Exchange Commission (SEC). Upon being declared effective by the SEC, the registration statement will allow the sale of up to $80 million of common stock. Too Smart By Half, Inc. has not made any decision about the timing, amount or type of any public offering, which may be made in the next two years under the registration statement.[The] president and chief executive officer of Too Smart By Half, Inc. commented: "We have concluded that the filing of a shelf registration statement would increase our flexibility and reduce the regulatory costs (in time and money) if we should conclude that Too Smart By Half, Inc. would benefit from increased funding. Too Smart By Half, Inc. has been growing rapidly. We want to make sure we have access to any financing we may need to fund continued growth. This would include funds for manufacturing expansion, working capital requirements, new product or market development, and/or acquisitions. However, we have not made any definitive plans for any offering, nor have we begun any process to select any underwriters to conduct such an offering.

That sent Pocket MBA scurrying for more information on these registrations that eventually bring money into a company's coffers, while diluting any current shareholder's investment at some unspecified time in the future. As often happens, life interceded, and Pocket MBA put the research on the shelf. Three months later, another press release issued from Too Smart By Half, Inc.:

> Too Smart By Half, Inc. today announced the filing of a prospectus supplement to its shelf registration statement for a public offering of 20,000,000 shares of common stock. The offering is being led by [an underwriter] and co-managed by [another underwriter]. Too Smart By Half, Inc. plans to use the net proceeds from the offering for working capital, general corporate purposes and repayment of a bridge loan.

Shelf registration is one of the more literally descriptive terms in securities law. When a company files to issue securities pursuant to SEC Rule 415, it is announcing that it has plans to conduct a public offering, but will do so later, thus putting the issue "on the shelf." Generally, as the above press release indicates, a company will file a shelf registration when it perceives it will need to raise money at some point, but can wait until (hopefully) market conditions are most optimal for it to do so. Having already registered the securities with the SEC, the company does not have to go through the time-consuming process of doing so (but must update the information in its quarterly and annual reports) and can thus act quickly. (Of course, delaying the actual sales of the securities can backfire on a company, as the result of Too Smart By Half, Inc.'s shelf offering, reported below, demonstrates.) Companies can also file a shelf registration for securities that are sold as part of a dividend or interest reinvestment plan or an employee benefit plan. The different types of offerings that can be made via shelf registration are specified by SEC Regulation C, Rule 415(i)-(x) and include:

    i.   Securities which are to be offered or sold solely by or on behalf of a person or persons other than the registrant, a subsidiary of the registrant or a person of which the registrant is a subsidiary;

    ii.   Securities which are to be offered and sold pursuant to a dividend or interest reinvestment

iii. plan or an employee benefit plan of the registrant;
iii. Securities which are to be issued upon the exercise of outstanding options, warrants or rights;
iv. Securities which are to be issued upon conversion of other outstanding securities;
v. Securities which are pledged as collateral;
vi. Securities which are registered on Form F-6;
vii. Mortgage related securities, including such securities as mortgage backed debt and mortgage participation or pass through certificates;
viii. Securities which are to be issued in connection with business combination transactions;
ix. Securities the offering of which will be commenced promptly, will be made on a continuous basis and may continue for a period in excess of 30 days from the date of initial effectiveness;
x. Securities registered (or qualified to be registered) on Form S-3 or Form F-3 which are to be offered and sold on a continuous or delayed basis by or on behalf of the registrant, a subsidiary of the registrant or a person of which the registrant is a subsidiary; or
xi. Shares of common stock which are to be offered and sold on a delayed or continuous basis by or on behalf of a registered closed-end management investment company or business development company that makes periodic repurchase offers pursuant to Rule 23c-3.

Also, Rule 415(a)(2) specifies that the company may only register securities "in an amount which, at the time the registration statement becomes effective, is reasonably expected to be offered and sold within two years from the initial effective date of the registration."

Now back to that example. At the time of Too Smart By Half, Inc.'s shelf registration, it was riding high in the market (its shares at a 52-week high of $7 or so; its products were being used on an increasingly widespread basis, and it certainly must have thought it would be selling those securities at a nice price, say somewhere north of $10/share). Certain things happened and then certain other things didn't happen. The next thing you know, the money to be realized from the shelf offering was needed immediately to keep operations going. Result? The company followed the second press release, in which its plans to use the funds to finance "manufacturing expansion, working capital requirements, new product or market development, and/or acquisitions" had morphed into "working capital" only, with press release number three:

> Too Smart By Half, Inc. announced today that the underwritten public offering of 20,000,000 shares of its common stock has been priced at $0.80 per share. This will result in net proceeds to Too Smart By Half, Inc. of approximately $14.6 million. The underwriters of the offering have a 30-day option to purchase an additional 3,000,000 shares of common stock from Too Smart By Half, Inc. to cover any over-allotments.

The moral of the story? While shelf registrations are a great option for companies, the old adage "never put off until tomorrow that which you can finish today" can be as applicable to securities offerings as it is to life in general.

PLI's Pocket MBA Vol. 2, No. 44   December 1, 2004

Poison Pill

Any of a number of defensive tactics employed by a company to avoid a hostile takeover.

POISON PILL IN THE REAL WORLD:

If last week's securities term, shelf registration, was the most "literally descriptive," then this week's is the most figuratively descriptive. Poison implies death, and the aim of any poison pill is to kill an unwanted takeover bid. In fact, Pocket MBA thinks the term could be even more descriptive if the Form 8-K's that companies filed when adopting various poison pills contained a picture of a skull and crossbones in the caption. Poison pill is one of those terms everyone hears or reads about in a law school corporations class, but ignores unless you have interest in actually becoming a securities lawyer. That is, until a company you or one of your clients has invested in files an 8-K stating that it is adopting something called a "stockholders rights plan," which seems to grant all sorts of hypothetical rights to buy preferred shares of stock at huge discounts, like the following one that stockholders of Autobytel, Inc. received earlier this year:

- On July 30, 2004, the Board of Directors of the Company approved the adoption of a Preferred Share Purchase Rights Plan (the "Plan"). Terms of the Plan provide for a dividend distribution of one preferred share purchase right (a "Right") for each outstanding share of common stock, par value $0.001 per share (the "Common Shares"), of the Company. The dividend is payable on August 10, 2004 (the "Record Date") to the stockholders of record on that date. Each Right entitles the registered holder to purchase from the Company one one-hundredth of a share of Series A Junior Participating Preferred Stock, par value $0.001 per share (the "Preferred Shares"), at a price of $65 per one one-hundredth of a Preferred Share (the "Purchase Price"), subject to adjustment. Each one one-hundredth of a Preferred Share has designations and powers, preferences and rights, and the qualifications, limitations and restrictions which make its value approximately equal to the value of a Common Share. The description and terms of the Rights are set forth in a Rights Agreement (the "Rights Agreement"), dated as of July 30, 2004, entered into between the Company and U.S. Stock Transfer Corporation, as rights agent (the "Rights Agent").

- Initially, the Rights will be evidenced by the stock certificates representing the Common Shares then outstanding, and no separate Right Certificates, as defined, will be distributed. Until the earlier to occur of (i) the date of a public announcement that a person, entity or group of affiliated or associated persons have acquired beneficial ownership of 15% or more of the outstanding Common Shares after the date of the adoption of the Rights Agreement, subject to certain exceptions set forth in the Rights Agreement (an "Acquiring Person"), or (ii) 10 business days (or such later date as may be determined by action of the Board of Directors prior to such time as any person or entity becomes an Acquiring Person) following the commencement of, or announcement of an intention to commence, a tender offer or exchange offer the consummation of which would result in any person or entity becoming an Acquiring Person...

And like the skull and crossbones, this type of release screams "stay away" to most suitors, who will not want the added expense of buying all of the additional shares created should they attempt a takeover. Of course, some pills are so toxic (by for instance lowering the trigger percentage of shares that have to be bought by a single purchaser) that a share purchaser can trigger the pill without having truly entertained any grand scheme to take over a company.

In any event, the Autobytel poison pill above is called a "flip-in" because it allows shareholders to purchase shares of the existing company at a discount. There are also poison pills that are "flip-overs," which grant stockholders the right to buy an acquirer's shares at a discount after consummation of a takeover. Of course, all of this is done because hostile takeovers, which seem so positive to the suitor, make the targeted company positively flip-out. After all, if your client is a fledgling technology company, what could be worse than losing control of the baby?

There are as many variations on the poison pill as creative lawyers can think up, and they all sport tremendously clever names. There are "suicide pills," in which the target company essentially adopts a plan of action that would destroy the company in the event of takeover bid. There are "scorched earth" pills, which entail a company liquidating valuable assets to make the takeover bid less attractive. And then there's Pocket MBA's favorite, "chewable pills," (how dastardly...chewables are so tasty, no one would suspect they contain...POISON) otherwise known as a "qualifying offer provision," which relieves the board of directors' of its ability to negotiate with suitors, leaving it to stockholders to decide whether to accept a takeover.

As the Autobytel plan demonstrates, most pills have a limited duration (generally ten years, though shorter periods exist if a short-term threat is being warded off) after which they expire. If the company doesn't renew the pill it has to fend for itself. Then again, who really likes to leave poison lying around?

Barriers to Entry

Any circumstance peculiar to a particular industry that acts to raise a bar to competitors entering the market.

BARRIERS TO ENTRY IN THE REAL WORLD:

As Pocket MBA makes the headlong rush into the holiday season, satellite radio is making a headlong rush into the public consciousness. And while Pocket MBA is not a satellite subscriber, it knows that if it becomes one it will choose either Sirius or XM as a provider. Of course, that's because they are the only two providers, thanks to an FCC-granted license duopoly. And even if the government were to rescind that duopoly, it hardly seems likely that another company would spend the billions of dollars to buy and launch the satellites required to beam the signal to wherever you had your receiver. Furthermore, if someone did launch the satellites, what is left to license when the two original entrants have secured and divvied up licensing deals with Howard Stern (a barrier to entry unto himself), CNBC, Rush Limbaugh (see comment on Howard Stern), Air America, Major League Baseball, the NFL, the NBA and whatever remains (not much) of the NHL? Add any restrictive intellectual property matters into the mix--any strategic alliances that give Sirius and XM access to the patented gizmos used to receive the signals, and you have some pretty serious barriers to entry. In fact, they encompass each type of barrier to entry: legal, patent and economic (e.g. high initial startup and marketing costs). Not a bad deal...as long as either can eventually make a profit.

There may be few subjects where business and law collide so heavily as on the subject of barriers to entry. That's because entrepreneurs love getting involved in ventures, like satellite radio, with as many barriers to entry to the rest of the world as possible, and antitrust law often seeks to redress the anti-competitive result of unnatural barriers to entry--those that monopolistic businesses may erect to keep their monopoly. Of course, Pocket MBA leaves that statutory/philosophical tug-of-war to the antitrust counsel among you. Here, the only thing that matters is the business side.

When starting a business, finding one with high barriers to entry is a good thing--in fact, the higher the better. Why? Because if barriers to entry do not exist, then the product or service you provide is already a commodity or will soon become one if you are successful, cutting into your ability to continue making profits. A good long-term business model is one where you can maintain or grow market share. And one of the things that can help you toward that is entry barriers.

You can tell which products don't have particularly high barriers to entry by following the price charged for the particular good. Most electronics gadgets are examples of industries where the barriers to entry are few. As long as manufacturers have spare capacity, they'll hop onto a trend to make a buck. That is why DVD players can now be had for under $50. It's also one of the reasons you get a fancy cell phone for next to nothing these days. Once electronics manufacturers saw the outsize profits being made by Nokia, Motorola and Ericsson, they sought their piece of the pie. Hence you can now get a phone by those three (although your Ericsson phone is now made by Sony), along with Kyocera, Samsung, Sanyo, LG (the latest "it" phone), V-Tech and others. The price of the phone has dropped accordingly (the fact that almost everyone has one is also a factor in the commiditization of the cell phone). Of course, the dominant companies seek to strike deals with the wireless providers that will tend to shut out smaller competitors.

Internet search engines are another classic example of a low barriers to entry industry; that's one of the reasons commentators question the valuation accorded to search engine Google after its recent IPO. There is little to stop someone else from creating a better search engine, with a cooler name. Time will tell whether that is a hindrance to the business model, though Pocket MBA senses that the fact that Google recently lowered its earnings estimates for the upcoming quarter has everything to do with the fact that everyone and their mother has a search engine. In any event, Pocket MBA's favorite example of a low (or no) barriers to entry venture is...email newsletters. Pocket MBA toyed with the notion of charging a nominal subscription fee for these weekly gems, but after doing a Google search on the number of newsletters, quickly concluded that it would be more likely to make a profit by launching a couple satellites and starting

Altman Z-Score

Statistical measure that quantifies the likelihood of a company's impending bankruptcy by compiling a variety of performance measures.

ALTMAN Z-SCORE IN THE REAL WORLD:

As this is the last issue of 2004, it only seems appropriate that this week's term contains both an "A" and a "Z." What's more, since bankruptcy in the U.S. can be an end and a beginning, the symbolic comparison between the Altman Z-Score and New Year's Eve was too cutesy to ignore. OK, enough preliminary, eggnog induced drivel. In 75 prior issues of Pocket MBA, the subject of how to determine the financial health of your clients, Vis à Vis the possibility of bankruptcy has come up, oh, 75 times. That's only a slight exaggeration, as these pages have covered liquidity ratios, debt-equity ratios, burn rates, EBITDA and related measures. One of the weaknesses of all of these is that they stand in isolation from the others. Back in the 1960s, Professor Edward I. Altman of New York University sought to formulate a statistical model of financial health employing a number of credit-based variables common to all companies. What resulted was the Altman Z-Score.

A Z-Score, generally speaking, is a measure of the distance, in standard deviations, of any sample from the mean. For the non-statistics versed among you, a standard deviation is a measure of volatility in a sample. If you take 30 people and give them a test, and they all score 15, there is no deviation; but if the mean score was 18, and the scores range from two to 26, you would conclude that the deviation from the mean score was high. Now if you took the same 30 people, gave them 15 tests, plotted the mean scores of all the tests and determined how far each individual score was from the mean, you would have a Z-Score. So, "a z-score is a measure of how far any particular score is from the mean of the entire set and ... the units of z-scores are standard deviations. So a z-score of 2.5 means that this value is 2.5 standard deviations above the mean; a z-score of -2.5 means that this value falls 2.5 standard deviations below the mean."

See "The Correlation Coefficient" at TimeWeb:
www.bized.ac.uk/timeweb/crunching/crunch_relate_expl.htm.

Z-Scores can be figured for any set of numbers. Pocket MBA's favorite Internet posting on Z-Scores is one developed to determine which baseball homerun hitter had the best all-time season (Babe Ruth in 1920, but this was figured before Barry Bonds' feats of the past few years -- though revelations of the past few weeks about creams and salves may relegate those achievements to the ashbin of pharmaceutical history).

OK, back to business. Professor Altman studied 33 bankrupt companies and 33 solvent companies to build his model, which calculates five ratios, weights each, and then adds the resulting numbers to achieve "Z." In order to calculate Z, you need to know a company's (1) earnings before interest and tax; (2) total assets; (3) retained earnings; (4) net sales; (5) total liabilities; (6) market value of equity; and (7) working capital. Once you have these numbers, you need to calculate the following ratios:

(A) Working Capital/Total Assets
(B) Retained Earnings/Total Assets
(C) Earnings Before Interest & Tax/Total Assets
(D) Market Value of Equity/Total Liabilities
(E) Sales/Total Assets

Each of these ratios tells an investigator something about the way a company is handling its assets. For example, a company with positive working capital (ratio A) is a good credit risk. A high ratio of sales to total assets (ratio E) means a company is growing market share.

While Altman's work in determining how to weight each of these numbers is for a different forum, you can search his work on the

Internet to get a more complete explanation. Suffice to say, he weighted them as follows for the Z-Score calculation:

-Z = 1.2A + 1.4B + 3.3C + .6D + 1.0E

Altman's 66 companies rendered Z's ranging from -4 to +8. From these deviations, he concluded that, in general, if a company's Z-Score is above 2.99, it is in good financial shape. A Z-Score between 1.81 and 2.99 indicates possible trouble. And a score below 1.81 means an increasing risk of bankruptcy. In fact, Altman concluded that companies with a Z-Score of zero have a 50% chance of going bankrupt (and subsequent statistics have borne out his conclusions). And now, Pocket MBA offers a holiday break. So take a few hours and apply Z-Score analysis to your corporate clients. You might find that you want to bill some of them before 2005 kicks in. See you next year.

PLI's Pocket MBA Vol. 3 No. 1   January 5, 2005

Forensic Accounting

Discipline combining accounting, auditing and investigative skills used in fraud detection and litigation support.

FORENSIC ACCOUNTING IN THE REAL WORLD:

Don't Enron and WorldCom seem like a long time ago now? When lawyers look back at these scandals, their minds also turn to Sarbanes-Oxley. And the revolutionary legislation has, indeed, been the most visible and celebrated response to the mess that the 1990s left behind. But a less visible and perhaps more important, for the future in any event, vestige of the shenanigans has been the rise of the forensic accountant. In its 2004 Report to the Nation, the Association of Certified Fraud Examiners, see www.cfenet.com, estimated that occupational fraud (which it defines as using "one's occupation for personal enrichment through the deliberate misuse or misapplication of the employing organization's resources or assets") causes "the typical U.S. organization [to] lose 6% of its annual revenues." That works out to $660 billion in business loss during 2003 alone. So it's no wonder that forensic accounting is one of the hottest job fields in the country. And its practitioners are not just called into ferret out fraud after the fact anymore. They are now on the front line of fraud prevention. They're becoming the superheroes of the post Sarbanes-Oxley accounting world.

Historically, forensic accountants have combined an accounting background, knowledge of auditing, internal controls and risk assessment with investigative training and basic knowledge of the court system aimed toward building easily understood and legally admissible opinions on the existence (or not) of fraud at an organization. Typical investigative accounting work involves the uncovering of embezzlement, employee theft, securities fraud, general accounting fraud, kickback schemes and anything else that implicates money flow. They often take over for an audit committee when fraud is suspected, for they have an expertise in piecing together the various data possessed by a company. Indeed, The AICPA Audit Committee Toolkit, www.aicpa.org/audcommctr/toolkitscorp/homepage.htm, encourages audit committees to consult with forensic accountants when fraud is "asserted or discovered":

> Forensic accounting consultants, in particular, may be needed to provide the depth of skills necessary to conduct a fraud investigation, and if it is desirable to get an independent assessment. Forensic accounting consultants can also frequently provide audit committees with other related advisory services, namely, (1) evaluations of controls designs and operating effectiveness through compliance verification; (2) creation of special investigations units (SIUs); (3) incident management committees; (4) disclosure risk controls; (5) ethics hotlines; (6) code of conduct; and other antifraud measures.

Forensic accountants delve into a company's books, files, computer records, even employee records. Hence, they work closely with in-house or outside legal counsel to avoid violating federal and state law.

There is a raft of information on forensic accounting available online and elsewhere. Pocket MBA's favorite nuggets are "the red flags" of financial crime that forensic accountants look for to confirm suspicions that fraud is afoot. These include individual employee behavior, such as overworking and inappropriate lifestyle changes (so much for buying a Porsche on the Pocket MBA subscription revenue), and organizational behavior (including unrealistic performance compensation packages, unprofitable offshore operations and low staff morale, high staff turnover and an abundance of whistleblower complaints). So, the next time you visit a client's office and you hear a lot of grumbling in the halls, you might want to check your Rolodex (how quaint) for your favorite forensic accountants. They might be needed.

PLI's Pocket MBA Vol. 3 No. 2   January 12, 2005

Profit Margin

A company's profitability, expressed as a percentage, arrived at by dividing net earnings after taxes by revenues.

PROFIT MARGIN IN THE REAL WORLD:

Pocket MBA's first job was a summer position as a stock clerk at a national retail pharmacy (or at least they used to be called pharmacies--to call Walgreens or Rite-Aid or any of their competitors pharmacies seems rather silly when you can buy DVDs and motor oil along with your ibuprofen). It was the first in a long series of short-term retail grocer/pharmacy positions, but as best as Pocket MBA can remember, the first day at any of these jobs included a video in which theft prevention was a primary topic. And in that section of the video, the company always stressed that just 2.5 cents of every dollar of sales was profit to the store. Pocket MBA had no idea what this meant because it seemed as if each of these retail companies was making millions upon millions of dollars in sales, so the "we're poor" speech didn't truly resonate. Nonetheless, the plea worked, as store clerks were generally vigilant in policing shoppers because, by golly, the company was on the verge of bankruptcy. What Pocket MBA didn't realize (because the video didn't explain it) was that the "2.5 cents presentation" was an introduction to the concept of profit margins. And Pocket MBA should have realized, after watching a number of first-day videos, that all retailers make about 2 or 3 cents on the dollar. That is a normal profit margin for them. And just because the typewriter dealer (hey, that was a high-end business back in the day) down the street made 40 cents on the dollar didn't mean that the retailer was in financial trouble.

So what does that tell you about profit margins? Profit margins, like most financial measurements, are only useful (although very useful) when comparing competitors in the same industry. To say that Company A earned $10 million in 2004, and Company B made $20 million, both respectable amounts, tells you little about what it took to make that money. If they are both the average retail grocers, one could conclude based on Pocket MBA's experience that those amounts reflected actual sales of $500 million and $1 billion, respectively. If Company B was able to ring its profit out of the same $500 million as Company A, you could conclude that Company A had discovered a new paradigm for retailing. This paradigm doesn't exist. Just check out retail behemoth Wal-Mart's profit margin. It is around 2.9 percent. (No doubt Wal-Mart shows the same video that Pocket MBA watched all those years ago.)

By the same token, if Company A was earning its $10 million on the same $1 billion in sales as Company B, you might be concerned that Company A was doing something wrong in failing to achieve the time-tested profit margin of the retail industry. Now, it might be that Company A had just begun business in an area dominated by Company B and so cut its prices to get established. That would be a conscious choice to sacrifice margin to attract sales and would be of no concern if, once established, Company A could raise its margin toward the industry average. But if Company A was earning less because its costs were such that it had to show a "1 percent video" instead of a

"2.5 percent video," an analyst would be concerned that its cost structure was simply out of line and inconsistent with long-term success in the industry.

This little examination of the staid retail industry is an introduction to the concept that profit margins are measures of how efficiently companies use their revenues to generate earnings. Of course, most industries are not the retail industry and so examining the profit margins of competitors in non-retail businesses is a bit more interesting, as they can tell you who the dominant players are.

There is more than one profit margin ratio. This week, Pocket MBA will focus on gross profit margin. Later issues will delve into net profit margin and operating profit margin. As are all profit margins, gross profit margin (GPM) is expressed as a simple ratio

- GPM = (Sales - Cost of Goods Sold)/Sales

You can find these numbers in a company's income statements. (They will even do the subtraction for you and tell you the gross profit; all you have to do is the division.) The resulting ratio tells you how efficiently a company is using its labor and supplies to produce profits.

Back to the retailers. If Company A sold $500 million of goods, and its cost of labor and supplies was $480 million, it has a GPM of

- ($500 million - $480 million)/$500 million =
- $20 million/$500 million =
- 4%

Hey, wait a minute, Pocket MBA. You said retailers have profit margins in the 2-3 percent range. What gives? Does this company need a different video? No. The 4% figure represents only gross profit margin. There are some costs that are not expressed in this ratio. Pocket MBA will deal with that later in its discussion of net profit margin.

Deferred Revenue

Income a company records as a liability until such time as it may be recorded as earned.

DEFERRED REVENUE IN THE REAL WORLD:

How can income received possibly be a liability? Only in the dark recesses of the accounting world, although in fact, the recesses are neither very dark nor very recessed. Deferred revenue is one of the simplest concepts in accounting. In essence, it symbolizes the reality of business transactions that are incomplete when consummated--things like subscription and license deals--because the product has not been delivered, even though the money for it has been paid.

Think about it this way. Let's assume that a year of Pocket MBA costs $150. (After you stop laughing, read on.) In 2004, there were 46 issues, so $150 annually works out to about $3.26/issue. In order to receive any issues, you had to send Pocket MBA $150 in advance, but in reality, Pocket MBA hasn't actually earned the entire $150 until after the final issue is zipped out through cyberspace. In the interim, any number of things might occur that would warrant return of a *pro rata* portion of the subscription fee. You might cancel your subscription; Pocket MBA might be bought out by a free publication, such as Wallet MBA, Purse MBA or PDA MBA; Pocket MBA could cease publication altogether for reasons other than bankruptcy. The list goes on. For accounting purposes, the balance sheet reflects this uncertainty by requiring that the $150 be recorded in a liability account that is drawn on at $3.26/issue. That $3.26 is then moved over to the asset side of the ledger, and the $150 is decreased accordingly.

This type of transaction goes on everyday, in any circumstance where pay now, receive service or product later applies. It gets a little more complicated when the income received overlaps a company's fiscal year. For example, assume you signed up for Pocket MBA on June 30, 2004, and your subscription lasted until June 30, 2005. Pocket

MBA, as a December 31 fiscal year entity (and Pocket MBA is really pushing things now, as it has no fiscal anything) would have to accrue the remaining $75 on the next year's balance sheets.

Note that deferred revenue has a mirror opposite concept, deferred charge. Deferred charges are expenditures like R&D expenses or even prepaid rent to some extent, which will benefit a company for reporting periods beyond the period in which the actual expenditure is incurred. So these expenses are recorded as an asset, and as each portion of the expenditure is used, it is written down--think of it as a sort of depreciation, and you'll get the idea. For example, the cost of setting up a business itself, incurred in one fell swoop, can be written down over time.

And now that the assuming is over, just think, all that cost you nothing.

PLI's Pocket MBA Vol. 3 No. 4   January 26, 2005

FAS 151 & Accounting Divergence

November 2004 enactment by FASB amending Accounting Research Bulletin (ARB) No. 43, Chapter 4 to clarify that "abnormal amounts" of "idle facility expense, freight, handling costs, and wasted materials (spoilage) should be recognized as current-period charges" and to require "the allocation of fixed production overheads to inventory based on the normal capacity of the production facilities."

FAS 151 IN THE REAL WORLD:

Don't worry, readers, what follows will not be a drawn out exegesis of allocation of inventory costs, although Pocket MBA is the first to decry the crisis in "idle facility expense." No, the reason FAS 151 caught Pocket MBA's eyes was the rationale behind FASB's action in amending ARB No. 43, namely its continuing effort to address divergence in cross-border financial reporting by working with the International Accounting Standards Board (IASB) "towards development of a single set of high-quality accounting standards." And when it came to idle facility expense and other inventory costs, the prior wording difference between ARB No. 43 and IAS No. 2 "could lead to inconsistent application of those similar requirements." FASB concluded "that clarifying the existing requirements in ARB No. 43 by adopting language similar to that used in IAS No. 2 is consistent with its goals of improving financial reporting in the United States and promoting convergence of accounting standards internationally."

Pocket MBA invites any of you to go ferret out the differences that previously existed in the two standards; since it will no longer be of moment in the very near future, Pocket MBA won't delve into such details. (FAS 151 "is effective for inventory costs incurred during fiscal years beginning after June 15, 2005," but "[e]arlier application is permitted for inventory costs incurred during fiscal years beginning after November 23, 2004.")

But what about this drive toward international convergence of accounting standards? Search the web; it's a big deal these days because globalization and the concomitant increase in cross-border financial reporting have made consistent international standards crucial to smooth business function. Pocket MBA likens it to the myriad different ways in which people balance a checkbook. You may have a method that makes perfect sense to you, but pick up that of a friend who uses a different method and forget it. But that doesn't matter until you become responsible for some of the numbers in the other checkbook. Of course, a business is more than a checkbook, but that's the reason convergence is so important--both for companies that do business around the globe and for investors who attempt to determine the soundness of one company versus another.

Currently the IASB and FASB, along with the blessing of the SEC, are feverishly working on trying to converge U.S. and European standards. *Accountancy Age,* see www.accountancyage.com, reported on August 12, 2004 that the two would begin by working on a draft to converge standards on business combinations. Pocket MBA will keep you posted on their progress. Suffice to say that as of this year, at least nobody will have to worry about what method companies use to account for that messy "idle facility expense."

AUTHOR UPDATE: Like the EU constitution demonstrated,

sometimes it's just not that easy to converge differing systems. On August 4, 2005, *Accountancy Age* reported that the initial efforts by FASB and IASB are being criticized "for failing to provide an improvement on the existing standards." See http://www.accountancyage.com/accountancyage/news/2140756/convergence-goes-awry.

PLI's Pocket MBA Vol. 3 No. 5	February 2, 2005

Return On Equity (ROE)

Measure of efficiency with which a company generates profits. Determined by dividing a company's net income by its stockholder's equity.

RETURN ON EQUITY (ROE) IN THE REAL WORLD:

Like most everything else in corporate finance, the propriety of using ROE as a determinant of corporate efficiency is relative--relative to the ROE of other companies in the same industry and relative to a host of factors, such as the amount of debt a company carries, that, not taken into account, can make it a useless exercise in simple mathematics. At its base, ROE measures the efficiency with which an entity uses the assets it has on-hand to generate profit. Generally speaking, a company that uses assets efficiently will have a long-term competitive advantage over one that does not, even if both companies generate the same amount of profits over the short term, because the efficient operator will not have to issue new equity. Think of it as bang for the investor buck.

To take a common example, look at an industry whose competitive arc most readers are familiar with: the PC industry. Go back to the 1990s and try and list all the companies that were successfully making and selling PCs on a mass scale. Pocket MBA's list includes Dell, IBM, Gateway, Toshiba, Hitachi, Acer, Compaq,

Hewlett-Packard, Packard-Bell and Sony. With a few exceptions (for instance, Packard Bell no longer exists; Compaq is part of HP; IBM is getting out of the business soon; and there are some boutique additions, like eMachines), this list is the same in 2005, but the visibility and mass-market ability of the players on the list has changed. Whereas in 1999, it was a bunch of equals slugging it out, today, it is basically Dell, maybe HP, and everyone else. Dell's rising supremacy had everything to do with forward thinking on the subjects of distribution and online sales, but if you just look at the company's ROE over the period and compare it to its competitors, you could predict that it would be the leader without knowing anything else about it. In fact, Dell's average ROE between 1999 and now hovers near the 40% range, with HP in the 12% range and Gateway lagging back at 2-3%. ROE is expressed as a percentage:

- Net Income/Stockholder Equity

These numbers are easily snagged from, respectively, a company's income statement and balance sheet.

Dell, in its most recent fiscal year ending January 30, 2004, had net income of $2.645 billion and stockholder equity of $6.28 billion for a ROE of 42 percent. This means that for each dollar invested in Dell, Dell generated a return of 42 cents. For its last fiscal year, Hewlett-Packard generated $2.539 billion in net income, almost equal to that of Dell, but had $37.746 billion in stockholder equity, rendering a ROE of 6.7 percent. (This number is lower than HP's historic average, due in large part, no doubt, to HP's purchase of Compaq, which raised the amount of stockholder equity. Of course, HP sells (or gives away) a lot of printers, as well, and that can't be helping.

ROE has limitations, as Pocket MBA alluded to at the outset. If a company borrows a lot of money, its ROE will be deceptively large. Why? Because stockholder equity is made up of total assets less total liabilities, and debt is a liability. Assume two companies similar in all aspects except one has more debt. The company with the higher level of debt will have less stockholder equity and hence a higher ROE.

Return on Investment Capital (ROIC)

Generally, the percentage return a company earns on all capital (equity and debt) it invests.

RETURN ON INVESTED CAPITAL (ROIC) IN THE REAL WORLD:

Pocket MBA's discussion of Return on Equity (ROE) last week was quick to offer caveats to using the formula to determine company profit-generating efficiency. But ROE is one of the more popular metrics, along with price/earnings ratios and profit margins, for people to do so. ROIC is not a popular metric, and there is a reason. While ROE, P/E ratios and profit margins are all relatively easy to figure out from a quick glance at balance sheets, ROIC is a big pain to determine--there's not really even a single method that everyone agrees should be used to get a definitive report on ROIC. Nonetheless, it is probably the most accurate measure of the four, and it is the one many companies use internally to determine how well they are using the capital at their disposal relative to others in similar industries--especially companies in capital investment-intensive industries like oil and gas which are constantly using the money they have, and borrowing more, to try and generate profits. (There's nothing worse for a company's ROIC than a dry well.) So, in Pocket MBA's inimitable, shorthand way, what follows is the lawyer's guide to ROIC.

First, think about the 2003 Florida Marlins. They beat the New York Yankees to win the World Series while sporting a team payroll (players being a capital investment of sorts) of $48.75 million, one of the lowest in all of baseball. The Yankees payroll for the same year was $152.75 million. Let's assume that all the other investment expenses in running a baseball team are roughly equal, and you can conclude that, where the goal is playing in the World Series, the

Marlins got a far superior return on their investment than the Yankees. Pocket MBA is sure that somewhere, someone places a monetary value on playing in and then winning or losing the World Series, but assume it's an immediate windfall of $30 million for both teams. If you were to divide the $30 million by the Marlins total 2003 investment (payroll + whatever else) and the $30 million by the Yankees, you easily see that the Marlins earned a higher percentage return on their investment. Knowing how efficient the Marlins were at creating profits in 2003, you would be smart to think about investing in them.

Now, Pocket MBA is not claiming that this is how to figure ROIC (the value of the Yankees franchise is such that the reality is they are probably a superior investment--just ask Yankees owner George Steinbrenner, who paid $10 million for the team back in the 1970s and has seen its value explode to near $1 billion), but that is essentially what ROIC is in a nutshell: how much you invest and borrow to earn a return. Obviously, companies with a high ROIC are better investments than those with a lower ROIC, and companies monitor their ROIC to make sure they are using capital wisely. Furthermore, to indicate value, a company's ROIC must be greater than its working asset cost of capital (WACC--in and of itself worth a future Pocket MBA issue). After all, it costs money to raise money, and companies that have an ROIC less than WACC are often referred to as "destroyers of value." If a company has a ROIC of 10% and its cost of capital is 12%, it is still losing two cents on every dollar of capital investment.

So getting away from lucky baseball teams (the Marlins did, after all, have the fortune of playing the Cubs in the playoffs--blasted fans and their gloves), not to mention diversions from the difficult computation ahead, how do you figure ROIC? Simple. Divide net operating profit after taxes (NOPAT) by invested capital. That is:

- ROIC = NOPAT/Invested Capital

But you say, "Pocket MBA, how do you figure NOPAT and invested capital?" NOPAT is determined by reference to a company's income statements. You can refine the calculation to the nth degree, but essentially, you can figure NOPAT by subtracting a company's operating expenses and taxes from its net income:

- NOPAT = Sales - Operating Expenses - taxes

Real sticklers suggest the more refined calculation:

- NOPAT = Reported Net Income - Investment and Interest Income - Tax Shield from Interest Expense (effective tax rate x interest expense) + Goodwill Amortization

As to invested capital, the denominator in the equation, you can figure that simply by taking a company's total assets and subtracting current liabilities and cash:

- Invested Capital = Total Assets - Current Liabilities - Cash

Now you understand why people prefer P/E ratios, profit margins and ROE. And those will give you a good sense of where a company is headed, but ROIC is the most exacting ratio, primarily because it includes debt. The others do not. So, next time a client tells you about her company's ROE, just raise an eyebrow, chuckle and remind yourself to check out their debt ratio.

PLI's Pocket MBA Vol. 3 No. 7   February 16, 2005

Naked Short

Short selling a stock without first "locating" (determining if the shares are available) the shares to be borrowed.

NAKED SHORT IN THE REAL WORLD:

The term naked short conjures all kinds of images, but of course it has nothing to do with a lack of clothing or a lack of height. It has to do with a stock trader finding a stock that is not available to be borrowed and then borrowing it anyway. True, in light of Rule 203 of the SEC's new Regulation SHO, which went into effect January 3, 2005, naked shorting has been earmarked for extinction, at least insofar as the retail investor is concerned. (It lives on for your broker-dealer clients.) But, as Monday was Valentine's Day, Pocket MBA thought it should take its cupid's bow and shoot directly at the concepts of nakedness, unavailability, along with matching buy and sell orders--concepts intricately intertwined with lonely hearts worldwide.

In order to understand why the SEC moved to get rid of naked shorting, you have to understand what it really is by distinguishing it from garden variety shorting, which is a time-honored and respected (in some circles) part of the market. Most Pocket MBA'ers have a fundamental notion of what short-selling a stock (or "going short") is. What follows is the simple version for anyone who does not. Most stock trades are "long," that is a seller offers shares for sale and a buyer purchases them at a price determined either by the market or by the parties via price limited buy and sell orders. For example, if you have 50 shares of Starbucks (that's shares not cups) that you want to sell, for whatever reason, you'll place an order to sell the shares, either at market or for a specific price. If Pocket MBA is simply itching to buy 50 shares of Starbucks (having already consumed 50 cups), it would place an order to buy the shares, either at market or for a specific price. (This ignores the machinations that match these orders, but you can read up on that in Pocket MBA, Volume 2, No. 7, the Specialist System. Suffice to say, it's more Yente from "Fiddler on the Roof" or even eHarmony.com than Cupid.)

Traders go long stocks because they think the price of the shares will rise. But, sometimes, a trader thinks a stock is overpriced already. That trader thinks the share price will go down and should be sold, but the trader owns no shares to sell. As a result, that trader may attempt a "short sale." Short sales are the blind date of stock trading.

Assume you have those same 50 shares of Starbucks in a margin account (that means you borrowed the money to buy them and the broker retains the right to sell them out from under you in certain circumstances), or you are a broker that holds 50 shares, but you have no intention of selling them. Pocket MBA is itching to sell those shares for you (having discovered that 50 cups of Dunkin' Donuts has the same effect as 50 cups of Starbucks at half the price). Pocket MBA can do so by locating the shares you have, borrowing them from you and selling them in the hope the price will decline over time. Later, when Pocket MBA concludes the share price has declined enough, Pocket MBA will step in and buy 50 shares long (known as "covering the short") and (oversimplifying the whole process) return them to your account, pocketing the difference between the sale and buy price as profit.

Now, let's get naked. What happens if Pocket MBA wants to sell a stock short but isn't sure there are shares to borrow? The short answer is it can't be done in the U.S., at least not legally. But people do it anyway. They borrow shares and put a receipt in the kitty saying they sold the shares short and that they'll find the shares later. That is a naked short. Problem is, when the shares never turn up, the trader who later bought the shares from the naked shorter does not ever rightfully own them. (Talk about getting stood up!) It's a big semi-Ponzi scheme whose primary purpose is to create downward pressure on a company's stock price, all to the benefit of the naked shorter. The companies affected by the practice are primarily small, and it can have a disastrous impact on their ability to tap capital markets. If you do a quick Internet search, you will see that some have dubbed as "Stockgate" an avalanche of naked short selling that has roiled small companies in recent years.

Enter the SEC with Regulation SHO, unveiled in July 2004, and Rule 203 of which, "regulation of short sales," went into effect a few weeks ago. Now when brokers hook up a buyer and seller, they have to designate the relationship as long, short or short-exempt. (This is roughly equivalent to marriage, casual dating and one-night stand.) Rule 203 of Regulation SHO combats naked short selling by enacting a "locate and delivery" requirement on short sales. According to the

SEC's release on Regulation SHO, see www.sec.gov/rules/final/34-50103.htm#V:

> [T]he rule prohibits a broker-dealer from accepting a short sale order in any equity security from another person, or effecting a short sale order for the broker-dealer's own account unless the broker-dealer has (1) borrowed the security, or entered into an arrangement to borrow the security, or (2) has reasonable grounds to believe that the security can be borrowed so that it can be delivered on the date delivery is due. The locate must be made and documented prior to effecting a short sale, regardless of whether the seller's short position may be closed out by purchasing securities the same day.

The rule provides exceptions, "including for short sales effected in connection with bona-fide market making," which you can read about on the SEC's website. And so Pocket MBA bids adieu to another Valentine's Day, feeling a bit more secure in a trading world where naked is out except for those who really should be, and where the rest of us have to hook-up the old-fashioned way - locate and deliver.

PLI's Pocket MBA Vol. 3 No. 8	February 23, 2005

FAS 123r

Statement of Financial Accounting Standard (SFAS) 123 (Revised 2004): December 16, 2004 revision of previous share-based compensation rule to require that all such transactions "be recognized in the financial statements."

FAS 123r IN THE REAL WORLD:

Pocket MBA first visited the issue of expensing stock options on June 30, 2003. That was way back in Volume 1, No. 10, and Pocket

MBA was pretty sure that it would revisit the issue sooner than the last week of February 2005, having declared at the time that FASB was likely to implement something in 2004. Well, at least the GAAP arbiter rewrote the rule in 2004 (December 16 to be exact) for implementation in the third quarter of 2005 (financial statements subsequent to June 15). This isn't Psychic MBA, after all. So after two years of work, let's see what FASB came up with.

To briefly review, share-based compensation became a hot-button issue in (when else) the late 1990s, as more and more small, cash-poor technology companies snagged the best and the brightest employees with the lure of possible riches via stock options. This followed on the heels of all the formerly small and already large, cash-rich companies that had been engaging in the practice for years. The accounting issue with such options was that there was no requirement that companies reflect the issuance on their balance sheets. So when issued, they had no definable, certain value. They were just a piece of paper (or an online file by that point) entitling an employee to buy stock at a set price after a certain vesting period, regardless of the price of the stock at the time of the vesting. To many observers, this seemed quite disingenuous from an accounting perspective because, by definition, an option exercised must have had some value aside from "zero" from the moment of issuance. It was payment for services and, like other payments, was an expense of sorts. Yet the value of options did not show up as a compensation expense.

Original FAS 123 (adopted in 1995) encouraged (but didn't require) companies to account for options as an expense and offered a methodology for companies to do so if they chose. But although 750 public entities began or committed to begin accounting for their options in financial statements, most companies (particularly the go-go tech companies) preferred to report options in the notes to their financial statements (as was their right), where they would have no impact on bottom lines, many of which were none too stellar. Ethical watchdogs persisted that such reporting hid the impact of options on a company's financial condition since the uncertain, yet eventual, exercise date of those options kept analysts in the dark and had impact on regular shareholders, who had to buy stock at market value no matter that millions of unexercised options lurked in the background.

If 100 employees hold 1,000,000 options each to purchase shares for $1 in a company that has 100 million shares outstanding, and Pocket MBA bought shares for $15 and saw them rise to $20, after which those employees exercised their options and immediately sold, doubling the outstanding shares and causing the share price to drop by half--well you can see where it might bother people to not have a crystal-clear view as to how many of these options were out there. (Note that anyone who knew how to tear apart the notes to the financial statements could probably figure out a company's option situation, but not so easily as if the value were plainly stated on the balance sheet.) But nothing beyond grumbling occurred. In any event, you know the rest: 2000, 2001, 2002, market crash, market crash, market crash, scandal, scandal, scandal. FASB's hand was forced, and so it has acted.

FAS 123(r) replaces FAS 123 and supersedes Accounting Principals Board (APB) Opinion No. 25 on share-based compensation and imposes a "fair value" regime. It "applies to all awards granted after the required effective date" as well as those granted prior to the effective date to the extent those are "modified, repurchased or cancelled in periods beginning after the effective date." FAS 123(r) pars. 70-74. Even awards granted before the effective date, but which remain unvested on the effective date, must be recognized using fair value.

You can access FAS 123(r) at FASB's website, www.fasb.org, and it is 295 pages of heavy lifting. But in essence, it requires companies to recognize in their financial statements the compensation expense relating to most share-based payment arrangements. (ESOPs are, for the most part, exempted.) FASB offered four reasons for the new rule:

- Addressing concerns of users and others: "Financial statements that do not faithfully represent [share-based compensation] transactions can distort the issuer's reported financial condition."
- Improving comparability of reported financial

information by eliminating alternative accounting methods.
- Simplifying U.S. GAAP by requiring all entities to use the same accounting method.

Convergence with international accounting standards (see Pocket MBA Vol. 3, No. 4): The IASB already requires accounting for share-based compensation and applies a methodology similar to SFAS 123(r).

So, from June 15 on (for large companies; smaller companies have until December to comply), your clients who issue share-based compensation will have to measure the cost of such compensation based on the "grant-date fair value of the award." And how will they measure that? Well, according to FASB, "The fair value of an equity share option or similar instruments shall be measured based on the observable market price of an option with the same or similar terms and conditions, if one is available." FAS 123(r), par. 22.

When such a value is not available, companies should determine value by estimation "using option-pricing models adjusted for the unique characteristics of" the particular instrument. See FASB news release, 12/16/04; FAS 123(r), par. 22. FAS 123(r) does not specify what options pricing model must be used. Indeed, Appendix A recommends the use of any model that renders the most accurate fair value. See FAS 123(r), pars. A13-A17. In extreme cases, when it is simply impossible to arrive at a valuation due to the complexity of the instrument, FASB allows use of intrinsic value, "remeasured at each reporting date through the date of exercise or other settlement." FAS 123(r), par. 24. Appendix A offers illustrative examples of how the new rule will work under various circumstances and varying degrees of instrument complexity, and Pocket MBA recommends you to it. In fact, FASB urges that Appendix A is "an integral part" of FAS 123(r).

Of course, it's up to you and the accountants you work with to determine how this affects your clients, but there are some interesting wrinkles that transition to the new rule will cause. One is that since this is a mid-year transition for many companies, their financial statements may be out of whack, as those subsequent to June 15 will show the impact of options grants (e.g., because expenses are higher, earnings will be lower) and those prior to June 15 will not. FASB is permitting companies some leeway (modified retrospective application) in restating prior quarters financial statements so as to present consistent data. See FAS 123(r), pars. 76-77. When Microsoft announced it would start expensing options back in 2003, it restated several years of previous earnings for the sake of consistency.

And now, Pocket MBA sends you off to FASB land to check out the entire text of FAS 123(r), fully hoping it has tied the bow on options expensing. Of course, hope springs eternal, and many who are unhappy with FAS 123(r) may well try to undo it. Indeed the House of Representatives has already passed a bill (which has gone nowhere) limiting the application of FAS 123(r). So it's possible we may convene again to talk options expensing. Until then, on to more settled topics. See you next week.

PLI's Pocket MBA Vol. 3 No. 9   March 2, 2005

Road Shows

Traditionally, a multi-city marketing blitz undertaken by companies and their underwriters to drum up key-investor interest in an IPO.

ROAD SHOWS IN THE REAL WORLD:

Recently Pocket MBA was lucky enough to meet, by chance, some of the principals of a freshly minted public company the day of their IPO, after they had "rung" the closing bell on NASDAQ (or turned off the lights or servers or whatever it is they do over at the NASDAQ studio in New York City to herald the end of a trading day). The company's stock had soared 30% on the first day of trading and PMBA jokingly asked the group why they hadn't called to let it in on the action. They replied that PMBA should have showed up to their road show events in Chicago and New York. Of course, PMBA was not invited because PMBA is just a member of the investing lumpen and hence not privy to road shows and the resultant IPOs. That may be beginning to change. And as PMBA has said before, chalk up another one for the Internet.

The road show has long been the smoke-filled backroom of investing. It's where fledgling companies, under the watchful eye of their underwriters, sold their business plans to select, wealthy institutional investors cherry-picked by the underwriters. The interest garnered during these events helped the underwriter to determine how much stock would be sold and at what price. The presentations were tightly planned (and tightly regulated by the SEC) as management told these potential investors about its lofty dreams a couple weeks before the registration statement became effective and everyone clammed up. And, typically, road shows made pit stops in only the five largest markets (e.g. New York, Chicago, San Francisco, Boston and Los Angeles).

If you weren't one of the favored investors invited to the show, you could never be someone who boasted "I bought Microsoft at (a split-adjusted) 10 cents per share." You had to wait for the shares to actually come on the market, where you could use your spare $500 to buy shares that had already appreciated 30 or 40 percent, or in the 1990s that had already appreciated 200 to 300 percent, in some cases, only to see your investment fail as institutions bailed, having profited handsomely and knowing that the shares had quickly become tremendously overvalued. And in some respects, a lot of the retail investor excess of the late 1990s probably resulted from an innate desire to be in on the ground floor. The problem was, even if investors bought the shares on day one, they were never in on the ground floor, and hence they bought shares at inflated prices without much information to back up their purchases.

But just as it did with the smoke-filled backrooms of political conventions, as the 20th century drew to a close, advances in communications had begun to render the IPO road show more and more anachronistic in its undemocratic distribution of investment information and riches. As more and more investors "did it themselves" with online accounts, the clamor to be able to get involved on the ground floor (meaning getting in on the IPO) grew louder and louder. And in an era of Regulation FD and Sarbanes-

Oxley, where communication and disclosure are the SEC's watchwords, how fair is it to give select people and institutions pre-IPO information that can just as easily be disseminated to everyone?

Indeed, in the late 1990s the SEC began to issue no-action letters that allowed broadcast of some road shows over the Internet. Charles Schwab was a notable example, and it proceeded to let some of its retail account holders into the backroom of the IPO process. And once you open the floodgates...

On November 3, 2004, the SEC published proposed rules "that would modify and advance significantly the registration, communications, and offering processes under the Securities Act of 1933." According to the SEC, the rules are designed to:

> eliminate unnecessary and outmoded restrictions on offerings. In addition, the proposals would provide more timely investment information to investors without mandating delays in the offering process that we believe would be inconsistent with the needs of issuers for timely access to capital. The proposals also would continue our long-term efforts toward integrating disclosure and processes under the Securities Act and the Securities Exchange Act of 1934. The proposals would accomplish these goals by addressing communications related to registered securities offerings, delivery of information to investors, and procedural restrictions in the offering and capital formation processes.

And one result of the proposed rules would be to make the webcast road show a standard option that would allow companies to enlighten investors who wouldn't ordinarily be in attendance at a traditional road show. Now does this mean that the average investor will get those "cheap" shares? No, not yet anyway. But at least when Pocket MBA runs into the principals of a fledgling NASDAQ company on the day before they light up the wall to celebrate their IPO, Pocket MBA can say "I logged onto your road show--exciting business. I'm in."

The comment period on the SEC's proposed rules ended on

January 31, 2005. So there'll surely be an update on the road show in the near future. Until then.

PLI's Pocket MBA Vol. 3 No. 10   March 9, 2005

Efficient Market Hypothesis (EMH)

Theory that all market participants receive and absorb all relevant, available market-related information, which is reflected immediately in the price of securities, thus rendering futile any attempt to outperform the market.

EFFICIENT MARKET HYPOTHESIS (EMH) IN THE REAL WORLD:

Pocket MBA decided to take a break from balance sheet formulas and new rules and regulations to ruminate about a controversial, largely discredited view of markets. So you may be asking yourself, "Why is Pocket MBA discussing a subject that has been largely discredited?" And if you didn't know that EMH has been largely discredited, you could look it up. And don't let the fact that plenty of financial scribes still write about EMH allow you to think that it hasn't been discredited because even those who subscribe to it recognize it is limited in its practical application. (Of course, what Pocket MBA is really saying here is that, like all theories, you can take EMH or leave it--it's up to you.) In any event, after giving the subject some thought, Pocket MBA has a take on this (you'll find it way at the end) that relates EMH to all the regulatory and rulemaking initiatives fostering transparency and good governance that have been legislated by the government and passed by the major exchanges. This means everything from Reg. FD to Sarbanes-Oxley to the latest proposed NASD broker-dealer rule on selling variable annuities. But first, back to the beginning.

EMH surfaced back in the 1960s and was popularized in the 1973 book by Burton Malkiel, "A Random Walk Down Wall Street"

(W.W. Norton & Co., Inc.). This is from whence arose the hypothesis that a blindfolded monkey could randomly throw darts at the stock pages of a newspaper and achieve as good a return as any money manager. Notice that the example uses a blindfolded monkey and not a typical investor--at the time, Joe Average didn't invest in the stock market, and probably nobody imagined that the time would come when over 50% of Americans would have unmanaged stock market holdings, as is the case today. Taken together, EMH and the "Random Walk" theory suggest it is futile for an investor to attempt anything other than trying to match the performance of the market in the long run without taking on extraordinary risk--risk that would as likely bankrupt as enrich an investor.

EMH and "Random Walk" enjoyed great currency for many years (years that were, perhaps not coincidentally, very stagnant for the stock market). So how does EMH work? Well, it assumes a rational, informed investor. (And if, having read that, you have already concluded that EMH is hogwash, you wouldn't be alone.) Because all investors are rational, they will investigate, absorb and immediately take advantage of all of the important information that is available and reflect it in the price of securities. (Some of these investors will absorb certain information and others will absorb other information, but all of it gets absorbed, like the Borg in "Star Trek: Next Generation," into the whole of the price.) As a result, at any point in time, the price of a security is the best barometer of its actual value. Thus to buy a security because you think it is undervalued or sell it because you think it is overvalued (which is what most investors do) is really just a crapshoot at what might occur after future information is absorbed. Hence the monkey.

There are three versions of EMH--weak, semi-strong and strong--each of which argues to a greater or lesser extent against trying to predict the market:

- Weak Form - assumes a stock price reflects all historical information including past returns. This form torpedoes any notion that technical analysis can predict price movement. See PMBA, Vol. 2, No. 41.

- Semi-Strong - assumes a stock price reflects both historic and currently available information. This form torpedoes the notion that fundamental analysis can help predict price movement.
- Strong - assumes stock price reflects historic, current and insider information. This is pure EMH and augurs in favor of indexing because you simply can't get ahead of the market (or behind) by any method other than by begging to pay more or less than a security is fetching.

Academics have challenged each of these by showing various patterns ("anomalies") independent of "important, relevant information" that seem to play out in the market (e.g. Dogs of the Dow Theory, which posits that if you buy the 10 highest yielding Dow stocks at the beginning of every year, you will outperform the market).

EMH author Burton Malkiel wrote a paper in 2003 to defend against all the challenges to EMH and Random Walk theory. See Malkiel, "The Efficient Market Hypothesis and Its Critics" (CEPS Working Paper No. 91, 2003)

Malkiel argues that none of the anomalies persist over the long run because, in part, once everyone discovers a pattern, it disintegrates. He also notes that analysts are so busy mining data that they are bound to find market patterns that have no real significance. (Any sports fan can relate to this after rolling their eyes at the latest statistic found by sportscasters--like most hits in a row to start off a season--it's insignificant.) Accordingly, he insists that EMH is as valid as the day it first surfaced.

But what about stock market crashes and the experience of the late 1990s and early 2000s? You might conclude that an efficient market shouldn't become massively overbought or be able to crash. Malkiel argues that even efficient markets "make mistakes." Pocket MBA wonders if, perhaps, EMH simply cannot survive situations in which the irrational investor (i.e. the masses) begin to become involved in the market, as was the case in the 1987 crash and even more so recently.

One monkey may be able to duplicate the market, but can efficiency withstand millions of monkeys? Maybe efficiency yields to the law of supply and demand. (Malkiel even pays lip service to this notion.) Viewed from this perspective, despite its blindfolded monkey conceit, EMH can be viewed as tremendously elitist in that it never really took into account the possibility of you, your clients and Pocket MBA logging onto E*Trade and buying stock whenever the mood struck. Malkiel has an answer for this, too: since professional money managers performed no better than the irrational masses, it proves that the masses had no discernable impact on the market.

Alert, here comes Pocket MBA's pet theory. Assuming that EMH didn't take into account the impact of the "average" investor becoming involved in the market, let's accept that the markets became wildly inefficient during the late 1990s. Enter the government to do what it often does best, whether advisably or not--level the long-term playing field. If you assume that the bubble burst of 2000-2003 was an efficient market correcting a mistake, then much of the regulatory action since can be seen as a government effort to encourage future market efficiency. SEC Regulation FD and Sarbanes-Oxley are all about making companies more transparent by forcing the disclosure of important, relevant information to the average investor who is now in the market. This in turn ensures that market efficiency isn't just for those who know how to read every line of a balance sheet or who read Investors Business Daily. So perhaps the unintended consequence of all the new regulation will be a rebirth of EMH. There, that was a long way to go for an observation that has no more validity than EMH is perceived to have. You might say it was a random walk down the page. But it was really just food for thought.

FAS 95 (Statement of Cash Flows)

Requirement instituted in 1987 that requires companies to classify separately, as part of their financial statements, cash receipts and payments as having stemmed from operating, investing and financing activities.

FAS 95 (STATEMENT OF CASH FLOWS) IN THE REAL WORLD:

It's earnings season! Actually, it's almost finished. By this time of the quarter, most companies have reported their recent results and produced financial statements. In looking at financial statements, and in particular the statement of cash flows, it struck Pocket MBA how much they look like the scribbling that Pocket MBA does when trying to determine what purchases it can make in the coming months. For instance, Pocket MBA was thinking of buying a condo, and started to write down a list of monthly inflows and outflows of cash, potential gains from investment portfolios and recurring debt. Roughly speaking, these correspond to a company's statement of cash flows. FAS 95 is that easy; it's all about how much excess cash (or not) you have at the end of whatever period you're dealing with. Back in Volume 1, No. 18, PMBA addressed the concept of free cash flow and its importance in determining a company's true liquidity. At that time, PMBA didn't address the actual report from which cash flow is determined. And as two years seemed like a long time to leave something hanging, today is all about FAS 95 and the statement of cash flows from whence a determination of free cash emanates.

The statement of cash flows is a relatively new creature of the accounting world, having been born of FASB's implementation of FAS 95 in 1987 (for complete text, see www.fasb.org). Until that time, Accounting Principals Board (APB) Opinion 19 reined over the ledgers and required that companies report only changes in financial position. APB permitted, but did not require, companies to report cash flow information. In erecting FAS 95, FASB's intent was to require companies "to provide relevant information about the cash receipts and cash payments of an enterprise during a period" to enable investors, creditors and others to better assess:

- The enterprise's ability to generate positive

future net cash flows
- The enterprise's ability to meet its obligation, its ability to pay dividends, and its needs for external financing
- The reasons for differences between net income and associated cash receipts and payments
- The effects on an enterprise's financial position of both its cash and non-cash investing and financing transactions during the period

The bottom line is that whereas a company's balance sheet gives you "the bottom line" at a point in time (the end of the period) and an income statement includes all manner of non-cash esoterica that can exasperate a non-expert, a statement of cash flows includes only inflows and outflows of cash (something anyone can understand) over the entire period. It is derived from the income statement and its bottom-line numbers are reflected on the annual increase or decrease of the cash & cash equivalents portion of the company's balance sheet.

In fact, the periodic change in cash & cash equivalents is what the statement of cash flows is all about. When the number is positive, that's free cash flow.

A statement of cash flows is reported in three sections:

- Cash flows from operating activities - this includes how much money a company's actual business generated in a period
- Cash flows from investing activities - this shows the money a company earned or lost investing cash in various instruments or in buying and selling subsidiaries, plants and equipment
- Cash flows from financing activities - this is where the company records activity related to its issuance of stocks and bonds, including dividends paid out and stock buybacks

If you think back to PMBA's scribbling, or your own for that matter, you will recognize all of these sections from your own budgetary process. That's why the statement of cash flows is not only useful, but easy to read. Everyone does something like it in their everyday existence. And that's the kind of accounting term Pocket MBA likes the most.

FAS 117

Standards that govern the contents of financial statements of not-for-profit organizations.

FAS 117 IN THE REAL WORLD:

Pocket MBA has paid so much attention to the various ways that companies count profit and the equally various ways that analysts and investors evaluate those profits that it's easy to forget that not all companies exist for the enrichment of shareholders or venture capitalists. And though Volume 2, No. 39 was dedicated to not-for-profit organizations, it was more structural paean than examination of how not-for-profit companies satisfy their equivalent to shareholders-- and those would be donors. After all, a not-for-profit doesn't simply spring from thin air. It has to be established and maintained like any other entity. And as that process involves the intake and expenditure of often-enormous sums of money (think Red Cross), not-for-profits have to, at some point, account for all that money. Still it wasn't that long ago (1993 to be exact) that not-for-profit accounting was a hodge-podge of tradition and play-it-by-ear.

As a result, prior to 1994, different types of not-for-profit organizations accounted for and reported financial information in different ways. For instance, according to FASB, in its introduction to FAS 117, most hospitals, trade associations and membership organizations provided financial information for the entity as a whole, while universities, museums, and religious organizations reported financial positions for individual units within the organization. FAS

117 changed all that by establishing uniform reporting requirements governing all not-for-profits. And the reality is that but for the unique characteristics of not-for-profits that must be reflected, the reports that they must make are roughly analogous (one is exactly the same) to those of for-profit companies, and they must follow GAAP. So briefly, here is the terminology that accompanies not-for-profit financial reporting pursuant to FAS 117.

FAS 117 requires that all not-for-profits issue three reports at the end of every reporting period, as follows:

Statement of Financial Position. A statement of financial position is roughly equivalent to a public company balance sheet. Thus, its "primary purpose...is to provide relevant information about an organization's assets, liabilities and net assets and about their relationship to each other at a moment in time." FAS 117, Par. 9. FAS 117 requires explicitly that a statement of financial position "shall focus on the organization as a whole." FAS 117, Par. 10. This did away with the sub-unit reporting that had existed. One significant difference between not-for-profit statements of financial position and for-profit balance sheets is in the characterization of assets. Whereas balance sheets include assets, liabilities and stockholder equity, the statement of financial position is most notable for the requirement that it classify its net assets depending on whether they are restricted as to how the entity may use them.

A not-for-profit's assets can be permanently restricted, temporarily restricted or unrestricted. The restrictions are erected by donor agreements. Each statement of financial position will contain line items detailing the various restrictions. For instance, land, artwork and buildings might be donated to a not-for-profit with the stipulation that they never be sold. This makes the asset permanently restricted. Or assets might be donated with the intent that they be invested to create a permanent income source or endowment. Donors might also place temporary restrictions on assets by, for example, asserting that an asset be used in a certain way for a specified term. Unrestricted assets are generally those that come to the organization as a result of ongoing business operations such as the production and sale of goods or services.

Statement of Activities: The statement of activities is sort of the income statement for not-for-profits. It contains information about "(a) the effect of transactions and other events and circumstances that change the amount and nature of net assets, (b) the relationships of those transactions and other events and circumstances to each other, and (c) how the organization's resources are used in providing various programs and services." FAS 117, Par. 17. The statement of activities reports the net change in permanently restricted, temporarily restricted and unrestricted net assets for the reporting period. It also includes revenues, expenses, gains and losses.

Statement of Cash Flows: The statement of cash flows is, well, the statement of cash flows, and FAS 117 specifically amends FAS 95, see last week's Pocket MBA, to include not-for-profits in its purview. A not-for-profit's statement of cash flows is, in all material aspects, the same as that of a for-profit entity, except insofar as for-profit statements of cash flow reflect investor related activity (such as dividends paid) and not-for-profit reflect the impact of those restricted assets.

So there you have it--everything you need to go out and start your own not-for-profit, or at least to monitor one for your clients.

PLI's Pocket MBA Vol. 3 No. 13   March 30, 2005

SEC No-Action Letter

SEC staff assurance that under a given set of circumstances, SEC will not pursue enforcement action against a market participant who undertakes the specified course of action.

SEC NO-ACTION LETTERS IN THE REAL WORLD:

Many readers may have looked at this week's term and said, "Why include 'SEC' as part of it; 'no-action letter' would have sufficed." Well, so many agencies, both federal (e.g. the CFTC) and state (the Arizona Securities Division) issue no-action letters that Pocket MBA wanted to be sure to focus on the one of greatest import to readers. The no-action letter is the "Mother may I," of the securities world. It's like going to ask your father for approval to do something "edgy," and he tells you "I don't know. Go ask your mother. If it's alright with her, it's alright with me." Your mother approves and you're home free on the planned activity. Of course, your sister could probably thereafter get away with doing the same thing, but if she asked, mom would not be bound by what she had previously told you. That's the family no-action letter. So it is with securities. Market participant clients will ask counsel if there are any legal impediments to pursuing a particular course of action regarding a proposed transaction that may be somewhat novel or may impact investors in an unusual way. Counsel will respond, "I don't know. Go ask the SEC. If it's alright with them, it's alright with me." And when the SEC says, "We won't make life tough for you if you do this," it only applies to you, though others similarly situated might rightly conclude that they could do likewise.

No-action letters are part of the SEC's inherent authority (granted by Congress) to interpret both the securities laws as well as its own rules. Because the securities laws are often so complex and also because the securities world is so complex, the SEC's official pronouncements on the law don't always apply to a situation presented by a specific transaction that had not been previously contemplated. But successful and orderly securities markets require that even under such circumstances, market participants enjoy some kind of certainty that their actions will not be referred to the Division of Enforcement. In these circumstances, the SEC historically encouraged its staff to "provide advice and guidance to those seeking assistance." Nagy, JUDICIAL RELIANCE ON REGULATORY INTERPRETATIONS IN SEC NO-ACTION LETTERS: CURRENT PROBLEMS AND A PROPOSED FRAMEWORK, 83 Cornell L. Rev. 921, 933 (1998).

No-action letters have their origins in the early days of the SEC. They developed as private responses from SEC counsel to parties who inquired whether a transaction implicated the securities laws. These answers were accompanied by the nowadays standard "these are the views of SEC staff and not an official pronouncement of the Commission," or something to that effect. As things evolved, SEC counsel didn't always offer a legal opinion; rather it simply opined on the likelihood of enforcement action. Id. at 936-37. These eventually became the no-action letter.

There are specific procedures that market participants must follow in requesting a no-action letter. Requests are generally directed to the chief counsel of the division implicated by the particular rules and factual scenario, after which staff attorneys work on draft responses that may be reviewed by various higher-ups before the no-action letter is issued. See Id. at 940-43 for an explanation of the procedure involved.

The interesting aspect of no-action letters is that although they are officially without precedential value (nor is the SEC or any court bound by them) and are intended to be relied upon only by the requestor(s), the legal community views no-action letters as a "source of law, and they are considered precedents by parties other than the recipients, providing a partial safe harbor and guidance to practitioners." Frankel, SYMPOSIUM ON THE INTERNET AND LEGAL THEORY: THE INTERNET, SECURITIES REGULATION, AND THEORY OF LAW, 73 Chi.-Kent. L. Rev. 1319 (1998). This transformation resulted from the 1970 decision by the SEC to publish no-action letters, which had been, until then, a matter between the SEC and the parties. You can visit the SEC website, www.sec.gov, and access thousands of no-action letters. Obviously when something is published, people will use it to compare, contrast and apply it to their own situation to determine whether a course of action is favored or discouraged by the SEC. And most commentators (including those cited here) argue that the SEC intends for parties to do so. Thus have no-action letters developed *a de facto* precedential value throughout the legal system. They're as good as your mother's word.

PLI's Pocket MBA Vol. 3 No. 14April 6, 2005

Down-Round Financing

Venture financing subsequent to initial venture financings in which investors pay less for the shares issued than previous investors.

DOWN-ROUND FINANCING IN THE REAL WORLD:

Down-round financing sounds complex, but it really isn't, although a company's decision to do a down-round can be. And because Pocket MBA likes to make things painfully simple and real-life, think about the following example as this discussion of down-round financing proceeds. You planned six months in advance to holiday at what had been projected to be the hottest vacation destination of 2005, the exotic, tropical island of Expensiva. You paid $1445 for an air/hotel package, knowing that if you waited, the price would surely double. Six weeks before your trip, an earthquake rocks Expensiva and, while your hotel is left standing, most of the attractions are ruined. You then see an ad in the newspaper trumpeting air/hotel packages to Expensiva for $599. You feel sick, having lost over half your vacation investment. That's what happens in a down-round, with the exception that it is conceivable that the early-bird investors in a company will recoup their investment dollars over time if they hold their shares.

Down-rounds were once seen as the financing option of last resort, to be exercised only when a company was in such dire straits that the only other options might be shutting the business or selling off the assets. They are more common today, especially among the survivors of the tech-wreck of the 1990s. Many companies that saw their values skyrocket to unrealistic levels (and also capitalized on that by selling shares in "up-rounds," which means at a price higher than the initial investors paid) only to watch them plummet in 2000-2002 have turned to down-rounds to weather the storm. These are the businesses that have demonstrated success and retain hope for the future, but lack cash to realize the hope. And they can often find investors willing to pony-up, but at prices significantly less than the company had been previously valued.

The most common side effect of a down-round is the dreaded dilution. (In fact, the dilution can be so severe that the new investors take effective control of the company--these types of down-rounds are called "washouts" or "cramdowns" because they obliterate the initial investors.) In any event, here is a typical down-round, minus all the technical provisions. Assume Risky Business, Inc. originally issued 10 million preferred shares to its venture investors for $10 each, but found subsequently that it needed another 10 million dollars either to keep the doors open or to finance the next leg of its march toward profitability. The new investors the company finds won't be willing to pay $10 per share. They might only be willing to pay $1 per share, which means the company has to double the outstanding preferred shares in order to get one-tenth the amount of capital that it originally received. Instead of the company being valued at $100 million (10 million * $10), it is now worth just $20 million (20 million * $1). And that makes the original investors want to pull their hair out. (Just like the impact of that $1445 vacation that is now worth just $599.)

The original investors often try to protect themselves by inserting anti-dilution provisions into their share subscriptions. These have the effect of increasing the number of common shares the investors can receive upon converting the preferred shares they received when they first invested. These provisions generally take one of two forms:

- Weighted Average - This method increases an original investor's share stake at a level proportional to the decrease in conversion price. This is accomplished by dividing the original share price by the conversion price and multiplying it by number of shares the original investor is converting to determine the number of common shares he will receive. Thus as the conversion price decreases, the number of shares the original investors receive increases.

- Full Price Ratchet - This method simply reduces the conversion price for initial investors to the down-round price. In the Risky Business example, this would result in the original investors receiving 10 times the number of shares they actually bargained for, resulting in an extravagant level of dilution.

The catch is that as a prerequisite to their participation, the down-round investors usually require the original investors to waive many, if not all, of their anti-dilution rights. These and other prerequisites, such as "pay-to-play" provisions (which require existing investors to participate in the down-round), put the down-round investors in the catbird's seat by making their shares more valuable relative to the other outstanding shares. As you can see, the typical down-round places the company in a financial vice, with the original venture investors on one side and the down-round investors on the other. And none of this guarantees that the company will succeed eventually and won't need to try further dilutive rounds of financing or even go belly-up. Of course, the investors who lose the most out of all this, as usual, are the common stockholders who bought shares on the open market after an IPO. They simply get to watch their investment shrink. And unlike the vacationer in the example at the beginning of this, they don't even have a hotel to stay in, just tickets to a place that may not be worth visiting.

Junk Bond

Bonds issued by entities with less than investment-grade credit ratings and that, in exchange for the higher risk of default, pay higher yields.

JUNK BOND IN THE REAL WORLD:

Pocket MBA was watching VH1 recently, and the cable network broadcast a marathon of its junk series, "I Love the '80s," which, like "I Love the '70s" before it, is a paean to all the wonderful and quirky pop-culture icons of the era. If you haven't seen the series, often during an episode (each of which focus on one year during the decade) the producers put together a fast-moving video montage, and PMBA is pretty sure that during one of them, images of Michael Milken, the king of junk bonds and the representative of everything that was supposedly bad about the '80s (though PMBA thinks Duran Duran would serve the same purpose), zipped by. And now you're asking yourself, "What does this 1980s nostalgia trip have to do with 2005?" Well, aside from the fact that '80s music has been playing everywhere PMBA goes, which means the '80s are back, if you take a look at the article, "U.S. Bankruptcies 'to Surge' Amid Junk Bond Deluge," published just a few weeks back by the Times (of London) online, see www.business.timesonline.co.uk/article/0,,16849-1497723,00.html, you will conclude that it's not just the music of the '80s that came back, but problem junk bonds. Next thing you know, Laura Bush will be having her horoscope read at the White House. Anyway, all that was a roundabout way of saying that since most people have forgotten what junk bonds are or never knew, a short Milken appearance in "I Love the '80s" just won't do them the justice they deserve.

In essence, a junk (or high-yield) bond is no different from any other bond. A bond is simply the physical embodiment of debt issued by a corporation or other entity. The debt is accompanied by a promise to repay the principal to the bondholder by a date certain (the maturity date), plus a bond usually specifies a rate of return, or interest (the coupon), that is also paid to the bearer. What makes a bond junk is the financial condition or creditworthiness of the issuer, as assessed by Moody's or Standard & Poor's, the two debt rating services. If a bond is not "junk," it is "investment grade." But these two designations tell you only the creditworthiness of the issuer--that is the likelihood that the issuer will default on payment of either the interest or the principal. Investment grade bonds are rated Baa3 (Moody's) or BBB- (S&P) or higher. See www.moodys.com; www.standardandpoors.com. Any entity issuing bonds with a credit rating lower than those is a junk bond issuer.

The fact that a bond is junk does not mean that it is bad (this isn't junk food or even junk TV, after all) or that there is a strong likelihood that it will not be paid. Rather, it means that the bond is of above-average risk, especially relative to its AAA (S&P) or Aaa (Moody's), AA and A cousins (filet mignon as opposed to a Big Mac). It's not until you get to ratings in the low B or C range, which, after all, is right above the D for "default" level, that Standard & Poor's and Moody's assess issuers as being at substantial risk of nonpayment.

Most financial institutions historically shied away from buying high-yield bonds, or established policies forbidding their purchase because of the added risk, hence the junk moniker. Still, in economic boom times, junk bonds are not necessarily all that risky. And that's why investing in junk bonds can be so attractive to high-risk players. In fact, absent crisis and economic dislocation, most are paid, which means that in exchange for the added risk, the investor ends up with more reward. The tradeoff is also attractive to the entities that issue junk. If your credit rating is relatively lower, attracting capital can be somewhat difficult; in such circumstances issuing higher-yielding bonds is the only way to do so.

The junk bond craze started in 1977, when they were first sold publicly to large pools of investors. Within ten years, a large percentage of issues were non-investment grade. And that led, eventually to the mass defaults of the 1980s that live on in legend and in short clips on VH1. The junk bond industry has recovered since Milken days, and it began to thrive again in the 1990s (watch VH1 if you love that decade, as well). In fact, there are now mutual funds and other portfolios that specialize in junk bonds. But, as PMBA alluded to earlier, there is potential trouble in junk bond land, and PMBA recommends you to the article link above. Of course, whether this decade becomes another 1980s in terms of junk bond defaults is yet to be determined. But if you turn on VH1 in 2020 to watch "I Love the '00s" and see a clip of this issue of Pocket MBA, you know it was.

PLI's Pocket MBA Vol. 3 No. 16   April 20, 2005

American Depositary Receipt (ADR)

U.S. security representing the publicly traded equity shares of a non-U.S. Company.

AMERICAN DEPOSITARY RECEIPTS IN THE REAL WORLD:

The development of a truly global economy is fascinating to watch, and ADRs, which are skyrocketing in popularity (30 to 40 percent annual growth), are the latest participants in this process that is inexorably turning the world into one huge shopping mall. But let's turn the clock back. Just a few years ago, the catchphrase "buy American" was a popular proxy for the notion that buying the actual goods made by foreign companies was bad for the U.S. economy. A prime accelerant in this movement was the growth of the Japanese auto industry, Toyota in particular. Who can forget the 1970s and 1980s images of shiploads of Toyotas being unloaded in Seattle or wherever? (If you weren't around in the 1970s, you are excused from this memory.) Xenophobia aside, one could have been forgiven for thinking the economic sky was falling.

Flash forward. Nowadays, if you buy a Toyota, it is as likely as not that you are buying a car that, while backed by Toyota's manufacturing methods and sporting a Toyota label, was assembled by the guy who lives down the street (or robot) at a factory a few miles from Anywhere, USA. And this process has made owning a foreign car a lot easier than it was when the cars arrived by container ship, and when spare parts were so hard to come by that if the car broke down, you had to either spend a fortune on repairs or junk it. Now it's almost as if you're buying an American car, which raises the rhetorical question: Is a Toyota built in Kentucky really a Japanese car, in the political-economic sense, or is it just an American car with a Japanese name?

Now, take the musings that result from that and apply it to the stock market, specifically companies that trade publicly on foreign exchanges, but who want and obtain access to investors on American exchanges. It's really part of the same process, except you don't hear anyone scream, "Buy American," when it comes to equities.

Before getting started, Pocket MBA offers a hat tip to the Bank of New York, which is currently the leading depositary bank and which offers an extremely in-depth examination of ADRs on its website, www.bankofny.com, in the event the following summary piques your interest. ADRs first appeared over 70 years ago, and they enable U.S. investors to access the publicly traded equities of non-U.S. companies, just as they allow those companies access to American investors. Of course, U.S. investors have always been able to access these equities; it's just that, like owning those "actually built in Japan" cars, it wasn't that easy.

Prior to the ADR, if you wanted to buy shares of, say Nokia, you would have had to call a broker on the Helsinki stock exchange and actually purchase the shares directly. (And Finnish is not an easy language.) You would have had to buy and sell the shares in Finnish Marrkas (the currency that predated the Euro), which of course raised the cost of trading the shares, as you would have to trade currencies first. And if a problem ensued, you would have to turn for protection to whatever the Finnish equivalent of the SEC was, if there was any such protection. With the advent of the ADR, you can buy and sell Nokia, along with several thousand other companies, on the NYSE, NASDAQ and AMEX. And while this process may make it seem as if you are trading actual shares of Nokia or India's ICICI Bank, in reality, like that American-built Toyota, it's something a little different, even if it represents the same thing. So how exactly do ADRs bring the equivalent of foreign equities to American exchanges?

Here's how the process works. In the most typical transaction, a U.S. broker (like an investment bank or whatever) will hire a broker to go directly to the foreign exchange on which a company's shares trade and buy a boatload of shares (as opposed to a boatload of Toyotas). The broker will direct that the shares be delivered to a custodian bank of a U.S. depositary bank located in the country where the shares are listed. Once the shares are delivered, the custodian will notify the depositary bank, which will then issue receipts for those shares. It is those receipts, rather than the actual shares, that are sold to investors. These receipts can then be traded between buyers and sellers in U.S. dollars using U.S. exchanges, as if they were the shares of stock of any registered company. The ADR holder receives dividends and votes the ADRs as would any other shareholder. If the shares represented by the receipts are eventually sold back into the home market, the receipts will be cancelled at the conclusion of the transaction, and the custodian bank will release the associated shares.

An ADR can be sponsored or unsponsored (though the latter option is considered obsolete). An ADR is unsponsored if it is issued without the formal agreement of the company whose shares the ADR represents. Sponsored ADRs can be Level I, Level II or Level III, the primary difference being that Level I shares are not registered with the SEC, and they trade in the over-the-counter market. One result of this is that the foreign issuer does not have to comply with the whole of U.S. securities law, including the requirement that financial statements be in accordance with GAAP. Level I is the fastest growing segment of the ADR market. Level II and III ADRs are associated with the foreign companies that want their securities listed on American exchanges. Those that do must register the ADRs with the SEC and must comply with the same reporting and disclosure rules as U.S. companies.

Now all that may seem complicated, but having purchased ADRs on several occasions, Pocket MBA can assure you that this all goes off without a hitch and in the blink of an eye. It's certainly easier than purchasing a new Toyota, wherever it was built.

PLI's Pocket MBA Vol. 3 No. 17   April 27, 2005

Asset Turnover Ratio

Ratio measuring the quantity of a company's sales to its average total assets for a given period.

ASSET TURNOVER RATIO IN THE REAL WORLD:

Like many of the ratios that Pocket MBA has explored, this is yet another that allows you to determine how efficient a company is-- in this case, it shows how many dollars of assets a company uses to produce a dollar in revenue. And along with net margins, which will be the subject of next week's issue, it is one of the numbers that go into determining a company's return on assets (to be discussed in two weeks). You can read about asset turnover all over the web, and everyone says pretty much the same thing. So, of course, Pocket MBA will try to be different.

Asset turnover, as a concept, is relatively simple. Let's go to your childhood lemonade stand. There were assets involved, some of which could be deemed long-term--a chair, a table, a big pitcher, a spoon--these are the equivalent of a manufacturer's production facility, a factory if you will. Then there were the short-term assets, the lemons, ice cubes and paper cups, along with the cash you collected as the summer days wore on. How much did you invest in all this and how much lemonade did you sell in a day, week, month, you pick the period. The ratio of lemonade revenue to the investment in assets is your asset turnover ratio.

Maybe your assets amounted to a value of $50, and at first, you didn't make much money, say $10 in your first period. That means you required $50 of assets to produce $10 of revenue. Let's say during your second period, you spent $5 on markers and cardboard to make some really cool signs that you posted in the neighborhood, and your other asset investment remained constant. Now your assets are valued at $55, but after you posted the sign, you were able to sell ten times more lemonade, which means you had to buy $10 more lemons, $5 more cups and $2 more ice during the period, raising your asset value at the end of the period to $72, for an average asset base during the period of $63.5 (($72 + $55)/2). So now you are producing $100 of revenue for every $63.5 of asset investment. Dividing the revenue into the assets gives you your asset turnover ratio.

Obviously, if you have a higher turnover ratio, the assets you have are generating more revenue--you are using the assets more efficiently. You can raise the ratio by charging more for lemonade, but maybe you'll lose customers to the neighbor's lemonade stand. You could also substitute cheaper lemonade powder for real lemons, but you might lose customers that way, too. So your asset turnover ratio is eventually going to reach a stasis, more or less, unless you figure out a revolutionary way to get more sales. Simple, right? And the concept is actually quite intuitive, but sometimes people let mathematical equations and the notion of running a big business cloud lessons they really did learn in kindergarten.

Figuring out asset turnover from a company's financial

statements is just as simple. All you have to do is find and divide a company's total sales in a period (you can find this number on a company's income statement--it is called total revenue) by the total assets (to be more precise, the average total assets). Average total assets can be derived from a company's balance sheet by averaging the sum of the total assets reported at the end of the period in question (PQ) and the total assets reported at the end of the prior period (PP). So,

- Average Total Assets = (Total Assets PQ + Total Assets PP)/2, and
- Asset Turnover = Total Revenue/Average Total Assets

Now what does it mean to be efficient with your assets? That depends on what industry you are in. What's efficient for one industry might not be efficient for another. That's why you can't compare a company in one industry with a company in another to determine which is more efficient. So let's do it anyway. Let's take two real companies in two different industries. Nike, the leading sports shoe manufacturer, sells a lot of shoes; ATP Oil & Gas Corporation is engaged in the development and production of oil and natural gas offshore in the Gulf of Mexico and the North Sea. Pocket MBA wants to compare the asset turnover of these companies and their industries, not to show which of these companies is better relative to the other, but to try and show two things: (1) some industries are, by nature "inefficient" users of assets; and (2) you already know this intuitively without all the math.

Here are some things Pocket MBA knows from reading and living. Everyone needs shoes, and they are generally easy to make from a variety of resources, so making shoes is a stable, and except for the TV commercials, not-too-exciting, cash generating business. All Nike does is rent the use of manufacturing facilities around the world, where it gets non-Nike employees to produce shoes and clothing for resale, either at its own retail outlets or someone else's. It can keep producing shoes and clothing in those same factories year in and year out--all it has to do is invest in new raw materials that it ships out the door as soon as they are assembled into the latest Air product, sign up athletes to make commercials and sell.

Everyone also needs oil and gas, but it is getting harder to find, extract and refine. Companies look in the ocean, in the desert and, increasingly, in places (Canada in particular) that are on top of something called oil sands. All this exploration is hit or miss--unstable, inefficient, risky and expensive. ATP Oil & Gas is constantly sinking oil and gas wells, which are the equivalent of Nike's factories. Whereas Nike can rent out factories and the cheap labor they employ indefinitely and simply invest in the current assets it needs to produce shoes (which raises its asset use efficiency and profit margins), ATP Oil & Gas has to spend capital to "build" new "factories" constantly. And whereas Nike's price increases fall to the bottom line, ATP Oil & Gas doesn't necessarily profit from the recent increases in oil and gas prices because its factories might produce nothing, and then it has to go build new factories in increasingly remote, lonely and dangerous corners of the earth (like the middle of the North Sea or under Northern Alberta). Based on this information, Pocket MBA bets that Nike and the shoe industry have a better asset turnover ratio than that of ATP Oil & Gas and its industry.

If you do the asset turnover calculation, you would find that for the most recent reporting period Nike's asset turnover ratio was 1.67 and ATP Oil & Gas's asset turnover ratio was .32. Remember, generally speaking, companies with high asset turnover are considered efficient users of their assets. And even though you can't compare companies from different industries, 1.67 seems a lot more efficient than .32. That doesn't mean Nike is good and ATP Oil & Gas is bad. That's where you have to compare within the industry. The shoe industry sports an average asset turnover ratio of around 1.7, so Nike is pretty average. The oil and gas industry average asset turnover ratio is around .8, so ATP Oil & Gas is below average in efficiency. It can increase its efficiency with a few really good, new production facilities, but in the long run, it's in an "inefficient" industry. But you knew that. So try pondering what you know about a few industries and decide whether they would be the kind that would be more or less efficient, in general. Then, take a few companies in the industry, do the math and see if you're right. Pocket MBA bets you will be.

PLI's Pocket MBA Vol. 3 No. 18   May 4, 2005

Net Profit Margin

A Company's profitability, expressed as a percentage, after allowing for all costs, expenses and taxes.

NET PROFIT MARGIN IN THE REAL WORLD:

Pocket MBA introduced profit margin ratios (specifically gross profit margin) back in January (see Vol. 3, No. 2) and promised to get to net margin at some undetermined date in the future. In last week's discussion of asset turnover, Pocket MBA promised to get to net margin this week because, together with asset turnover, it makes up a company's Return on Assets, which is scheduled for next week. Hands tied, the discussion of net margin has arrived. And really it's very simple.

Let's go back to last week's lemonade stand. If the lemonade stand sold $100 of lemonade and spent $20 on the supplies that went into the lemonade, its gross profit (GP) would be roughly $80, as GP is equal to sales less cost of goods sold. The gross profit margin (GPM), as described in Volume 3, No. 2, would be .8 because GPM = gross profit/sales.

Now, let's say Pocket MBA got tired of sitting under the hot sun selling lemonade to the neighbors and hired little Timmy from down the street at a commission rate of 10% of sales. Let's further assume that the municipality in which the lemonade stand was located, the Village of Confiscator, levied a 2% tax on every cup of lemonade sold. Finally, assume that PMBA's father charged $5 rent per day to use the family driveway. Those are all expenses that eat away at the gross profit, and a bigger entity might have additional expenses that Pocket MBA didn't have, such as depreciation and interest, professional bills and the like.

If you subtract all those expenses from gross profit, you are left with an entity's net profit (or net income or any of the various other names it goes by.) In the case of that $100, the net profit (NP) would be $63. That's a big difference, but all companies have these various expenses, and to determine which companies are the most efficient, you need to find out how much of their sales actually fill the company coffers. To determine the net profit margin (NPM) is as simple as dividing the net profit by sales, which in the case of the lemonade stand is .63. Before we continue, let's note that NPM of 63% would make this lemonade stand the envy of many businesses because, as far as NPMs go, it's pretty darned good. In any event, let's get the math in one place:

- GP = Sales - Cost of Goods Sold
- GPM = GP/Sales
- NP = Sales - (costs + expenses + taxes)
- NPM = NP/Sales

Now, just what is NPM good for? NPM measures operating efficiency better than any other single measure (with the possible exception of operating margin, which Pocket MBA will also get to--more promises). Though you should generally compare NPM only within an industry (using the average within the industry as a baseline), as PMBA noted last week regarding asset turnover, cross-comparing NPM will at least tell you which industries are prone to produce high margin businesses, in general. Companies with relatively high NPM are those that maintain strict controls over the expenses they can control, which gives them wiggle room in light of those they cannot. And those companies with the highest net margins in any industry are generally the dominant players in that industry. Take a quick gander at the net margins of companies like Dell, Intel and Cisco Systems to verify this.

You can also determine companies on the verge of stardom by their rising margins (maybe they have found new, efficient manufacturing or distribution processes); likewise, fallen angels will telegraph their fall from grace by their falling margins. (Maybe nobody wants their product anymore, the product has become a commodity or their cost structure is such that they cannot compete with the rising star referenced above.) A company with high NPM can withstand upstart competition better than low NPM companies because it can lower prices to meet the competition without fatally wounding its bottom line.

Beware, however, that net margin is one ratio that can be affected severely by short-term influences, like a rise in the cost of raw materials (which would reduce margins), and which we may be witnessing in the near future with soaring raw material prices (oil, iron ore, timber, metallurgical coal). Likewise, a one-time event like a tax write-off can artificially boost NPM in a given period. So when you look at NPM to determine company efficiency, make sure you use a long enough period of time to smooth out the inevitable factors over which companies don't have strong control, like commodity prices (though super smart companies might have hedged rising prices) or general economic downturns (though companies with high NPM have the pricing power to weather these better than those with lower NPM, as well).

Next week, Pocket MBA will marry asset turnover and net margin in the crescendo known as return on assets. No doubt the lemonade stand will come in handy then, as well.

PLI's Pocket MBA Vol. 3 No. 19   May 11, 2005

Return on Assets (ROA)

Ratio that measures a company's profitability relative to its total assets.
RETURN ON ASSETS (ROA) IN THE REAL WORLD:

Asset turnover measured a company's efficiency in using its assets by comparing the quantity of a company's sales relative to its average total assets for a given period, and net profit margin measured operating efficiency by comparing a company's profitability relative to all its costs. ROA measures the two married together to give you a picture of a company's total earning efficiency--that is, its profitability relative to its assets, or how much money a company is making on every dollar of assets it owns, be it a dollar of plant, purchase of other companies, investments or whatever.

At bottom ROA, as a concept, is really as simple as looking at yourself as a business. If you invest $1,000 and earn $150 in a year, you can determine that your return on that investment was 15 percent, and you would probably be pretty happy--certainly happier than if you'd made the same $150 on a $2,000 investment for a return of 7.5 percent. So would most companies. ROA is that easy as a concept. Of course, in that example, you're only looking at investment assets; you probably have other assets, like your car, that don't return 15 percent, or you might have some, like your house, that returned more than 15%. Then there are the assets that it takes to earn a salary--suits, computers, food. If you combine all these and measure them relative to your net income (salary, dividends, interest, etc. less costs), you could conclude that you made $X using $Y amount of assets or $X for every $1 of assets. That's all we're talking about here, except ROA involves the results of a business doing it. A company owns assets so it can sell its products, and the amount of money it earns relative to those assets is its return on the assets.

Companies with a high or rising ROA are generally better at earning money than those with a low or falling ROA. Of course, as with the other ratios we've been examining the past few weeks, it helps to compare companies within an industry. Some industries (like oil and gas) are so asset intensive that their ROA is booby-trapped, while others (like software) that don't tie up money in hard assets have the easy road to high ROA. Still, regardless of a company's ROA, you want to determine whether its return on its investments is higher than its debt costs. If so, the company is on the right track.

The most basic, acceptable way to determine ROA is to divide net income (or net profit or whatever you want to call it--let's call it (NP) by average total assets (TA) in the period:

- ROA = Net Profits/Average Total Assets
- ROA = NP/TA

That's all there is to it, except now you're asking, "What does this have to do with asset turnover and net profit margin?" Let's have a look.

Recall our useful lemonade stand, which we learned last week had a NP of $63, and which we learned two weeks ago, had TA of $63.5, you can determine that the lemonade stand's ROA was a seemingly astounding 99.2 percent, meaning that it made 99.2 cents per dollar of assets. Of course, if Pocket MBA told you that most lemonade stands have an ROA in excess of 100 percent, you would ask what is wrong with the way this particular lemonade stand is doing business? Are its assets bloated or are its sales weak or both? For instance, we know from last week that Pocket MBA hired little Timmy, who gets a 10 percent commission on his lemonade sales. Maybe that's holding the lemonade stand back. Or maybe the company is spending too much on lemons or too little on pitchers, which slows the production process. There's no way to get inside the numbers in the equation ROA = NP/TA. But we need to know what's inside them to understand the lemonade stand better. So we need a better equation.

There may not be two subjects that seem more mutually exclusive than childhood lemonade stands and algebra. But if we are to determine what is going on with the lemonade stand's ROA, we have to brush up on simple algebra. If Pocket MBA were to tell you that Company G had NP of $5 and TA of $10, you would be able to say that its ROA was .5 (ROA = 5/10). But when you make the equation ROA = 5/10, what you are really saying, algebraically is:

- ROA = 5 * 1/10, or
- ROA = 5/1 * 1/10

It's just that the "1s" cancel each other out to give you

- ROA = 5/10

In fact, any time you place the same number in place of the "1", it will cancel out to give you 5/10. Watch:

- ROA = (5/4) * (4/10) = 20/40 or 5/10 = .5

Now, here's where the last three issues of Pocket MBA, this one included, come into play. From Issues 3-17, 3-18 and 3-19, respectively, we know:

- Asset Turnover Ratio = Total Revenue/Average Total Assets (AT = TR/TA), and

- Net Profit Margin = Net Profit/Total Revenue (NPM = NP/TR)

Back to ROA:

- ROA = Net Profit/Average Total Assets

Do you see where we're headed?

- ROA = Net Profit * 1/Average Total Assets
- ROA = Net Profit/1 * 1/Average Total Assets

The "1" cancels out. So, as in the example above, you can also substitute "Total Revenue" for the "1" without changing the equation, which gives you the following:

- ROA = (NP/TR) * (TR/TA)

Voila! In reality,

- ROA = Net Profit Margin * Asset Turnover Ratio

When you look at ROA in this manner, you can more incisively determine where a company is strong and weak relative to its competitors.

If we look at the lemonade stand and determine its profit margins are equal to or above average for the lemonade stand industry, then it's not little Timmy dragging the enterprise down. We might find that the lemonade stand's asset turnover is relatively poor. And when we look into the matter, we might learn that it spends far more on ice than its competitors because it never instituted an efficient mechanism for keeping ice from melting. Investing in an icebox might improve its asset turnover, which could save little Timmy's job. Or the stand could decline to buy the icebox and unload little Timmy's per glass commission expense to increase its net profit margin, which would, in turn, bump up its ROA. Thus, the more advanced equation also demonstrates that a business can make up for low profit margin with high asset turnover, and vice versa.

And that concludes Pocket MBA's brief, three-part series on efficiency ratios. You are now fully equipped to dissect a lemonade stand, entire retail chain, sport-shoe manufacturer, even oil and gas concerns. Next week, no math.

PLI's Pocket MBA Vol. 3 No. 20   May 18, 2005

12b-1 Fee

Annual charges to mutual fund shareholders resulting from SEC adoption of Rule 12b-1, which permits mutual funds to pay distribution costs and fees out of fund assets.

12b-1 FEE IN THE REAL WORLD:

When Pocket MBA bought its first share in a mutual fund ten or so years ago, the part of the prospectus that beckoned most was the graph showing the "hypothetical growth of a $10,000 investment in the fund" that you can find in all the prospectuses of all funds. Observing the line shoot up into the stratosphere was enough to convince PMBA that this was a worthwhile venture. PMBA does recall glossing over the fees section of the prospectus: no upfront sales load, although if you sold the shares before the end of a certain amount of time, there was a redemption fee of 1.5%; management and other fees of 1.2% and something labeled a 12b-1 fee of a small amount, probably around .25%.

Being callow in the ways of mutual funds, Pocket MBA engaged in the following thought process: well, the fund has demonstrated great long-term performance, meaning it's a keeper, so the short-term redemption fee won't be a problem; a fund has to pay its managers, so whatever it takes to maintain the great performance is reasonable; .25% is close to zero, and since it's a small amount, it doesn't matter that it is unclear what that .25% is for, so let's round down and pretend it doesn't matter. This is how most investors approach the 12b-1 notations in a prospectus. And that is why 12b-1 fees are controversial. It's not because they are "hidden fees," as some contend. To the contrary, they are always right there in the prospectus. It's just that funds don't always explain what they are in detail, and in reality, according to the funds themselves, they are just an alternative to the front-end load. So a fund can sell itself as no-load and still have the load via the 12b-1 fees. That's like not having your cake and eating it, too. And, in fact, that performance graph that seduces the new investor might actually look better if there were a front-end load rather than the annual drip-drip of the 12b-1 fees.

Pocket MBA is not here to take sides. Funds charge what they charge, and consumer advocate groups complain about what they complain about. (And they complain loudly about 12b-1 fees, so loudly that the consensus seems to be that the SEC may look at them anew, even as the agency has already made a recent amendment to Rule 12b-1 prohibiting funds from using brokerage commissions to compensate a broker for selling a fund's shares.) The focus here is more of where did these 12b-1 fees come from, and what were they originally for and what are they for now?

12b-1 fees did not exist prior to 1980. That's when the SEC adopted Rule 12b-1 pursuant to its authority under section 12b of the Investment Company Act of 1940. Before 1980, fund advisors were compensated for all services solely via the sales load--those front-end charges that range anywhere from 3% to 6% and higher. That meant for every $1,000 you invested, you really started with somewhere in the middle to high $900 range. In turn, that load supported all the current and future services of the advisor with regard to the fund, including things like advertising and printing prospectuses, compensating brokers. The fund could not use fund assets to pay for these things. It came from the loads and that was it. If a fund didn't sell many shares, too bad. Of course, that wouldn't be good for a fund's existing investors--the idea is to expand a fund's holdings and to do that, a fund needed new investors. Funds' inability to use fund assets to advertise and build business is asserted as one of the reasons that, prior to 1980, mutual funds were not really all that popular with the investing public.

In stepped the SEC with Rule 12b-1, which "permits funds to use their assets to pay distribution-related costs." According to the SEC, distribution fees "include fees paid for marketing and selling fund shares, such as compensating brokers and others who sell fund shares, and paying for advertising, the printing and mailing of prospectuses to new investors, and the printing and mailing of sales literature." See http://www.sec.gov/answers/mffees.htm#distribution. In order to rely on Rule 12b-1, a fund must adopt a written plan, approved by shareholders and the fund's directors, that explains what the fees will be used for.

With the advent of Rule 12b-1, funds were able to aggressively market themselves. After Rule 12b-1, the sales loads went to the brokers, and the 12b-1 fees went into the ad market. And after 1980, the mutual fund industry exploded, due in part, no doubt, to all those "advertising" dollars that came from fund assets via the 12b-1 fee. But as competition increased, a new pressure was exerted on funds--that of the no-load fund, the new breed of funds that charged no upfront sales charges. An investor who puts up $1,000 likes to think that the entire $1,000 is going to work, and like Pocket MBA's initial experience, doesn't concern himself with future charges that seem relatively small. So more funds became no-load or carried a smaller load. But how do funds compensate the brokers who sell the funds to the mom and pop investor if there are no longer sales charges? Well, brokerage is part of distribution; so 12b-1 fees became the backdoor way to do so.

However, some statistical studies show that investors get better returns with flat upfront fees, as opposed to annual fees that continue to chop away at their returns. If you could show that 12b-1 fees were used primarily for brokerage, rather than advertising, wouldn't an investor be better off with the front-end load instead of the 12b-1 fees? In fact, according to a late-2004 study by the Investment Company Institute (ICI), which represents the fund industry, 40% of 12b-1 fees are used to compensate financial advisors for initial assistance and 52% is used for ongoing shareholder services. Only 2% goes to advertising. See HOW MUTUAL FUNDS USE 12B-1 FEES, *Fundamentals, Investment Company Institute Research in Brief*, Vol. 14, No. 2, Feb. 2005, available at www.ici.org/pdf/fm-v14n2.pdf.

This became a hot-button issue as mutual fund fees skyrocketed in the wake of Rule 12b-1, along with the market meltdown and the recent mutual fund scandals. And critics blame 12b-1 fees, in part. Although the SEC doesn't limit the amount of 12b-1 fees, the National Association of Securities Dealers (NASD) does place restrictions on them, for instance, 12b-1 fees used for marketing and distribution expenses (as opposed to shareholder service expenses) cannot exceed 0.75% of a fund's annual net assets. The rule, and the industry, has its defenders, such as the ICI, which points to the increased number of shareholders over that time period to conclude that the actual fund costs per shareholder has decreased. See TOTAL SHAREHOLDER COST OF MUTUAL FUNDS 2003, *Fundamentals – Investment Company Institute Research in Brief*, Vol. 13, No. 5, Dec. 2004, available at www.ici.org/stats/res/fm-v13n5.pdf. Still there are many that want the SEC to take a much more in-depth look into Rule 12b-1 than it already did when amending it last year. Until such time, just remember that graph of the hypothetical investment might look a lot better were it not for those 12b-1 fees.

Stock Appreciation Rights (SARs)

Non-stock compensation award that gives an employee cash equal to the appreciation in a company's share price over a period of time.

STOCK APPRECIATION RIGHTS (SARs) IN THE REAL WORLD:

With all the headlines that stock options garner, one tends to forget that companies don't dole them out to everyone. Some employees in the dynamic domestic workforce don't get any fancy bonuses; rather they just participate in a variety of 401(k) or ERISA plans or ESOPs. And if their employers cannot or don't want to afford such plans, well, they might try to make their fortune the old-fashioned way – by winning lotto. But some companies want to reward certain employees without the attendant ownership that stock entails or because they are not in a position to offer stock. That's where the unfortunately named SARs (along with their cousin, "phantom stock") can come into play. Think of SARs and phantom stock as a kind of contingent bonus that offers companies a way to allow employees to share in the appreciation in its equity without having to issue publicity-drawing stock options. And it was thought they might become more prevalent (because accounting for them is easier) in light of the revolution in accounting for stock options brought on by FASB's adoption of FAS 123r. However, as often happens, other legislation interceded and has reduced that potential. The American Jobs Creation Act passed in late 2004 created new IRC Section 409A, which broadened the definition of non-qualified deferred comp to include SARs and makes them considerably less attractive. Still, they exist, and Pocket MBA would be incomplete without examining them.

SARs are really quite simple. A company will issue a SAR on date "x," and give it a vesting date of "y." Anytime after date "y," the employee can exercise the SAR and receive the difference between the share price at vesting and the price at issuance. SARs can be paid in cash or stock. Phantom stock, on the other hand, is exclusively cash-based, and can be set up the same as a cash SAR or can be set up as the payment, in cash, of the value of a specified number of shares after the vesting period.

So let's look at a SAR, payable in cash. Assume you were working at Nike (be like Mike and just do it) on January 2, 2003, when the price of the company's stock is $46.10, and the company decides to issue you 500 SARs, payable in cash, with a vesting period of two years. On January 3, 2005, you exercise your SARs with the company stock valued at $90.60. This entitles you to 500 * $44.50 = $22,250--even Nike doesn't have a pair of sneakers that cost that much. (Of course, if the stock declines, you'll have to shop at Payless Shoes.) There is no exercise cost to the employee, as there would be with a stock option. (Of course, the amount of the theoretical payout above suggests one of the drawbacks to SARs from the company's standpoint--liquidity; issue too many SARs, and you have to pay out an enormous amount of cash.) The tax consequences for the employee are quite simple--it is taxable in the year of exercise as ordinary income. (If the SAR is payable in shares, the amount of any gain is taxable at exercise, and then any future gain is taxed when the employee sells the shares.)

You would be correct in assuming that the tax and accounting considerations for the issuer of the SAR are more complex. First, the issuer does not receive any tax benefit (in the way of a deduction for salary) until the SAR is paid upon exercise. Second, the new FASB rules under FAS 123r governing accounting for stock options apply to SARs and phantom stock. See Pocket MBA, Vol. 3, No. 8. Companies have to account for the issuance of the SAR on an annual basis until exercise. In the example above, and this is the simplest example, Nike would start by recording a compensation charge on the income statement of $46.10 and then would adjust it annually to track the value of the SAR as it increased (or decreased) so that at exercise the full $22,250 would be reflected in the company's financial reports. Most SARs are issued for longer periods than the two-year period Pocket MBA used in the example, so the vicissitudes of the market can make the accounting much more difficult. Also, note that when SARs are payable in shares, they carry along much of the same accounting baggage as stock options.

Inventory Turnover

Ratio that indicates how often a company sells and replaces inventory in a given period.

INVENTORY TURNOVER IN THE REAL WORLD:

Pocket MBA seems to recall an adage to the effect of "it takes money to make money," implying that there are always out-of-pocket expenses in any venture. The concept of inventory turnover modifies that adage so that it reads, "the less money out-of-pocket it takes to make money, the more efficient you are at using that out-of-pocket money."

If you are in the business of selling doodads, defined by Merriam-Webster Online as "an often small article whose common name is unknown or forgotten," you have to keep X amount on-hand in inventory to satisfy buyers and to maximize your use of company resources. When you start to run out, you have to buy more. So how much do you need to keep on-hand? This is just another way of asking how many times can you run through your average investment in inventory over a period, be it month, quarter or year. And like most other efficiency measures, the only way to really know whether you are maximizing your company resources is to look at how much inventory other doodad sellers run through in similar periods.

So say you buy, wholesale, $50,000 worth of doodads in a particular period, let's use a year. You sell the doodads for $120,000, which results in a gross profit of $70,000. Let's also assume that you sell the doodads at a constant rate of $10,000/month. Now, you could buy all the doodads at the beginning of the year, and you would sell the inventory by the end of the year. That is to say, you would have turned over your inventory one time. But that would cost you $50,000 up front. That money would be lost to you for the year, or to put it in investment terms, you would have an initial rate of return on that money of zero. Seen in that light, investing in a year's worth of doodads in January doesn't seem like a very wise investment.

But is it really necessary to do that? What if the price of doodads drops during the year? You've lost money by investing in inventory that is not worth as much as when you bought it. (Even if the price of doodads rises, you can hedge the rise by buying more as you see the price rise--also the sales price might well rise along with the wholesale price; but once you've bought the whole boatload of doodads, you're out $50,000.) On the other hand, you could buy just two months of inventory for $10,000 out-of-pocket, sell the inventory and before it runs out, buy another two months using some of the $20,000 revenue from the doodads you sold. By the end of the year, you would have bought and sold the same $50,000 of doodads, and grossed the same $70,000, but your initial investment, out-of-pocket, would have been only $10,000. And you could use that other $40,000 for something else. Doesn't that seem like a better use of cash? And if you look at the investment, you will have sold five times more than you invested, as opposed to selling exactly what you invested--that is, you will have turned your inventory five times--you sold $50,000 worth of doodads after investing $10,000 initially. So, in a nutshell, inventory turnover is the number of times you run through your average investment in inventory.

Of course, using an example with a lot of round figures always makes for easy computation. But how do you determine inventory turnover when the numbers aren't so pretty? We can use the pretty numbers to help us figure that out. In the doodad example, we concluded that, depending on how we decided to spend our money, we had either a turnover ratio of one or five by dividing the average amount in inventory into the total cost of doodads sold: 50,000/50,000 or 50,000/10,000. Accordingly, inventory turnover =

- Cost of Goods Sold/Average Inventory Investment

The higher the turnover relative to other players in an industry indicates better sales. And of course, a low turnover indicates that a company is investing too much in inventory or has a poor sales force. You can also look at a company's current assets and compare that to how much a company has in inventory--a company with heavy asset investment should have a high turnover ratio.

You can refine inventory analysis further by dividing the number of inventory turns into the number of days in a year to find out how many days it actually takes a company to run through inventory. In the doodad example, that would be 365/5 = 73. As with the other efficiency ratios that Pocket MBA has reviewed, you can pretty much intuit which industries will have high relative turnover ratios: fast food, retail and grocery. Pocket MBA is not sure what the average inventory turnover of the doodad industry is.

Exchange Rate

Rate at which one country's currency is converted into another's.

EXCHANGE RATE IN THE REAL WORLD:

Many of you are thinking to yourself right about now, "I went to Europe; I know all I need to know about the exchange rate--it stinks right now, but not as much as it did last month. What's coming up next week?" But do you know why it stinks? Well, sit tight, and Pocket MBA will try and make you forget about that bad dollar/euro conversion you got. And who knows, now that the French and the Dutch have scuttled the EU constitution, the Euro may be finished--a dubious but nice thought. In any event, understanding the exchange rate beyond the cost of a hotel room in Firenze is especially important if you have clients that sell into international markets, do business abroad or are just plain involved in the currency markets.

Think of the currency market as you would any clothing store, but instead of different brands of jeans, you have different currencies. Like the jeans, they have their plusses and minuses and so sell at different prices. The other big difference is the size of the market. The currency market makes Wal-Mart look like a mom-and-pop operation. Indeed, the foreign currency exchange market (or Forex) is the largest market in the world. Nobody seems exactly sure how much currency trades hands on a daily basis, but estimates begin in the $2 trillion range and go up. Now you see how your hotel room was just a drop in the bucket.

Exchange rates can be either "fixed" (also known as "pegged") or "floating." Most of the currencies issued by developed countries float, that is they are subject to the law of supply and demand on a daily basis and fluctuate accordingly. Developing countries will often peg their currency to the dollar (or whatever currency) in the interest of providing stability. This is done to attract foreign investment and reign in inflation. Thus the Chinese Yuan is pegged to the dollar at the rate of 8.28 Yuan to the dollar. The Chinese central bank maintains this level by buying and selling Yuan in exchange for dollars in varying amounts, depending on what frequency will maintain the peg. For the past several years, as its economy has sprinted along, China has maintained the value of the Yuan by buying dollars on the Forex when demand for the dollar is weak. China is under pressure to revalue the Yuan because the strength of its economy and its cheap currency create imbalances of trade, as cheap goods flood Western markets. Hence many argue that the current astronomic trade deficits of the United States are directly related to the fact that the Yuan does not float.

As noted, simple supply and demand calculi determine most exchange rates. Some of the factors that affect supply and demand for currencies are political upheaval, inflation and recession. In general, as with any other product, when demand for a currency exceeds supply, the currency will appreciate. If supply exceeds demand, the currency will generally depreciate. So if there is a growing supply of a certain currency and a constant (or even falling) demand for that currency, the price of the currency will decline. If you want to know a basic reason for the price of that Firenzian hotel room, look no further than the open spigot of cash provided by low interest rates in this country since 2001. The Federal Reserve consciously provided liquidity to the U.S. economy so that Americans would spend freely to disentangle the country from recession. At the same time, low interest rates tend to repel foreign investment in U.S. Dollar-backed instruments; hence the falling dollar and the expensive hotel room. (Pocket MBA opts not to get involved in a discussion about how the federal deficit plays into all this; suffice to say that there are some economic commentators who believe that the dollar is headed for a long-term crash.) As the Fed has continued to raise interest rates over the past year, you will note that the dollar has stopped its slide and begun to appreciate against other major currencies as investors begin to see that they can make money on their cash here.

Of course, the Federal Reserve is not the only player that impacts exchange rates. Your clients who export or import to and from other countries constantly convert dollars into the currencies of those countries and vice versa. And one trend that has ramped up in the last couple years is the increase in commodity prices. Commodities--oil, coal, copper, timber, sugar--while they are found here, are often found in even greater abundance elsewhere. Look no further than our neighbors to the north, with their vast untapped oil reserves stuck in the tar sands of Alberta. As the prices of these items produced in other countries rise, American businesses must convert or sell more dollars to buy commodities sold in other currencies. This pushes the dollar down as well. Also, companies that sell a lot of goods abroad, like Nike, benefit from cheap dollars because it can sell more of its expensive shoes abroad. This goes directly to Nike's bottom line, and if you dissect Nike's earnings over the last couple years, you'll note a spike in earnings, which has been attributed in large part to the falling dollar.

A small, but significant part of the currency market is comprised, not of tourists seeking a good time or business converting currency to run their operations, but of traders who, just like participants in equity markets, bet on the direction of particular currencies. These traders toss around millions, taking advantage of arbitrage opportunities. (An arbitrage permits a relatively risk free profit on minute differences in the exchange rates of varying currencies. An arbitrageur does this by starting with, say $1, and serially converting it into various currencies until he is able to convert it back to dollars having earned a few pennies for his trouble. Multiply those pennies by millions of dollars, and you get a nice chunk of change.)

To show you how volatile all of this is, as noted the dollar has been steadily rising from the dead over the past several months. But, as of today's writing, the dollar is plunging against foreign markets because U.S. payroll growth for May was just 78,000. Why? Because slowing job growth might mean that the Fed will stop raising interest rates sooner rather than later. This means that foreign investors cannot count on a rising rate of return. What's the take away from all this? Take your vacation in Seattle, where a dollar is worth a dollar.

AUTHOR UPDATE: In July 2005, the Chinese indeed revalued the Yuan. It is no longer pegged to the dollar, but rather to a basket of currencies. The experts are currently haggling over whether this is a good or bad thing, but the truth is we probably won't know for a while.

Beta Coefficient

One measure of a security's volatility (or systematic risk) relative to that of the market as a whole.

BETA COEFFICIENT IN THE REAL WORLD:

When the stock market rises, some stocks tend to soar, while others meander, regardless of any company fundamentals or news warranting the one or the other. Conversely, when the market drops some stocks fall off the cliff, while others hold their relative value. The stocks that act in these ways tend to be the same stocks (or at least stocks in the same industries) over and over again. When professional investors talk about a stock's, a mutual fund's or an industry's "beta," they are referring to the relative place of that stock, fund or industry on the continuum of general market volatility.

Volatility is what often enables "traders," as opposed to "investors," to make (or lose) vast sums of money in short-term market swings. That volatility can inform a decision about when to get in and when to get out of a position. For instance, a stock that has a high beta, that is, it is volatile relative to the market as a whole, will tend to rise faster out of a market bottom (absent any company fundamentals that would prevent it) than a stock with a beta that is equal to or less than the market as a whole. Furthermore, beta can inform conservative investors what stocks are better for holding long-term due to their lack of volatility. Likewise, it can be useful to value-oriented investors as a beacon to know which stocks, having fallen hard and thus become good bargains, are likely to spring back fastest.

You can calculate beta by simply paring the daily percentage movement in a stock over a yearlong period with the same movement of an index in the same period and then plotting the number pairs on a graph, with the slope of the resultant line equating to beta. But statisticians prefer complex "regression analysis," of which there are various formulations, none of which is simple enough to explain in Pocket MBA format. And if you search for these formulae on the Internet, you will see why Pocket MBA left them out of this discussion. And it's really not necessary. Mutual fund companies and analysts maintain their own beta books, and you can get the beta of any stock from a number of news and financial websites, including Reuters. When you look up a company--let's use Nike, as PMBA often does--you will find beta for the company itself, its industry, market sector and the market as a whole (in this case the S&P 500). For Nike, those numbers are as follows:

- Nike = .48
- Industry = .65
- Sector = 1.05
- S&P 500 = 1.00

The market as a whole is always pegged at 1.0. So relative to the market as a whole, Nike is .48 times as volatile as the market as a whole. That is to say, generally speaking, Nike is less volatile or less risky than the market. If the market has fallen 10%, Nike has tended to fall only 4.8%. Of course, this hurts you on the upside, for if the market has risen 10%; Nike has tended to rise 4.8%. You can also see that Nike has been less volatile than its industry and market sector as well. Someone interested in a stable portfolio would tend to be attracted to Nike. Swing traders don't find stocks like Nike sexy or profitable.

You'll note that PMBA writes in a past tense when writing about Nike's beta. That is because beta, while a predictive tool, is a backward-looking indicator. It only takes into account what a stock, mutual fund or industry has done in previous market cycles. It is unable to factor in current events in the life cycle of a business that might undermine its predictive utility. Thus, if it were to be determined that wearing sneakers was detrimental to human health or that to ward off skin cancer people needed to wear sneakers on their hands, Nike might plummet or soar at a rate far exceeding its .48 beta. Because beta is backward looking, you will not find a beta for newly trading companies due to lack of data. Therefore, beta cannot help you judge the trend of a stock like Google, though anyone who has paid attention in the last several months can tell you that it jumps around tremendously. Thus, you can conclude that it has a relatively high beta thus far. That may or may not change as Google matures.

The different beta scores can be categorized as follows:

- Beta = 0: this is the theoretical volatility of cash without inflation
- Beta < 1.0: the stock is less volatile than the market --think utility stocks and solid, but staid, companies that provide the everyday necessities of life, like Nike
- Beta = 1.0: the stock moves in tandem with the market--index mutual funds are geared to have betas of 1.0
- Beta > 1.0: the stock is more volatile than the market--the higher the beta, the more likely you are dealing with technology or emerging industry stocks

Theoretically, beta can be less than zero and can be as high as 100, though it cannot be more than 100 because the stock would be statistically likely to fall to zero any time the market declined. You would be hard pressed to find companies with betas much higher than 4.5, though they exist. PMBA has been looking for an hour now and has only found one--it sported a beta of 4.66 and shall remain nameless. Suffice to say that in the market sell-off of about 5%-6%

that occurred in March and April 2005, its price dropped about 60%; then when the market rebounded a couple percentage points in early May, it shot up 67%. That would make it the alpha-dog of beta.

Appendix A

From PLI's Course Handbook
Asset Based Financing 2004
3240

2

INVENTORY FINANCING

Scott A. Lessne
FleetBoston Financial Corporation

Copyright © 2004
All Rights Reserved

Biographical Information

SCOTT A. LESSNE is an Assistant General Counsel at FleetBoston Financial Corporation in Hartford, Connecticut. He is responsible for managing and providing legal services to the workout division of the Corporation. Before joining the Bank in 1992, Mr. Lessne represented institutional clients including commercial finance companies in connection with the documentation of commercial finance transactions, restructurings, workouts and bankruptcies. Mr. Lessne is President of the Association of Commercial Finance Attorneys and is a Fellow of the American College of Commercial Finance Lawyers. He is a member of the adjunct faculty of Suffolk University Law School where he has taught Secured Transactions. He is a graduate of Trinity College, Hartford and Western New England College School of Law where he was the Research editor of the Law Review. Mr. Lessne is a regular speaker on topics relating to commercial finance, creditors' rights and bankruptcy.

Table of Contents

A. COLLATERAL AND PARTIES..............................1
B. FINANCING STRUCTURES................................7
C. PERFECTION AND PRIORITY..........................11
D. DOCUMENTATION...15
E. OPERATING RISKS...21
F. LENDER REMEDIES..24

INVENTORY FINANCING

by

Scott A. Lessne

April 21, 2003

A. COLLATERAL AND PARTIES

    1.   Definition: 9-102(a)(48) defines inventory as goods which "... are leased by a person as lessor; are held by a person for sale or lease or to be furnished under a contract of service; are furnished by a person under a contract of service; or consist of raw materials, work in process, or materials used or consumed in business":

    a. "Goods" includes all things which are movable when a security interest attaches..." 9-102(a)(44).

    b. Goods become inventory based on how they are utilized, and by whom. CNB v. Douglas, 17 UCC Rep. Serv.2d 999 (Conn. 1992); Cooperative Fin. Ass'n v. B & J Cattle Co., 32 UCC Rep. Serv.2d 808 (Colo. App. 1997); Morgan County Feeders, Inc. v. McCormick, 18 UCC Rep. Serv.2d 632 (Colo. App. 1992) (distinction significant in that ordinary course buyers of inventory take free of perfected security interest). A truck held by a dealer for sale or lease is inventory. A truck used by the dealer to deliver parts is not inventory. Gasoline held by the dealer to fuel its delivery van is inventory. A truck owned by a moving company is not inventory, notwithstanding that it may at some time be offered for sale. The cardboard cartons used for packaging the materials being moved are inventory

    c. "Equipment" is defined in 9-102(a)(33) as "goods, other than inventory, farm products, or consumer goods". The fact that equipment may under some circumstances be sold does not convert it to inventory. On the other hand, a purchase money creditor described collateral as "inventory" in the security agreement and the financing statement. The collateral, computers and related items, did not fall within the definition of inventory and therefore were classified as "equipment". Notwithstanding the incorrect classification, the court found that the purchase money creditor had an attached and perfected security interest in the collateral. Fifth Third Bank v. Comark, Inc., 794 N.E.2d 433 (Ind. App. 2003).

d. Since "goods" must be movable, unmined ore or petroleum is not inventory, but will become such upon extraction. 9-102(a)(44) Martin Marietta Corp. v. New Jersey National Bank, 505 F. Supp 946 (D.C.N.H. 1981). Special rules apply when personalty and realty interests intersect, e.g. fixtures; minerals; crops; and timber.

e. If a unit has two uses (e.g., a demonstrator model which will be sold eventually) it is the primary purpose that controls. First State Bank vs. Producers Livestock Marketing Ass'n Non-Stock Corporation, 23 UCC Rep. Serv. 500 (Neb. 1978). 9-109, Off. Com.2; "Goods" as defined in 9-102(a)(44) and are broken into four mutually exclusive categories: "consumer goods", "equipment", "farm products", and "inventory". McFadden v. Mercantile Safe-Deposit and Trust Co., 8 UCC Rep. Serv. 766 (Md. 1971). "The generally accepted rule is that the debtor's stated intended use, at the time of attachment of the security interest, defines the nature of the goods for purposes of ascertaining the proper place for perfecting the security interest." In re Rex Group, Inc., 80 B.R. 774 (E.D. Va. 1987). But see, In re AvCentral, Inc. 289 B.R. 170 (D.Kan. 2003) holding that a creditors lien on aircraft properly filed with the FAA remains perfected under 9-311(b) without a subsequent state UCC filing notwithstanding that the intent of the debtor at the time the security interest was granted was to disassemble the plane for parts resale and that the parts constituted inventory in the hands of the debtor. Note that under revised Article 9 the place for perfecting a security interest by filing will be governed not by collateral classification, but rather by location of the debtor. See 9-301; 9-307.

f. Under revised Article 9, software embedded in goods is considered part of the goods together with any supporting information if the software is customarily considered part of goods. 9-102(a)(44).

g. Inventory is a wasting asset. It is intended to be used up quickly, i.e., sold. Its proceeds are the source of repayment. Land and equipment are not sources of repayment in the ordinary course. Accounts receivable are a direct source of repayment, the accounts receivable loan being a cash anticipation transaction.

The different transactional consequences explain the different Art. 9 rules.

2. Parties: Inventory financing is generally a two party transaction.

a. The borrower is a seller or lessor of goods (who may, or may not, be the manufacturer of the goods).

b. The lender may be a bank or finance company. Or it may be a manufacturer who is providing purchase money credit to its customers.

c. If the manufacturer does not want to tie up its funds, it may borrow against the security of its purchase money financing arrangements with its customers. Such borrowings may be on a notification (i.e., direct collection), or non-notification (i.e. indirect collection) basis. This transaction involves two related, but independent UCC classifications. As between the manufacturer and its distributor it is a purchase money loan. But as between the manufacturer and its lender it is a loan secured by, or a sale of, chattel paper.

d. Accurate characterization of collateral (e.g., equipment or inventory) is an essential element of effective documentation, and most particularly, perfection. See, North Ridge Farms, Inc. v. Trimble, 37 UCC Rep. Serv. 1280 (Ky. App. 1983).

3. Types of Inventory Collateral: There are two basic types of inventory collateral.

a. One type is a pool of goods which is identified in mass, through accounting procedures. It may be a combination of raw materials, work in process and finished goods, e.g., bolts of cloth; cloth being dyed, cut and sewn; finished garments. Or it may just be finished goods, e.g., finished garments. The individual units cannot be identified, and are continually changing their form and/or being sold and replaced with new goods. The loan is secured by the pool of inventory.

b. The second type is new or used hard goods, generally identifiable on a unit basis by serial number. The loan is often secured by individual units, and not by the aggregate of inventory. This type of inventory financing is referred to as floor planning and is most widely known in the auto dealer finance world.

c. Where a manufacturer takes a purchase money lien on the goods it supplies they may be identified by the manufacturer name, e.g., all steel or all machine tools manufactured or supplied by X. Purchase money financing by a vendor is one type of asset based financing. The vendor's position may be assigned to a financer. Alternatively, a third party financer may function as the purchase money financer for a vendor, with (perhaps) some recourse to the vendor, as well as to the purchase money obligation of the vendee. This is common with retail vendees such as furniture, appliance, and computer stores.

d. The lender's security interest will extend to proceeds, which may be cash, open accounts receivable, trade-ins, or installment sales contracts. 9-102(a)(64). Proceeds of proceeds may also be covered. Generally a security interest in proceeds is perfected via a perfected security interest in the underlying collateral 9-315(c). Under 9-315(d) such perfection will terminate 21 days after the security interest in the proceeds attaches unless (1) the following conditions are satisfied: (a) a filed financing statement covers the original collateral; (b) the proceeds are collateral in which a security interest may be perfected by filing in the office in which the financing statement has been filed; or (c) the proceeds are not acquired with cash proceeds; or (2) the proceeds are identifiable cash proceeds; or (3) the security interest in the proceeds is perfected other than under subsection (c) [of 9-315] when the security interest attaches to the proceeds or within 20 days thereafter. See, e.g., In re Weber, 29 UCC Rep. Serv. 690 (Bankr. W.D.N.Y. 1980) (as possession was required to perfect in type of proceeds received, failure to obtain possession of a "certificate" received as proceeds rendered security interest in proceeds of sale of inventory unperfected).

e. In the case of a borrower/manufacturer, "products" will be included, e.g., the shoes manufactured from the leather. The lender will share ratably with other lenders based on the ratio that the cost of the original goods on which they have their respective liens bears to the cost of the finished product, 9-336. The same approach applies to a fungible mass (e.g. heating fuel commingled in storage tanks).

f. Accessions, defined in 9-102(a)(1) means "goods that are physically united with other goods in such a manner that the identity of the original goods is not lost". 9-335 governs creation and perfection of security interests in accessions. <u>In re Aztec Concrete, Inc.</u> 177 UCC Rep. Serv.2d 288 (Bankr. SD Iowa 1992) (failure to perfect under state motor vehicle law rendered security interest in mixer element of cement mixer avoidable by bankruptcy trustee as mixer was not an accession but an integral part of the truck).

g. The complexities and potential for conflict inherent in dealing with commingled goods, products and accessions are not susceptible to practical resolution. Therefore, lenders typically do not rely on the Code provisions for their protection. Rather, they take an exclusive security interest in the goods throughout the manufacturing process. The lender's goal is to structure the loan so it works, i.e. so it can be enforced without conflict or delay. The question is not whether we can enter the deal, but whether, on default, we can gracefully exit.

4. Consumer Goods: Inventory collateral may be of a kind sold for business use (e.g., machine tools) or for "consumer" use (e.g., mobile homes). It may have both business and consumer attributes (e.g., light aircraft), in which case the primary use governs. <u>McGehehee v. Exchange Bank & Trust Co.</u>, 561 S.W.2d 926 (Texas Civ. App. 1978)

a. "consumer goods" are defined in 9-102(a)(23) as goods "used or bought for use primarily for personal, family or household purposes." This is a fairly universal formula for identifying consumer transactions.

b. Special Code rules apply to consumer goods, e.g., non-enforceability of waiver of defense clause, 9-403(e). <u>See, e.g., Unico v. Owen</u>, 4 UCC Rep. Serv. 542 (N.J. 1967)

c. Consumer transactions are not here addressed because they present an array of unique regulatory concerns wholly unrelated to commercial usage.

d. In the seller's hands inventory is not characterized as "consumer", although it may be such once it is sold to the end user. However, the inventory lender must be sensitive to consumer issues because as the inventory converts into proceeds in the form of accounts, and more significantly chattel paper, the lender may become subject to consumer laws.

5. Farm Products: Farm products are not "inventory". The term is defined in 9-102(a)(34) as "goods ... with respect to which the debtor is engaged in a farming operation and which are: A) crops grown, growing, or to be grown... B) livestock, born or unborn, including aquatic goods... C) supplies used or produced in a farming operation; or D) products of crops or livestock in their unmanufactured states."

a. For the most part, agricultural financing is governed by the same Code rules as apply to other types of collateral. However, farm products are an independent classification of goods and are subject to some special provisions. Farm products are not classified as inventory or equipment, although under changed circumstances they would be so characterized, e.g. milk is a farm product when held by a dairy farmer; inventory when held by a cheese maker.

b. Perfection of a security interest in farm products generally follows the rules for "goods" under 9-310 and shall be filed centrally under 9-501(a)(2).

c. Under Article 9, buyers of farm products in the ordinary course of business do not take free or prior perfected security interests, as is the case with inventory, 9-320(a). This distinction would be significant if one is lending to a food processor on the security of its farm product inventory.

d. Most agricultural states have modified the farm product exception so that it conforms to the general bona fide purchaser rule (e.g., Cal. 9-307(1); Ind. 307(1)(a); Iowa 554.9307(4)).

e. The Food Security Act of 1985, provides that purchasers from farmers take free of a security interest created by the seller unless the purchaser has received actual notice of the security interest. Such notice is not effected by Article 9 compliance, but is dictated by a complex set of rules detailed in the Act and its regulations (7 USC 1631; 9 CFR Ch II, Part 205).

f. The Federal statute supplants state law. However, it provides for a state system of actual notice, which system may be incorporated in Article 9, perhaps via regulations establishing a central farm products filing system (e.g. Title 67, Ch 2 Idaho Code and Regulations adopted by Idaho Secretary of State).

g. The Packers and Stockyards Act of 1921 gives the unpaid cattleman an interest in the inventory and its proceeds superior to that of an inventory financer. 7 U.S.C. 196j(b). The Perishable Agricultural Commodities Act does the same for an unpaid farmer. 7 U.S.C. 499e(c). Both Federal laws utilize a trust funds concept. Their impact is to render impractical the financing of meat packers and food processors in reliance upon their inventory or accounts.

h. An involuntary bankruptcy proceeding may not be commenced against a farmer, 11 USC 303(a). A Chapter 11 proceeding initiated by a farmer cannot, without his consent, be converted to a Chapter 7 liquidation, 11 USC 1112(c).

i. Chapter 12 - Adjustment of Debts of a Family Farmer with Regular Annual Income was enacted in October of 1986. It gives the farm debtor unique rights to dispose of mortgaged property, and to use the proceeds.

j. These protective rules for farmers illustrate the sort of atypical provisions that the secured lender must anticipate when it deals with some class of persons who, for policy reasons, are granted preferential treatment.

B. FINANCING STRUCTURES

1. Revolving Loan: Loans are made on an "evergreen" revolving basis secured by all of the inventory, including after-acquired inventory, which is expressly provided for, 9-204(c). Advances are based on a percent, usually 50% of "eligible" inventory.

a. The advance ratio and eligibility concepts are the same as apply to accounts receivable financing. Inventory eligibility is based on the lender's evaluation of its liquidation value. Work in process is almost always ineligible. Stale goods are ineligible, or their advance ratio is sharply reduced. Any inventory as to which there is a question as to the debtor's clear title is ineligible. Goods in the hands of third parties who may have adverse claims, or as to which the costs of assembly and disposition are high, are ineligible. Goods that meet eligibility standards initially may become ineligible, e.g., because of technological obsolescence.

b. For advance purposes, inventory is generally valued at the lower of cost or market. Actual values, rather than accounting conventions (e.g. LIFO) are used. Often a ceiling will be set on inventory loans, stated as a dollar amount or a percentage of the total borrowing base. This is a safeguard against a growth in inventory that reflects an inability to sell the goods.

 c. The lender is continually repaid from the proceeds of the pool of inventory, e.g., accounts receivable. Therefore, this sort of inventory financing is tied to accounts receivable financing.

 d. Sometimes the inventory is taken as extra collateral to back up a receivables loan, and no advance is made against it. Sometimes the inventory loan is maintained at a constant dollar level (subject to a collateral ratio) and does not revolve. Borrowing base certificates are used.

 e. An inventory loan which does not include proceeds is generally unsound. Since inventory is always being sold, the lender who lacks a claim to proceeds will see its collateral decline. In theory, new inventory replaces the old. In practice, when a debtor is in financial difficulties, that will not be the case. A declining inventory level, with no right to proceeds, forces the inventory lender to immediately foreclose, despite the fact that orderly sales in the normal course of business are the best way to maximize inventory values.

 f. An inventory loan can be structured on an amortizing term basis. This generally does not, however, meet the borrower's need to have funds to carry the inventory, i.e., the inventory level remains constant, or even increases, but the loan steadily decreases.

 g. In order to control the collateral and avoid conflict, this sort of inventory lending involves only one lender, and conflicting or parallel security interests are not permitted. If they do exist, they must be tightly limited by intercreditor agreements.

 h. The equitable doctrine of marshalling is a particular problem where there are multiple inventory liens. "The equitable doctrine of marshalling rests upon the principal that a creditor having two funds to satisfy his debt, may not by his application of them to his demand, defeat another creditor, who may resort to only one of the funds." Meyer v. United States, 375 U.S. 233, 236 (1963). The purpose is to prevent the arbitrary action of a senior lienor from destroying the rights of a junior lienor or a creditor having less security. Id. at 237.

9

  i. Interest will be charged monthly at a fixed or floating rate (more likely the latter) based on the average daily balance outstanding. This approach is the same as for accounts receivable financing.

 2. Floor Planning: The loans are made against the security of specific identifiable units of hard goods inventory (e.g., tractors).

  a. The loan is paid off when the unit is sold. An outside payment date is fixed. If the collateral is of a kind that requires a long sales period, periodic amortization ("curtailments") will be required. They may be satisfied through receipt of rental proceeds.

  b. As to new equipment the lender will advance the full dealer cost, or close to it. As to used equipment, the ratio is more likely to be around 75% of the dealer's book value.

  c. Interest is most often charged monthly on the average balance outstanding. It may be at a fixed or floating rate. Fixed is not unusual because the term is short.

  d. The security interest extends to proceeds, but unlike the revolving inventory loan, the lender requires payment on sale of the unit. The acceptance of "paper" proceeds in lieu of payment is a separate economic decision for both the lender and the borrower. The lender's interest in proceeds tends to be asserted only on default.

  e. Unlike a revolving loan, there may be more than one lender involved. Because the collateral is identifiable, and the loan does not flow into proceeds, it is entirely practical for there to be multiple lenders. This gives the dealer-borrower the advantage of rate and credit competition. However, a single lender with a blanket security interest in all inventory is not unusual.

  f. Each lender will require cross collateralization of all of its loans. However, in the normal course of business, they will permit the sale of an individual unit provided they are paid their advance against that unit. The cross collateral provision is activated upon default. The debtor is entitled to adequate notice of this change in the ground rules. Cross collateral is not an issue in revolving lending since the lender's lien covers all inventory, as a mass, and repayment is via proceeds.

g. Rental proceeds are paid to the lender, even in the absence of default, because the collateral is depreciating. The rental stream is analogous to the accounts arising in a revolving loan situation. The lender will not, absent default, claim 100 percent of the rents because the borrower needs to retain a sufficient amount to cover its operating costs. Alternatively, the lender may require fixed monthly amortization without reference to the rental income, or some combination of the two concepts may be utilized.

h. A variation from the typical loan format is for the loan to be structured as a lease. The lender "owns" the unit, leases it to the dealer, who in turn subleases it to his customers. The prime lease is usually on a full payout basis, i.e., the rentals are sufficient to repay the lessor's investment plus a market interest rate. This structure, which may include a sale-leaseback, is always a reflection of tax and accounting considerations.

3. Document Financing: Article 7, as well as Article 9, applies to documents of title. Inventory in the possession of a bailee such as a warehouseman or carrier is evidenced by some document of title, e.g., warehouse receipt, bill of lading. Loans can be made against the security of these documents, which are the equivalent of the inventory they represent, 9-102(a)(30); 1-201(15). Note that motor vehicle certificates of title and like evidences of ownership are not "documents of title" for Article 7 purposes.

a. Goods in a public warehouse or a vessel can be advanced against upon the same basis as if they are in the borrower's possession. However, they are subject to the charges of the bailee. If imported, they may be subject to customs duties. A bank opening letters of credit will routinely take a security interest in the imported inventory.

b. Field warehousing is a means of maintaining control of the inventory. The warehousing facility is established on the debtor's premises, as by fencing off part of a storage facility. The arrangement is managed by an independent warehouse company, but the actual custodians may be the debtor's employees. However, the warehouse company must set up controls, and monitor them, so that it can meet its responsibility to the lender of ensuring that the inventory is, in fact, present.

c. Field warehousing is a mechanism for perfecting by possession. It was legally useful under pre-UCC law. Today, a lender will perfect by filing and not rely solely on possessory interest. In part, this reflects the potential to challenge the possessory nature of a field warehousing arrangement on grounds that its controls were not sufficient to constitute possession.

d. The warehouse company leases the warehouse premises from the debtor, and pays the employees. These expenses are reimbursed by the debtor, and can add materially to the financing cost.

e. The lender will want to verify that the field warehouse company has the financial capacity to respond to any failure by it in monitoring and controlling the inventory e.g., release of inventory without substitution of replacement inventory, or payment. Field warehouse companies often carry insurance that backs up their financial responsibility.

C. PERFECTION AND PRIORITY

1. Filing: Aside from documentary transactions, or where perfection is by possession or control, perfection is by central filing. 9-501(a)(2) (all filings, other than fixture filings to be central). Under 9-301 and 9-307(b) Financing Statements are to be filed at the location of the debtor; location is determined to be the jurisdiction where an entity must register to commence entity existence. If the debtor is an individual, the debtor is located at its principal residence. If the debtor is an unregistered organization, then it is located at its chief executive office.

a. Prefiling is permitted, 9-502(d). The filing is generally effective for 5 years, 9-515. The 4-month rule for perfection applies if the debtor changes its location. 9-316(a). Provisions in Security Agreements designating locations of inventory for enforcement purposes together with representations as to maintenance of location of the debtor and representations not to remove collateral to another jurisdiction outside of ordinary course sales without Secured Party consent are important items. In short, aside from farm products the standard Code rules apply.

b. Financing statement contents should conform to standard Code requirements. 9-502; 9-503 and 9-504. Since "inventory" is a Code classification, it suffices as a description.

However, better practice is to take advantage of the notice system by giving record searchers a fuller description. 9-502 and 9-504(1) only requires an "indication" of the collateral sufficient to satisfy 9-108, but note that 9-504(2) permits the financing statement collateral description to read "all assets" or "all personal property"; this broad description will not be sufficient for the security agreement. 9-108(c) and Comment 2. Specific reference should be made to packaging and shipping documents.

   c. If the collateral is on lease, filings should be made at the lessee "locations", as well as those of the debtor to which the units may be returned. Filings should be made at third party warehouse and processor "locations", and the third party should be directed to abide by instructions from the lender.

   d. Possession should be taken of long-term (e.g., 6 month) leases. This is an alternate form of perfection and, unlike the financing statement, provides protection against a third party financer to whom the paper is transferred for value, 9-330. The possession alternative reflects the fact that chattel paper is often sold, or borrowed against, to a Lender other than the floor planner.

   e. Particular care should be taken in identifying floor plan inventory because other lenders may be financing similar equipment, the only distinction being the serial numbers. 9-322 to 9-324 governs priorities. It is a "race" statute.

   2.   Purchase Money Priority:

   a. 9-324 establishes rules for obtaining purchase money security interests (defined in 9-103) in inventory or in collateral other than inventory although there are few situations where a PMSI in intangibles may be achieved. See, In re Woodworks Contemporary Furniture, Inc., 39 UCC Rep. 1842 (Bankr. W.D. Wis. 1984); Mbank Alamo, N.A., v. Raytheon Co., 886 F.2d 1449 (5th Cir. 1989). 9-103(b)(3) and (c) and 9-324(f) will permit a PMSI in software sold or licensed together with goods which are PMSI collateral if the software is acquired principally for use with the goods. Under revised Article 9, the PMSI inventory lender's security interest will continue in chattel paper proceeds of the inventory. 9-330(e); 9-324(b). A purchase money priority in inventory may arise from a credit sale or a loan which enables the debtor to acquire an item of inventory, 9-103 and Comment 3. A purchase money lender, upon following the purchase money rules, will achieve priority over a pre-existing lien in the same collateral type.

b. Achieving purchase money priority in inventory requires that prior to the debtor receiving possession the purchase money interest be perfected and the conflicting lienor will have received an authenticated notification within 5 years before the debtor receives possession of the inventory which notification states that the PMSI creditor has or will acquire a PMSI in the inventory described. 9-324(b).

c. In general, inventory lenders do not rely on purchase money priority. It presents difficult problems of proof, see, Southtrust Bank, N.A. v. Borg Warner Acceptance Corp., 760 F.2d 1240 (11th Cir. 1985); contra, In re Pan Am Corp., 124 B.R. 960 (Bankr. S.D.N.Y. 1991), In re Ionosphere Clubs, Inc., 13 UCC Rep. 2d 1276 (S.D.N.Y. 1991), and may limit freedom to restructure the loan at a later date. More broadly, an inventory lender will not want a purchase money lien, or even a junior lien on inventory collateral to exist because it does not want to have to deal with a conflicting claim in the event of default, e.g., it does not want to be exposed to marshalling claims. 9-103(b)(2) will permit cross-collateralization of PMSI inventory advances such that the total of all PMSI inventory advances from the same supplier or lender may be secured by successive shipments of collateral from the same supplier or financed by the same lender. Further, in non-consumer transactions, 9-103(f) provides that PMSI status is not destroyed because it also secures non-PM obligations, non-PM collateral or it is renewed or refinanced.

d. Where conflicting liens do exist, they are best resolved by an intercreditor agreement which is broader than what can be achieved via purchase money priority, e.g., the lien subordination covers all advances, not just the purchase money component. At the "go in" the lenders can usually reach agreement, including utilizing operating controls to ensure that each lender's collateral is identifiable. At the exit, accommodation may be impossible. 9-324(g)(1) grants priority to a PMSI supplier over a PMSI lender financing the same collateral.

3. Record Searches: Record searches must be conducted. They are made in the same places where financing statements will be filed in the given circumstances, as well as locations at which filings may have been made in the past based on then existing facts. The search

identifies prior liens that must be released or subordinated. If the collateral unit is used equipment, it is subject to liens against the original seller/user. The lender will generally rely upon the dealer/borrower to get clear title. But if the used equipment dealer is financially weak, prudence may dictate conducting a search against the seller. The search should also cover judgment and tax liens, which must be cleared. Such liens, even if paid off, may indicate serious credit problems that would militate against making the loan.

    a. The potential for possessory liens should be kept in mind. These include storage fees, custom duties, third party processor liens and mechanics liens. The last category may arise in a fleet rental situation where the equipment is being repaired.

    b. Federal tax liens are a particular risk in the case of revolving loans because, after 45 days, they can take priority over the revolving loan, I.R.C. 6323. In re Dorough, Parks & Co., 185 B.R. 46 (E.D. Tenn. 1995)

    4. Possession: Perfection can be effected by possession, 9-313, but inventory lenders rarely use that approach. It is inconsistent with the borrower's need to sell, and impractical for the lender except for high value inventory such as diamonds.

    a. Perfection by possession may be achieved, through the creditor's agent (e.g. field warehouseman) who issues documents of title under 9-312 or perfection can be accomplished by notice to a bailee who does not issue a negotiable receipt if the bailee acknowledges that it holds possession, 9-313, although the bailee is not required to provide such acknowledgment. However, the lender will almost invariably rely on filing. Perfection by possession invites controversy, See, In re Kontaratos, 31 UCC Rep. 1124 (D.C. Maine 1981). Also the lender's security interest in proceeds is only good for 21 days after the debtor receives the proceeds, 9-315(d), unless the lender has satisfied the conditions of 9-315(d).

    b. If the inventory is evidenced by a negotiable document, perfection can be effected by filing or possession of the document since the lender's interest would otherwise be subordinate to that of a party to whom it is negotiated. 9-312(c).

    5. Statutory Background: The Article 9 provisions governing revolving loans have their antecedents in Factors Lien statutes. The first such law was enacted in New York in 1911, and by 1950, they

had become widespread. Floor planning has its statutory roots in the Uniform Trust Receipts Act (U.L.A. Vol. 9C), which was promulgated in the 1930's and adopted by 39 states. Its complexities illustrated the need for adoption of Article 9.

    a. UTRA terminology lingers, e.g., "sale out of trust" (SOT) to describe a sale by a borrower who has not paid off the loan against the unit sold.

    b. Floor planning documentation for motor vehicles sometimes includes "Trust Receipts" as the mechanism for identifying the vehicles coming under the floor plan arrangement. Better practice is to use Code terminology. Trust receipts do make transactional sense when the 20-day grace period of 9-312(f) is being relied on.

    c. While Article 9 has special rules for collateral subject to Federal law, 9-109(c) and state titling requirements, such collateral tends to be subject to the Code provisions regarding inventory, e.g., perfection against motor vehicle inventory is by UCC filing.

D.   DOCUMENTATION

    1.   Security Agreement (S/A): The operative terms of an inventory loan with respect to, among other things, collateral, are found in the credit agreement and/or security agreement. A security agreement (9-102(a)(73)) is an agreement that creates or provides for a security interest 1-201(37). Creation of a valid and enforceable security interest under 9-203 is a prerequisite to perfection. The agreement takes three basic forms:

    Revolving Security Agreement: This form covers a revolving pool of inventory and may be incorporated in, or be an adjunct to, a factoring or accounts receivable financing agreement. It will include reference to documents of title, if they are part of the financing.

    Wholesale Security Agreement: This form covers the typical floor planning arrangement in which the inventory is held for sale.

Fleet Rental Security Agreement: This form covers the situation in which the inventory is held for rental. It differs from the "wholesale" form in that it provides for a security interest in the rental proceeds.

a. The S/A includes a standard granting clause, including leases and rental payments if appropriate. If cross collateralization is being relied upon that fact should be expressly stated since the typical floor planning agreement permits sales without reference to cross collateralization, unless the debtor has defaulted. Activation of the cross collateral clause, on default, should be effected by a written notice. Proceeds are referenced. While the S/A may state that proceeds are held "in trust", this provision has little value vis-à-vis third parties. Respective rights will be governed by the UCC and Bankruptcy Code, and not by equitable doctrines.

b. Patents and trademarks should be included in the S/A if they have value in relation to the inventory. If inventory is produced under a license, the lender should seek an agreement with the licensor permitting it freedom to dispose of the inventory. If a customer's name is imprinted on the goods, they cannot be sold to third parties. Agreement between lender and licensor is most often possible at the "go-in"; but not at the exit.

c. Advance ratios and eligibility standards (if not discretionary with the lender) should be stated in the S/A. Inventory subject to any conflicting lien, albeit junior, should be treated as ineligible. Other types of eligibility criteria set forth in the S/A may be one or more of the following non-exhaustive list:

(i) Inventory must be subject to the lien of the lender and no other creditors:

(ii) Inventory located on leaseholds as to which the lessor has not, within 60 days of the date of the initial extension or credit, entered into a consent and agreement providing the lender with the right to receive notice of default, the right to repossess such inventory at any time and such other rights as may be acceptable to the lender;

(iii) Inventory that is obsolete, unusable or otherwise unavailable for sale through normal trade channels;

17

(iv) Inventory with respect to which the representations and warranties set forth in the S/A applicable to inventory are not true and correct;

(v) Inventory consisting of promotional, marketing, packaging or shipping materials and supplies;

(vi) Inventory that fails to meet all material standards imposed by any governmental agency, or department or division thereof, having regulatory authority over such inventory or its use or sale;

(vii) Inventory that is subject to any licensing, patent, royalty, trademark, trade name or copyright agreement with any third party from whom the borrower has received written notice of a dispute in respect of any such agreement if, in the lender's reasonable judgment, such dispute would adversely affect the ability of the borrower to sell such inventory;

(viii) Inventory located outside the United States;

(ix) Inventory that is not in the possession of or under the sole control of the borrower or any of its wholly owned U.S. subsidiaries;

(x) Inventory consisting of work in progress;

(xi) Inventory in respect of which the S/A, after giving effect to the related filings of financing statements that have then been made, if any, does not or has ceased to create a valid and perfected first priority lien or security interest in favor of the Secured Parties securing the Secured Obligations and as to which no other liens exist, other than Permitted Liens; and

(xii) Inventory not meeting all standards imposed by any governmental agency having regulatory control over such inventory, its sale or use including statutes such as the Federal Labor Standards Act.

d. In a revolving loan S/A, the lenders "commitment" to lend, if any, should be stated. Discretionary advances are common, and "loans pursuant to a commitment" have enough "outs" to be, as a credit matter, tantamount to discretionary.

e. Interest and amortization (if any) provisions are standard. A floor planning S/A includes late payment penalties. Prepayment penalties do not apply in floor planning since it is contemplated that payment will be made upon sale and the borrower, typically, has no obligation to make further borrowings. In the case of a revolving loan, there may be minimum borrowing requirements for the term of the loan agreement. The penalty for underborrowing should be based on a formula that covers the lender's "spread" not its gross income.

f. The S/A includes extensive provisions regarding the preservation of the collateral. It will be well maintained and insured. No adverse liens will be permitted, and its location will not be changed. In floor planning, the debtor agrees not to sell the unit for less than the debt due on it. If rented, the leases will be subordinate to the lender's security interest (a covenant honored by its breach). Also, the borrower/lessor will perfect a security interest against its lessee if the lender requests. This requirement addresses the risk of the lease being deemed a credit sale. The lender may take physical possession of any lease as a means of perfection.

g. The S/A will list events of default, e.g., nonpayment; failure to preserve collateral. Financial covenants are not typical in asset based lending except for loans to be made pursuant to a commitment.

h. The S/A will give the lender a right to conduct audits (a revolving loan term) or commodity checks (a floor planning term). Enforcement rights will be detailed. One could rely on a simple reference to the Code rights (and that reference is made), but it is preferable to articulate to the borrower and his counsel what those rights are.

2. Promissory Notes: Promissory notes are never necessary, and are impractical in revolving loans (except for grid notes). They may be used in floor planning as a convenient means of stating the repayment and interest provisions applicable to each unit, the S/A being a standard all-purpose form.

3. Financing Statement: The contents of the financing statement is governed by 9-502.

4. Corporate Formalities: In revolving loan situations Board resolutions will be required. In some jurisdictions stockholders consent may also be necessary. The same practice applies to floor planning if all, or most, of the debtor's inventory is covered. Such action is most likely not necessary when floor planning only a few units, and such financing is commonly engaged in by the debtor.

    a. Resolutions and consents should be stated in broad enough terms to cover future transactions. Unanimous stockholder consent can replace Board action.

    b. Charter and by-laws should be reviewed to determine that they do not restrict the corporation's power to enter into the transaction, or impose any unusual approval or execution requirements. An opinion from the borrower's counsel may substitute for this review.

    c. It can be fairly argued that reliance can be placed on a certified resolution and execution by a proper officer, without reference to charter or by-law restrictions. That approach suggests not conducting a charter and by-law review. Any such review must be done thoroughly since the lender will be deemed to have full knowledge of that which it has reviewed, and can no longer rely on the resolution or apparent authority.

5. Execution. Documents should be executed by the President or a Vice-President. Since the transaction is financial in nature execution by the Treasurer may also be acceptable. The Board Resolution may confer signing authority upon some other person. The Secretary, having certified to the Board Resolution, should not sign the security agreement even if he carries some other corporate title such as Vice President.

6. Pay Proceeds Letter: This is a colloquially phrased document which states who is to receive the loan proceeds. It is used in floor planning and fairly frequently with revolving loans. In part, it serves the practical function of providing payment instructions and preserving a record of the "value" given by the lender. In part, it is a device for verifying that the borrower has paid for the collateral. This ties into clearing any adverse lien claimed by the supplier. It also helps prove that the loan proceeds were applied to the purchase of the collateral and are therefore entitled to purchase money priority.

7. Proof of Ownership: Copies of invoices, title certificates and delivery records are required to verify that the Borrower has title and possession.

8. Landlord's Waiver: A landlord may assert a statutory lien against the collateral for unpaid rents. While this claim may have little legal merit, the issue can be obviated by a waiver. This instrument will also expressly provide that the lender may remove the collateral from the premises. If the goods are difficult to remove the lender can try to get the landlord to agree that it may take over occupancy for a brief period of time, paying rent for that period. Landlord's waivers may not be available. The economic consequences of their omission should be estimated. Often, the amount at issue is not material.

9. Mortgagee's Waiver: The holder of a real estate mortgage (including a leasehold mortgage) generally has no basis for claiming an interest in the borrower's inventory. Absent special circumstances, a "waiver" of this nonexistent interest is not necessary or desirable.

10. Insurance: Proof of casualty insurance is a routine part of the loan documentation, along with an endorsement to the policy naming the lender as an insured as its interest appears. This endorsement should provide that the lender will be paid notwithstanding defenses the insurer may have against the borrower. Also, the lender must receive prior notice of cancellation, so it can protect its interests. Lenders often carry single interest coverage to protect them if the borrower's insurance fails. Provision should be made for the application of insurance payments, i.e., to replace inventory or to repay the debt. The lender may require that it have the right to adjust the claim.

11. Miscellaneous: Guaranties, debt subordinations, etc., may be part of the loan transaction. They will be no different in form and substance from what would apply to any other loan.

12. "Factory" Recourse: In floor planning the manufacturer may have accepted a degree of liability for non-payment of the lender by the dealer. This recourse frequently takes the form of an agreement by the "factory" to purchase the collateral from the lender for an amount equal to the direct loan against the collateral. The lender has the burden of getting possession of the collateral, which is not always feasible.

a. A method of fixing the factory liability is a bookkeeping "reserve". As each unit is financed, a percentage of the price is set as the factory's liability. This amount is applied to the "ultimate net loss" suffered by the lender. While it is a small amount as to each unit, the pooling of the reserve results in a material recourse.

b. A variation of the repurchase agreement is the remarketing agreement. In that case the "factory" agrees to use its best efforts to sell the repossessed collateral, but does not undertake to realize any particular price.

c. Revolving loan arrangements may include a "put" to the inventory supplier. It will generally relate to an existing arrangement between the borrower and its supplier whereby the borrower can return unsold inventory. "Take or pay" contracts are another alternative. An inventory lender may take an assignment of this right, but is better served by a direct contractual agreement which is not subject to defenses the supplier may have against the borrower.

E.   OPERATING RISKS

1.   Sales Out of Trust: The most significant risk attendant to inventory financing is that the borrower will sell the collateral, and wrongfully retain the proceeds. A purchaser of inventory in the ordinary course of business will take free of the lender's lien, 9-320(a). See 1-201(9) for definition of "buyer in the ordinary course of business". Note that transfers in total or partial satisfaction do not constitute purchases in ordinary course. See, U.S. v. Handy & Harmon, 750 F.2d 777 (9th Cir. 1984). Since inventory is intended to be sold, the transaction has no earmarks of impropriety. The lender's main protection is simply the integrity of the borrower. Audits and commodity checks will eventually identify the missing collateral, and permit the lender to take such steps as are available to protect its interests, e.g., foreclosing on the remaining collateral; locating the proceeds of the unaccounted for collateral. The borrower's awareness of these controls serves as a deterrent to sale out of trust. If the lender lacks the competence or manpower to conduct audits or commodity checks it can hire that service from companies specializing in that form of collateral control.

22

2. Loss of Proceeds: A revolving inventory loan generally flows into the accounts receivable, with the borrower delivering remittances, in kind, to the lender. Often the invoices instruct the account debtors to remit to a lock box which, in fact, is controlled by the lender.

a. In floor planning, the debtor will typically deposit the cash proceeds in its bank account for subsequent remittance to the lender. These proceeds may arise from a cash sale, a sale on open account, or an installment sale (conditional sales contract) which is discounted with a financial institution. A material gap of time often exists between the transfer of the collateral to the buyer, and receipt of payment. This creates a risk that the payment will not be made. Or a creditor of the borrower may attach the proceeds. An especially likely event is that the depository bank will offset against the deposit of the proceeds. The lender may have superior rights in the proceeds if they can be traced. But at best this means litigation. If the proceeds are "chattel paper", the party purchasing the paper for value, and taking possession, has superior rights. The lender has a security interest in the value, if it can be found.

b. Some revolving inventory arrangements only require periodic (e.g. monthly) settlements in which case these same problems arise.

c. A prudent lender will not rely on its ability, factually or legally, to recover proceeds deposited in its borrower's bank account. It will adjust its advance ratios to cover its estimate of these amounts, and will regularly verify that its estimate of their magnitude is correct.

3. Used Equipment: If the collateral is used equipment the lender may have difficulty in establishing its value. This is particularly true if the borrower accepted the used equipment as a "trade-in", thereby possibly ascribing an arbitrary value to it. A second exposure is that the collateral is subject to a lien against the seller. Since the seller was most likely a user, the dealer/borrower does not take free of such liens. Inventory acquired via a bulk sale is subject to claims of creditors of the seller if there has been no compliance with bulk sales law. Note that the bulk sales law (Art. 6 of the UCC) has been repealed in a number of jurisdictions.

4. Accessions: Accessions are goods that are affixed to, or installed in, other goods, 9-335. In some factual circumstances floor planned inventory may be enhanced by accessions already subject to a security interest. These accessions are subject to removal by the prior

secured party. This is, in general, a minor or nonexistent hazard for the floor planner. But as to certain collateral (e.g., construction equipment) it may constitute a material portion of the unit's value, and should be kept in kind.

     5.   Statutory Liens: Inventory is subject to an array of statutory liens that prime the lenders Code security interest. These include possessory claims of warehousemen, processors, repairmen, landlords, common carriers and bailees, 9-333.

     a. Federal tax liens, after 45 days prime an Article 9 interest. Some state tax liens, especially for unpaid payroll taxes, will have a similar impact.

     b. Unpaid wage claimants may have prior rights to the debtor's assets under state or Federal law, Donovan v. TMC Industries, Ltd., 20 B.R. 997 (N.D. Ga. 1982).

     c. Secret liens, such as those of a seller of livestock or perishable agricultural commodities, may give the supplier a superior right to the inventory and its proceeds, e.g. Packers and Stockyards Act, 7 USC 181 et seq.; Calif. Ag. 55.631 et seq.; Perishable Agricultural Commodities Act, 7 USC 499e.

     d. Violation of the Fair Labor Standards Act minimum wage requirements may result in goods being enjoined from sale in interstate commerce, 29 U.S.C. 213(a)(1). While unpaid employees do not have a lien on the goods ahead of a perfected security interest, the application of the "hot goods" provision may result in the lender having to pay the employees in order to dispose of the inventory. Citicorp Industrial Credit, Inc. v. Brock, 107 S. Ct. 2694 (1987).

     6.   Conflicting Consensual Liens: The S/A should forbid conflicting liens, even though junior, because of the difficulties they present upon liquidation. This is particularly true with respect to a pool of revolving inventory.

a. Sometimes purchase money liens must be allowed so that the borrower can get credit from a supplier. In that case the inventory lender should exclude the PM inventory from its collateral base, and should closely monitor its amount. It should also anticipate that on default it may, as a practical matter, have to pay off the PM creditor in order to maintain an orderly working off of the total inventory.

b. Suppliers may sell on "consignment", or "approval" or "sale or return". These types of sales are generally construed as secured transactions, and are subject to Article 9 perfection rules and priority, 9-109(a)(4) and 9-103(d). Even if the supplier fails to perfect, the inventory lender should treat its inventory as "ineligible" because it must anticipate conflict with the supplier in the event of default. For two inconsistent opinions by the same court in the same bankruptcy proceeding, See, Eastman Kodak Co. v. Harrison, 639 F.2d 1213 (5th Cir. 1981) and In re Sitkin Smelting & Refining, Inc., 648 F.2d (5th Cir. 1981).

c. Goods sold on "bill and hold" should be removed from the seller's eligibility, but not included in the buyer's eligibility, it not being clear who the inventory belongs to. See, In re Tambro, 385 NYS 2d 260, 350 NE2d 590 (N.Y. 1976).

d. "Tolling" arrangements are common in commodity processing. The owner of a raw material ships it to a processor with the understanding that title remains with the shipper/owner throughout the conversion process. In fact, the commodity may be commingled with that of others, and when returned to the owner is not literally the same material as was supplied. While the shipper/owner should perfect under Article 9, a lender to either party should not rely on how a court will treat the transaction. See, General Motors Corp v. Bristol Industries Corp., 38 UCC Rep. 989 (Bankr. D. Conn. 1981), rev'd on procedural grounds 690 F.2d 26 (2d Cir. 1982) and the Kodak and Sitkin cases cited in E(6)(b), supra.

7. Impediments to Liquidation: The sale of inventory by the secured creditor may be subject to various impediments, such as:

a. The inventory being subject to the rights of a licensor.

b. The need to provide warranties, e.g., aircraft parts, as to specifications.

c. Statutory requirements regulating the sale, e.g., liquor; firearms; drugs.

d. Rights of third parties whose name or trademark are affixed to the inventory, e.g., tools manufactured for Sears and bearing its trade name.

e. Patent violation claimants seeking to enjoin the sale of the inventory.

F. LENDER REMEDIES

1. Enforcement Rights: The inventory lender, on default, has the same set of rights as is typical of secured lending generally, UCC Article 9, Part 6.

a. Every contract under the UCC "imposes an obligation of good faith in its performance or enforcement," 1-203. "Obligations of good faith, diligence, reasonableness and care prescribed by [the UCC] may not be disclaimed by agreement but the parties may by agreement determine the standards by which the performance of such obligations is to be measured if such standards are not manifestly unreasonable," 1-102(3).

b. A declaration of a default should be based on demonstrable facts in order to avoid counterclaims, Sahadi v. Continental Illinois Nat'l Bank & Trust Co., 706 F.2d 193 (7th Cir. 1983); K.M.C. Co., Inc. v. Irving Trust Co., 757 F.2d, 752 (6th Cir. 1985).

c. Insecurity clauses should not be relied upon, although 1-208 expressly provides that they may be enforced if the creditor "in good faith believes that the prospect of payment or performance is impaired. The burden of establishing lack of good faith is on the party against whom the power has been exercised." This burden can be all too easily met by such anecdotal "proof" as that the loan officer was motivated by personal anger at the debtor.

2. Approaches to Liquidation: There are two general approaches to inventory liquidation. One is to take possession of the inventory as quickly as possible, and dispose of it. The other is to permit the debtor to sell it in the ordinary course of its business, with the lender perhaps providing some additional financing to enable the debtor to continue in operation.

a. As to floor planned inventory, the lender will tend to want to take possession and sell the units itself (publicly or privately), place them for auction in a sale involving other unrelated equipment, or arrange for their sale by a dealer who handles such equipment.

b. If the debtor is still in operation, the floor planner may permit it to continue to sell the units. However, since the floor planner is not generally the sole inventory lender, or the source of working capital funds, it is unlikely to provide any supplemental financing. It may permit the borrower to retain a percentage of the sales proceeds to recompense it for the direct costs of sale, including salesmen's commissions.

c. A mid-ground approach is for the floor planner to place the units in a facility under its control, but for a period of time permit the debtor to do the selling.

d. The inventory pool lender will be inclined to leave the inventory with the debtor so that work in process can be completed, orders met, and sales made by the debtor at, or near, its usual prices. In general, a pool of inventory consisting of many different items in various stages of manufacture will lose much of its value if removed and sold in bulk.

3. Taking Possession: Possession can be effected by self-help, voluntary surrender, or judicial proceedings.

a. 9-609 permits self help after a default if done without breach of the peace. Such action is constitutional. See, Adams v. Southern Cal First Nat's Bank, 492 F.2d 324 (9th Cir. 1973), cert. den., 419 US 1006 (1974); Crouse v. First Trust Union Bank, 448 NYS 2d 329 (App. Div. 1982). However, as a practical matter, in inventory financing it is usually not possible to exercise a self-help remedy.

b. Voluntary surrender is a realistic alternative, especially if the lender makes some realistic concessions such as (i) discontinuing interest charges, (ii) providing its own insurance, (iii) allowing the debtor an opportunity to sell the inventory. The lender should attempt to obtain a written agreement from the debtor evidencing a voluntary surrender. The lender should be carefully to negate any implication that it is taking the collateral in satisfaction of the debt, although if certain steps are taken, a lender may accept collateral in partial satisfaction of its debt without compromising its deficiency. 9-620, 9-621 and 9-622.

 c. 9-601 also authorizes proceeding by judicial action. The Code does not set out the procedure, which is left to state law and which goes under such names as Claim and Delivery - Writ of Possession (Cal. Civ Proc Code 511.010 et seq.); Replevin (Ohio Rev Code 2737 et seq.); Rules 696 et seq.); Sequestration (Tex Civ Proc Rules 696 et seq.). Constitutional requirements of due process call for notice and a hearing. Snaidach v. Family Finance Corp., 395 US 337 (1967); Fuentes v. Shevin, 407 US 67 (1972).

 4. Disposition of Collateral: The creditor may sell at public or private sale. "Every aspect of the disposition ... must be commercially reasonable." 9-610(b). "The fact that a greater amount could have been obtained...is not of itself sufficient to preclude the secured party from establishing that the ... enforcement, disposition or acceptance was made in a commercially reasonable manner. 9-627(a).

 5. Notice: Unless the debtor after default has waived the right of notice, or the collateral is perishable, rapidly declining in value or sold on a recognized market (e.g., stock exchange), the creditor must give notification of the intended disposition to a variety of parties. 9-611. The contents of the notification is set forth in 9-613 which section also provides a "safe harbor" form of notice. Case law is inconsistent as to whether guarantors as "secondary obligors" 9-102(a)(71) can, prior to default, waive notice, see, Commercial Discount Corp. v. Bayer, 372 NE2d 926 (Ill. App. 1978); McNulty v. Todd, 276 SE2d 73 (`Ga. 1981). Notification must be sent to the debtor, to secondary obligors, other persons who have filed a financing statement or lien and to other persons who have notified the secured party of a claim of interest in the collateral to be sold. 9-611

Appendix B

From PLI's Course Handbook
Hot Issues in Executive Compensation 2004
#2879

2

A PRIMER ON STOCK-BASED COMPENSATION AND SELECTED RECENT DEVELOPMENTS

Max J. Schwartz
Sullivan & Cromwell LLP

Copyright © 2004 Sullivan & Cromwell LLP
All Rights Reserved

II. FINAL GOLDEN PARACHUTE REGULATIONS

On August 1, 2003, the IRS issued a final regulation (the "*final regulation*") under I.R.C. § 280G covering the denial of a deduction to a corporation for any "excess parachute payment." The provisions of the final regulation also apply for purposes of the 20% excise tax imposed by I.R.C. § 4999 on recipients of excess parachute payments. The IRS concurrently issued Revenue Procedure 2003-68, providing guidance on the methods that may be used to value stock options for purposes of these provisions.

The final regulation replaces the proposed regulations issued in 2002 (the "*2002 proposed regulation*") and in 1989 (the "*1989 proposed regulation*"). The final regulation does not depart significantly from the 2002 proposed regulation and includes a number of helpful clarifications. Certain of the controversial features of the 2002 proposed regulation, such as the valuation methodology for stock options, remain in the final regulation. Included as Annex A hereto is a reprint of an article from the October 2003 issue of The M&A Lawyer discussing the final regulation.

A. PRINCIPAL CHANGES/CLARIFICATIONS FROM THE 2002 PROPOSED REGULATION

The final regulation modifies the 2002 proposed regulation in a number of ways the most significant of which are noted below. In determining whether a change in control has occurred, the final regulation:

- retains the rule from the 2002 proposed regulation that prohibits taking into account overlapping share ownership to conclude that neither corporation has undergone a change in control;

- generally adopts the "one change" rule that if one corporation undergoes a change in control, the other corporation involved in the transaction does not undergo a change in control;[38] and

- provides that whether a sale of assets constitutes a change in control is determined by the gross fair market value of assets without regard to any liabilities associated with such assets.[39]

In exempting payments from the definition of "parachute payment," the final regulation:

- clarifies that a domestic corporation eligible to elect treatment as an S corporation under the I.R.C. may use the exemption for small business corporations, even if it does not elect S corporation treatment; and

- simplifies the private corporation shareholder approval procedures by permitting shareholders of record to be determined on any day within a six-month period ending on the change in control. The preamble to the final regulation also clarifies that a foreign corporation eligible to be treated as a private corporation may use the shareholder approval exemption.

---

[38] See the preamble to the final regulation.

[39] This rule is also applied in determining the voting requirements applicable to an entity shareholder of the payor corporation for purposes of the shareholder approval procedures. (These requirements depend on whether a substantial portion of the assets of the entity shareholder consist of the payor corporation's stock.)

In calculating parachute payments, the final regulation:

- provides that the full amount of a payment (instead of the portion attributable to acceleration of vesting or payment) pursuant to an agreement entered into or modified within one year of a change in control generally is treated as contingent on the change in control and potentially subject to excise tax;[40]

- provides that the portion of a payment treated as contingent on a change in control cannot exceed the amount of the accelerated payment or, if the payment is not accelerated, the present value of the payment; and

- clarifies that the base amount includes *all* amounts received by a disqualified individual for the performance of personal services for a corporation during the base period, potentially resulting in lower base amounts (and higher excise taxes) for individuals who serve the corporation variously as independent contractors and employees during the base period.[41]

---

[40] For example, assume that options were granted on January 1, 2004 with one-year cliff vesting on January 1, 2005 as part of a corporation's annual option program and pursuant to a plan that provides for full vesting on a change in control. Under the final regulation, if a change in control occurs on December 1, 2004 (and the presumption that the grants were contingent on a change in control is not rebutted), the full value of the options, rather than the portion attributable to one month of accelerated vesting, is presumed to be contingent on a change in control and potentially subject to excise tax.

[41] For example, if an individual earned $30,000 in director fees in 2004 and 2005 and then became an executive with annual compensation of
(continued. . .)

49

Additionally, the final regulation provides that the holder of an unvested option or a vested option that is exercisable only for restricted stock generally is not considered to own the underlying stock, such as for purposes of the rules on identifying disqualified individuals and determining if a change in control has occurred. The holder of a vested option exercisable for unrestricted stock is generally treated as the owner of the underlying stock, other than for purposes of the shareholder approval exemption.

B. BACKGROUND

Under I.R.C. §§ 280G and 4999, no deduction is allowed to a corporation for any excess parachute payments made to a "disqualified individual" and the recipient of the payment is subject to a non-deductible 20% excise tax in addition to any regular income tax (which may be incurred at a different time). In general, a payment will be treated as a "parachute payment" if (i) the payment is compensatory in nature and contingent on a change in control (as defined by regulation) of the corporation and (ii) the present value of the aggregate of all such payments received by the disqualified individual equals at least three times the individual's base amount.[42] Payments for this purpose are not limited to cash

---

(...continued)
$500,000 in 2006 and $600,000 in 2007, the base amount calculation with respect to a change in control occurring in 2008 would include all amounts earned as a director and as an executive ((($30,000 x 2) + $500,000 + $600,000)/4 = $290,000) instead of just amounts earned as an executive (($500,000 + $600,000)/2 = $550,000). Because excise tax is applied to parachute payments that exceed three times an individual's base amount, a smaller base amount increases an individual's exposure to excise tax liability.

[42] A parachute payment also includes any payment of compensation to a disqualified individual that is made pursuant to an agreement that violates any generally enforced securities laws or regulations.

(continued...)

payments but include the value of other benefits, *e.g.*, the accelerated vesting of stock options. The "base amount" is the disqualified individual's average annual compensation from the corporation which undergoes a change in control that is includible in gross income during the five complete years ended immediately preceding the change in control.[43] The amount of a parachute payment can be reduced if it is shown to be reasonable compensation for services performed, or to be performed, by the individual. The "excess" amount of any parachute payment is the amount by which it exceeds the allocable portion of the individual's base amount. The amount of a parachute payment can be reduced to the extent it is shown to be reasonable compensation for services performed, or to be performed, by the individual.

C. EFFECTIVE DATE

The final regulation applies to any payments that are contingent on a change in control occurring on or after January 1, 2004. The 2002 and the 1989 proposed regulations generally may be relied upon with respect to payments that relate to changes in control occurring prior to January 1, 2004.[44] Revenue Procedure 2003-68 (relating to option valuation) applies with respect to changes in control

---

(...continued)
    Certain payments that are approved by shareholders of certain private corporations are excluded from the definition of a parachute payment.

[43] If the disqualified individual has not been employed by the corporation for five complete years, the base amount is determined for the period of the individual's employment. Certain payments for partial years may be annualized for this purpose.

[44] The preamble to the final regulation states, however, that "clarification in the 2002 proposed regulations does not support reliance on the 1989 proposed regulations for a position contrary to the provisions of the 1989 proposed regulations."

51

occurring on or after January 1, 2004 but may be applied by taxpayers with respect to transactions that occur prior to such date.[45]

D. CERTAIN OBSERVATIONS

Although the final regulation does not fundamentally change the golden parachute rules, the following observations can be made:

- As discussed more fully below, the treatment of stock options upon a change in control should be carefully considered. In particular, accelerated vesting of an underwater option could result in excise tax liability even though the option might never be exercised because it remains underwater.

- Stock options and other awards with graded vesting are still favored over those with cliff vesting, and awards that vest on achievement of performance targets are subject to a separate regime.

- Certain limited events may provide an opportunity to redetermine an option's value and possibly recoup a portion of excise tax previously paid by claiming a refund, as discussed more fully below. This redetermination feature could reduce the cost of providing excise tax gross-ups, depending on how the excise tax gross-up provision is drafted.

---

[45] Revenue Procedures 2002-13 and 2002-45 (the predecessors to Revenue Procedure 2003-68 which were issued in conjunction with the 2002 proposed regulation) may be applied with respect to changes in control occurring prior to January 1, 2004 but are revoked as of January 1, 2004.

E. REVISED TREATMENT OF STOCK OPTIONS

Under the final regulation, the accelerated vesting of a stock option in connection with a change in control is treated as a parachute payment, which must be valued under the relevant facts and circumstances. Contrary to some previous practices, but consistent with Revenue Procedure 2002-45, Revenue Procedure 2003-68 provides that this value cannot be based solely on the option spread at the time of vesting. The IRS has retained the controversial yet simplified safe harbor approach from Revenue Procedure 2002-13 for valuing options. The safe harbor allows the value of a stock option to be established based on the option spread (if any), the remaining term of the option, and a basic assumption regarding the volatility of the underlying stock, all as determined at the time of the change in control. This safe harbor valuation method may be used without regard to whether the underlying stock is publicly traded.

Although it is helpful to have a safe harbor for calculating option values, it is worth noting that the safe harbor methodology:

- can yield values for options that differ markedly from the income actually realized on option exercise or cashout, including producing a value for underwater options;

- may overstate the value of the option relative to the conventional methodology used for financial and proxy reporting; and

- may result in a determination that excise tax applies to underwater options that employees perceive to have no financial value.

Revenue Procedure 2003-68 does, however, give taxpayers additional flexibility in choosing an alternate valuation method:

- Taxpayers that do not use the safe harbor must use a valuation method consistent with generally accepted accounting principles that takes into account the same factors used in the Black-Scholes valuation methodology. The IRS has not prescribed the option term or volatility to be used in determining an option's value outside of the safe harbor, other than requiring consistency with generally accepted accounting principles.

- The value of accelerated vesting of an option may be redetermined during the 18-month period following a change in control if (i) the term of the option is shortened due to a termination of the option holder's employment or (ii) the volatility of the underlying stock decreases. All other factors in the redetermination remain the same, although a different valuation methodology may be used in the redetermination as long as it is otherwise permitted under the Revenue Procedure. The parachute payment and the excess parachute payment will be recalculated, and an individual may claim any resulting adjustment to his or her excise tax liability by filing an amended return for the taxable year in which the excise tax was previously paid.

In addition, Revenue Procedure 2003-68 clarifies that if options are exchanged in a change in control for options based on a different stock, the valuation is based on the substituted option (as opposed to the original option).